THE
EVERYTHING
START YOUR OWN
CONSULTING BUSINESS BOOK

Love to give advice? Want to get *paid* to give advice? Consider starting a consulting business!

Consultants use their own knowledge and experience to help others solve problems. Consultants answer questions about adventure travel, advertising, aviation, biotechnology, business writing, college entrance, dog training, estate planning, event planning, fashion, fundraising, honeymoon planning, and hundreds of other personal and business topics. Chances are that if you are—or want to be—an expert in *anything*, you can sell your services as a consultant!

But where do you start? How can you develop your credentials? How and where do you find clients? How do you establish profitable pricing for your services? Should you work at home or from an office? How do you pay taxes? How do you succeed as a consultant?

This book answers these and many other vital questions to guide you into the growing field of consulting. Its twenty chapters and extensive glossary of consulting business terms will help you mold your own skills into a viable business that serves others and brings you an honest income.

Who am I? A successful consultant! I've helped many thousands of people start businesses of all types over the past four decades. And I've operated many successful service businesses myself. I am your guide.

So get ready to take the first step toward starting and profiting from your own consulting business.

To your success,

Dan Ramsey

Welcome to the EVERYTHING® Series!

These handy, accessible books give you all you need to tackle a difficult project, gain a new hobby, comprehend a fascinating topic, prepare for an exam, or even brush up on something you learned back in school but have since forgotten.

You can choose to read an *Everything*® book from cover to cover or just pick out the information you want from our four useful boxes: e-questions, e-facts, e-alerts, and e-ssentials.

We give you everything you need to know on the subject, but throw in a lot of fun stuff along the way, too.

We now have more than 400 *Everything*® books in print, spanning such wide-ranging categories as weddings, pregnancy, cooking, music instruction, foreign language, crafts, pets, New Age, and so much more. When you're done reading them all, you can finally say you know *Everything*®!

QUESTION

Answers to
common questions

FACT

Important snippets
of information

ALERT

Urgent
warnings

ESSENTIAL

Quick
handy tips

PUBLISHER Karen Cooper

DIRECTOR OF ACQUISITIONS AND INNOVATION Paula Munier

MANAGING EDITOR, EVERYTHING® SERIES Lisa Laing

COPY CHIEF Casey Ebert

ACQUISITIONS EDITOR Lisa Laing

ASSOCIATE DEVELOPMENT EDITOR Elizabeth Kassab

EDITORIAL ASSISTANT Hillary Thompson

EVERYTHING® SERIES COVER DESIGNER Erin Alexander

LAYOUT DESIGNERS Colleen Cunningham, Elisabeth Lariviere, Ashley Vierra, Denise Wallace

Visit the entire Everything® series at *www.everything.com*

THE EVERYTHING

STbrand

START YOUR OWN CONSULTING BUSINESS BOOK

Expert, step-by-step advice for
a successful and profitable career

Dan Ramsey

Avon, Massachusetts

*"Have two goals: wisdom—that is, knowing
and doing right—and common sense. Don't
let them slip away, for they fill you with living
energy, and bring you honor and respect."*
—Proverbs 3:21–22

An Everything® Series Book.
Everything® and everything.com® are registered trademarks of F+W Media, Inc.

Published by Adams Media, a division of F+W Media, Inc.
57 Littlefield Street, Avon, MA 02322 U.S.A.
www.adamsmedia.com

ISBN 10: 1-60550-365-7
ISBN 13: 978-1-60550-365-3

Printed in the United States of America.

J   I   H   G   F   E   D   C   B   A

Library of Congress Cataloging-in-Publication Data
is available from the publisher.

This publication is designed to provide accurate and authoritative information with regard to the subject matter covered. It is sold with the understanding that the publisher is not engaged in rendering legal, accounting, or other professional advice. If legal advice or other expert assistance is required, the services of a competent professional person should be sought.

    —From a *Declaration of Principles* jointly adopted by a Committee of the American Bar Association and a Committee of Publishers and Associations

Many of the designations used by manufacturers and sellers to distinguish their products are claimed as trademarks. Where those designations appear in this book and Adams Media was aware of a trademark claim, the designations have been printed with initial capital letters.

*This book is available at quantity discounts for bulk purchases.
For information, please call 1-800-289-0963.*

Contents

Acknowledgments

Any book is a compilation of the wisdom of many. This book was built upon the wisdom of Hal Wright of the Wright Track; Claire Rosenzweig and others of the Institute of Management Consultants; Bill Stinehart, Vito Tanzi, James Bickmann and others of the American Association of Professional Consultants; Donna-Jean Rainville of The Consulting Source, Inc.; and Herman Holtz, consulting guru. In addition, the Association of Management Consulting Firms, Business Marketing Association, and the American Management Association supplied information for this book. Thanks also to the staffs of Ramsey Business Strategies for past assistance. Thanks also go to my editor, Lisa Laing, and my agent, Bob Diforio, for their guidance and support.

Top Ten Things Every Successful Consultant Must Know

1. What your unique expertise is.

2. Who needs your expertise.

3. How you can build your credentials.

4. How you can make your prospects contact you with their problems.

5. How you can efficiently solve your clients' problems.

6. How you can expand the need for your services.

7. Who your competitors are.

8. What your competitors are doing right now.

9. Whether your business is profitable and, if not, what to do about it.

10. How to continue to enjoy what you are doing.

Introduction

"A CONSULTANT IS ANYONE who carries a briefcase and comes from more than 200 miles away." Funny, but not true. Actually, a consultant is someone who sells advice to someone who needs it. It's that simple. And this year, more than 100,000 consultants will sell advice for more than $20 billion. That's big business!

Consultants are simply experts for hire. They range from large investment firms to personal trainers. Their expertise ranges from accounting to zoning, acne eradication to zipper design, weddings to funerals. They operate from offices, briefcases, and their own homes. They are paid to know and to share. Management, scientific, technical, consumer, and lifestyle consultants are paid well for their advice—if they know how to start and run a successful consulting service. This book can help you decide if consulting is a smart career and lifestyle move for you.

This book is structured to guide you through the process of considering, planning, developing, and operating a consulting business in any one of a thousand fields. It assumes that your knowledge of business management is primarily from the outside, as a consumer or an employee. It helps you find and hone your expertise. It guides you in the structure of a profitable advice service that you can apply toward your own unique business success.

Sidebars offer additional information that you put to work right now as you plan or expand your consulting business. The sidebars include E-Fact (facts and statistics), E-Alert (cautions), E-ssential (tips), and E-Question (questions and answers), written to clarify and guide you as you start your consulting business.

CHAPTER 1

Opportunities for Consultants

Consulting is a multibillion dollar business. It includes everything from corporate investment consultants to child care advisors. But what is it that consultants do to earn their fees? What special knowledge or skills do they have that others don't? How much do they earn? And, most important, how can you start your own consulting business? This first chapter opens the door to the world of consulting so you can find opportunities that fit your skills and goals.

The Life of Consultants

It is said that a consultant is anyone who carries a briefcase and comes from more than 200 miles away. That's not quite true, but it reflects the image that a consultant is someone with objective knowledge.

Actually, a consultant is someone who sells advice to those who need it. Useful advice may be developed through the consultant's knowledge of a subject, the skill of problem solving, or the ability to research. To better understand what consultants do, following is a description of a typical consulting service.

FACT

Consultant, from the Latin word *consultare*, means "to discuss." Synonyms include counselor and advisor. However, the meaning has been diluted—for instance, a garbage truck driver can carry the title "waste management transportation consultant." A professional consultant offers valuable advice for a fee.

Typical Consulting Service

Communication Solutions is a business communications consulting service in the Pacific Northwest. President Walter Curtis had fifteen years of experience in the marketing communications field before striking out on his own. Actually, he was pushed.

As project manager for a training service, Walt was responsible for producing industrial training manuals in the pulp and paper industry. He had risen from writer to project coordinator to project manager. After four years, the training contract ended and was not renewed. Walt was out of a job. He had previously worked as a copywriter for a large regional advertising agency. Before that he had been a staff writer for a business publication. Walt knew business and he knew communications. He just didn't know what he was going to do next.

Fortunately, he heard about a small writing project through a trade association of which he was a member. The project would only last four weeks but would pay about twice what Walt previously made in a month. He took it. The small project grew into a larger project, as they sometimes do.

Fortunately, Walt's agreement required a per diem (per day) rather than a flat fee for the project. The longer the project lasted, the more Walt was paid.

Three months later, Walt decided that he couldn't count on an eternal project, so he took a day off to pursue other contracts. Walt came up with a business name—Communication Solutions—that sounded like he had been a communications consultant that solved problems, and had business cards made up. He wrote a short brochure listing his experience and qualifications. He set up four appointments for the day and started making the rounds. He soon had sufficient jobs to carry him for the next eight months. Walt was in business for himself.

QUESTION

What is it that consultants sell?
Solutions! Every client has a problem that needs to be solved. The best—and highest paid—consultants are those who clearly identify the problem, get agreement on it from the client, and help the client work toward the agreed solution. Your client's underlying question is: "Can you help me solve my problem—even if I don't know exactly what the problem is?"

Today, Communication Solutions consults with high-tech businesses in the Willamette Valley. It helps clients define their communication goals, find writers and other resources, and review their marketing documents to make sure they are efficient. Communication Solutions charges $155 an hour for consulting services. Writing projects are bid at $110 an hour. Walt has one full-time and one part-time associate who help him develop communication projects. Both work as independent contractors on a percentage of gross income.

After two difficult years, Walt has sufficient contracts to begin taking Friday afternoons off. He justifies it by saying, "I'm the boss!"

Business Consulting

There are two broad categories of consulting services, each with overlap: business consulting and consumer consulting. Let's look at the larger group first: business consulting.

The following is a list of common business consulting services. Each can be redirected into many more:

- Acoustics
- Advertising
- Architecture
- Auditing
- Automotive
- Aviation
- Biotechnology
- Body language
- Building management
- Business selling
- Business startup
- Business travel
- Business writing
- Communication
- Community relations
- Computer hardware
- Computer software
- Construction management
- Convention planning
- Data processing
- Direct marketing
- E-Business
- Economic research
- Editorial
- Employee benefits
- Engineering
- Environmental
- Etiquette
- Executive search
- Financial management
- Food services
- Foreclosure
- Forestry
- Franchising
- Fundraising
- Gaming
- Government relations
- Grant writing
- Graphic design
- Hospital administration
- Hotel management
- Human resource
- Immigration
- Information technology
- Insurance
- Inventory control
- Investments
- Labor relations
- Land-use planning
- Leasing
- Licensing
- Mail order
- Management
- Marketing
- Material handling
- Mergers and acquisitions
- Office management
- Online business
- Operations
- Opinion polls

- Organizational development
- Payroll management
- Performance
- Political
- Pollution control
- Product design
- Programming
- Public affairs
- Publishing
- Purchasing
- Quality control
- Real estate investment
- Recycling
- Rehabilitation
- Restaurant management
- Retailing
- Reunion planning
- Safety
- Salary administration
- Sales
- Sanitation
- Security
- Search engine optimization
- Shipping
- Small business
- Social services
- Stockholder relations
- Strategic planning
- Tax law
- Technical writing
- Telecommunications
- Traffic control
- Translation
- Trial
- Urban renewal
- Venture capital
- Wage administration
- Warehousing
- Waste management
- Website design
- Winery management
- Writing

In addition to a specialty, a business consulting service may decide to specialize in one of two approaches to advising clients. The service may emphasize the resolution of an issue or the transfer of needed skills to the client. For example, a restaurant with cash flow problems may only need advice on how to resolve that specific problem. Or the owner may need to be trained in advanced cash flow forecasting and other aspects of business management.

There are advantages and disadvantages to both approaches for the consultant and the client. Problem resolution is less expensive for the client, but it may not solve the underlying cause. Skill transfer is more expensive for the client, but it reduces dependence on the consultant. You'll learn more about these consulting methods in this book.

The Association of Management Consulting Firms (*http://amcf.org*) says that business consultants typically earn $65,000 to $300,000 a year in salaries and bonuses. Their employers charge clients much more in order to make a profit. Independent business consultants often charge by the hour; hourly fees range from $100 to $400 depending on the specialized knowledge and experience—and the value of the solutions.

Personal Consulting

Businesses aren't the only clients for useful advice. Consumers also need informed help making decisions. The following is a list of common personal consulting services. Add to this list the business consulting services that can be used by individuals, such as aviation, body language, communication, and recycling. Personal consulting services could include:

- Adventure travel
- Aerobics
- Beauty
- Career
- Child care
- College entrance
- Credit
- Cruises
- Dog training
- Estate planning
- Event planning
- Family relations
- Family travel
- Fashion
- Fitness
- Gardening
- Golf
- Health services
- Home buying
- Home remodeling
- Home repair
- Honeymoons
- Image
- Interior decorating
- Interior design
- Journal writing
- Landscaping
- Makeover
- Marriage relations
- Medical
- Music
- Party planning
- Personal image
- Personal trainer

- Pet selection
- Photography
- Poker
- Religion
- Relocation
- Resume
- Spiritual
- Studying

- Taxes
- Voice
- Wardrobe
- Wedding
- Weight loss
- Women's issues
- Woodworking

These are just a few of the hundreds of topics on which consumers want help.

FACT

Full-time consumer consultants typically earn $50 to $120 an hour and six-figure annual salaries. Others operate part time from their homes, bringing in $40,000 to $100,000 a year in gross income. Make sure there is a niche for your business in your market, but be wary of markets that seem saturated.

Within these fields, there are many areas of specialization that can be selected to fit your client's needs as well as your own interests and skills. For example, you may decide to specialize in advising clients how to select a pet that has the appropriate personality and temperament for their needs. Or you may specialize in helping college students manage their time more efficiently. Or you may have qualifications to offer advice on planning a Muslim wedding ceremony. What do you know that others would pay to know?

Consumer consultants aren't typically paid as much as business consultants. The primary reason is that a business can financially benefit from useful advice, so it is in a position to pay more for that advice. In addition, credentials for a business consultant are often more difficult and expensive to acquire that those for a consumer consultant. Even so, a consumer consultant with strong credentials and valuable advice serving a specific market can make an excellent income.

Consulting in the Information Age

Technology has influenced all aspects of modern life for both businesses and consumers. Technology offers many tools that help consultants gather information and help their clients. The Information Age—the wide sharing of information using technology—has expanded knowledge and opened up opportunities for problem-solving consultants.

Modern Consulting

Here's an example of consulting in the Information Age. A successful direct marketing consultant serves clients throughout the United States without ever leaving her rural home in South Dakota. Her office is in her house, which has three incoming lines for telephones, faxes, and broadband Internet access. She has an answering system that sounds like she has a receptionist and a computer system that allows her to quickly develop graphic layouts for clients. From her office, she can simultaneously send her monthly newsletter by e-mail to thousands of clients and prospects. She sends and receives dozens of e-mail messages from clients and resources each day. She even does her banking and orders office supplies online. She recently installed a video telephone conferencing system for face-to-face meetings with her primary clients in New York City, Chicago, and Los Angeles.

ESSENTIAL

The Internet that allows you to consult with out-of-town clients also allows your clients to develop business relationships with consultants in other countries—at lower fees. Make sure your service is not one that draws competition from consultants in countries where the cost of living is dramatically below yours.

Consumer consultants can also use the Internet to interface with prospective and regular clients. However, most rely on face-to-face relations, using the Internet as a marketing and communication tool. Their web page and e-mail addresses are included on business cards, but most of their consulting is done in person.

Computers and the Internet

The Internet has dramatically changed how all businesses manage their processes. It has been especially powerful in the past decade as consumers of all ages rely on the worldwide web and search engines such as Google to find useful information on any topic.

Computers are numerical machines, and the Internet began as a resource for sharing data. To help in decisions, data must be converted into information, then knowledge. That process requires knowledgeable human beings who can use data to develop solutions.

Fortunately, you don't have to be a computer wizard to use the power of computers and the Internet in your consulting business. This book describes and offers specific resources that you can use to help your clients. The Internet is one. If you are intimidated by the thought of using computers, you have two choices:

· Select a consulting business design that doesn't require computers
· Learn how to use computers, one step at a time

Remember that your competitors probably have an Internet presence and that not using the Internet may put you at a competitive disadvantage.

Primary Consulting Services

What is it that consultants actually do? They help clients solve specific problems. And they do so by using a process. A process is a series of operations required in making a product or furnishing a service. The process of making a hamburger, for example, requires knowledge (how to prepare), materials (meat, bun, pickle, special sauce), labor (cooking, assembling, packaging), and results in a specific output (a hamburger) in a form the client wants. Your consulting process will work the same way.

Consultant's Process

There is a process to producing consulting services. Understanding the mechanics of the process—the required knowledge, materials, labor, and expected results—will make you a better and more efficient consultant.

Consultants who solve specific problems for clients typically follow a four-step process:

- Diagnose
- Design
- Implement
- Measure

For example, a marketing consultant would diagnose the client's situation and its cause, design a marketing campaign to solve the problem, implement or help the client implement the campaign, and then measure the results to determine whether the expected results were achieved. The diagnosis may determine that sales are down because business has been lost to a competitor on pricing. In this case, the marketing consultant designs a campaign that stresses value over price, then implements the campaign by developing ads and sales literature. Finally, the consultant determines if sales to the target market—clients that had moved to competitors—have increased.

The exact process for your consulting may be different, depending on what services you offer, to whom you offer them, what results are expected, and whether you solve problems for them or transfer skills to them. However, most consulting processes follow the four steps.

The Consultant's Knowledge

The knowledge required for producing consulting services includes oral and written communication skills, fundamentals of business, and extensive knowledge within your specialty. Your consulting service will also be more efficient if you understand business management and the use of computers and software. Chapter 5 offers numerous resources for developing your knowledge and skills.

The materials you will need for many consulting services are basic: office equipment and supplies, communication tools, reference materials, marketing materials, and any specialized tools or equipment.

Of course, your consulting service will require labor. In fact, most consulting services are labor-intensive. That is, most of what the client is paying for is your time rather than a physical product. You may perform all the labor yourself or get help from employees, independent contractors, sub-contractors, associates, or other outside services. In each case, you must understand what the labor requirements of the process are to ensure that the job is being done properly and efficiently.

ALERT

How do clients know you have the knowledge they need? They depend on your credentials and your references. If you have extensive education in your field, promote it. If you have helped others solve similar problems, get references or referrals from them. Help prospective clients answer the question: Does this person have sufficient knowledge to help me solve my problem?

Result

Finally, you need to define the result you want. Actually, it is not the final step; it is the first one. Until you understand exactly what your client requires, you cannot define the other elements in your process: knowledge, materials, and labor.

For example, before you can develop the specific steps to reach the client's goal, you must decide that the client's need is to increase sales, have a successful event, or reduce employee problems. You cannot efficiently define the components of your process until you have defined your desired output. In our earlier example, you don't select beef as a material until you've decided that a hamburger is the output or end result you want. You can't make "hamburgers" using tofu.

This is where more new businesses get lost than anywhere else. They look at their solution before they've even discovered what a client's problem is.

Add-On Products and Services

Depending on what type of consulting you do, there may be other products and services you can provide to increase your market as well as your income.

For example, a construction consultant may offer a subscription newsletter, books, reports, and other documents to prospects and clients. In addition, the consultant may speak on related topics for a fee or at no charge to promote the business. Doing so makes the consultant an expert. It also brings the consultant into contact with potential clients.

ESSENTIAL

Many successful consulting services sell products as well as services. For example, a personal trainer may sell exercise equipment, training courses on DVD, and spa retreats in addition to advising individual clients. Not only do the products increase the consultant's income, but selling them to prospective clients can bring in new consulting clients.

Branch out. An image consultant can produce and sell videos on how to enhance beauty and image. You can also consider expanding your business to include clients outside your normal target range.

Selecting Your Field of Expertise

By now, you may have a number of ideas for consulting services you could offer.

To develop a list of potential fields of consulting, ask yourself:

- What training have I completed?
- What business experience have I had?
- What are my interests and hobbies?
- What skills and attributes do I have?
- What do I enjoy doing for others?
- Do I prefer working with people directly or indirectly?
- What knowledge and skills will I need to become an effective consultant?

The topic of assessing your personal goals, covered in Chapter 3, will offer additional focusing questions to help you decide both what you want to do and how you want to do it.

Finding the Tools You Need

Once you've selected your field of consulting, deciding what tools you will need will be relatively easy. For example, if you sell advice on increasing retail sales, you will need experience in this field and you will need to know what the latest statistics, tools, and trends are. The retail sales consultant will have numerous contacts within the field, subscribe to a variety of publications, gather and study books on retail sales and related topics, and develop experience and credentials in solving retail sales problems.

Chapter 5 offers resources for consultants, including professional associations, trade journals, and books.

How Much Will You Earn?

It's difficult to generalize about earnings for consultants. There are many variables, including experience, the marketplace, and the needs of clients. However, as an example, the typical independent consulting service operated by the owner without employees can soon sell about $80,000 to $120,000 in services in a year. That's earning a rate of $80 to $120 an hour, four billable hours a day, five days a week. The other four-plus hours a day will be spent on marketing and administration duties. Few consulting services start out the first year making that much, but most can do so by the second full year of operation.

ESSENTIAL

One successful consultant was asked how many hours she typically works. Her answer: "Oh, I only work half-time—just twelve of the available twenty-four hours in a day!" Many new consulting business owners work even more, though few hours are billable. They are building their knowledge, expanding their network, contacting prospective clients, and developing their consulting process toward the day when they can work "half-time."

How much profit should you expect to make? As a service business, much of your income will go to pay for labor. In a one-person office, that's you. During the second year of operation, your salary may be approximately 40 percent of income. That's $32,000 to $48,000 in salary for our example. Overhead expenses (rent, telephone, advertising, equipment) will take about 25 percent of your income. Direct expenses (books, subscriptions, office supplies) will typically take ten percent of your income. What's left over is profit: about 25 percent of income. Taxes come from this figure before you can call it net profit.

These figures are for your second year of operation when you have developed repeat and referral business, identified a target market, and purchased your primary equipment and supplies. Your first year will be more difficult as you build your business. During the first year, expect about 75 percent of your estimated second-year income and overhead to be as high as 40 percent of income. That is, if you estimate that second-year sales will total $100,000, estimate first-year sales to be 75 percent of that, or about $75,000. Your salary will be about $30,000 (40 percent), overhead will be higher at approximately $30,000 (40 percent), direct expenses of about $7,500 (10 percent), and profit before taxes of about $7,500 (10 percent) before taxes. Don't plan on getting it right the first year and you won't be disappointed.

You can build your consulting business part-time before going full time. You can select a specialty that pays better. You can set up your office in your home, which has numerous tax advantages. You can learn how to operate your consulting business even more efficiently than average. This book will show you how to use these and other advanced techniques for building profitability.

The numbers used in these examples are averages. During the first year, a business consultant may only bill 25 percent of available hours and a consumer consultant with both products and services to sell may be profitable after three months.

Overhead Expenses

Let's take a closer look at overhead expenses. The following estimates are guidelines to help you in calculating income, expenses, and profitability. For a typical consulting business, you should expect to spend about 40 percent of your income the first year and 25 percent in years after that. Where does it go? Rent will be about 10 percent of sales, office equipment and supplies will require another 5 percent, and your telephone/Internet connections about 5 percent. The remaining 20 percent the first year and 5 percent in subsequent years will go for advertising and promotion. The first year's advertising will cost more because you want to get your name out widely and because your advertising won't be as efficient. After the first year of advertising you'll know which media and messages work best for your market.

Making the Leap

Starting a business—any business—is similar to starting a long road trip. Before you head out on the highway, you must answer a few basic questions to make sure you will arrive at your destination. Consulting may be your dream job—or it could be a nightmare. This book offers an inside look at starting and running a successful consulting business. As you continue reading, keep the following four questions in mind:

- Where are you now?
- Where do you want to go?
- Why?
- Do you have what you need?

Consider your answers to each of these vital questions as you proceed toward success as a consultant.

Where Are You Now?

If you wanted to make a road trip from your current location to a distant location, you'd probably pull out a map and find your current location. In planning a consulting business, you will take a similar step: Identifying your present situation. Are you currently employed? Exactly what is your employer paying you to do? What knowledge or skills do you have for which others would pay a premium? If you're not employed—or not employed in your chosen field—what assets do you have now that you can use to advise and help others? What income or other assets do you have to finance your business venture?

Where Do You Want To Go?

Your road trip begins where you are. Where do you want it to end? What's your destination? This book will help you answer that question in detail; for now, think of your options. Are you looking for a career that offers independence, financial rewards, and opportunities to help others solve problems? Consulting may be for you. However, poor planning or inadequate assets can make consulting a frustrating business that eats away at your startup cash. Make sure you know exactly where you want to go before you start the trip.

Why?

A road trip may be planned to see new places, visit specific people, or attend a particular event. Each is a purpose. Your business venture must also have one or more primary purposes. Why are you doing this? Some knowledgeable advisors believe they can earn more money as independent consultants than as employees. Others want the prestige of being a consultant. Still others don't care as much about the money, but want the satisfaction of being their own boss. Many want a creative business they can operate from home. How about you?

Do You Have What You Need?

You're ready to start your car's engine and head off toward your destination. Will the car make it? Do you have enough money for fuel, food, lodging, and emergencies? If not, don't start. It's the same with a business: don't start until you know you have what you need to arrive at your career destination. You don't have to work out every detail, but you must know if you have access to what you absolutely need.

Starting your own consulting business is a journey. Fortunately, you will have guidance from experts and advice from those who have traveled this road before you.

CHAPTER 2

What Consultants Do

Before you make the leap and start your own consulting business, you should visualize what your life will be like and how it will change. You may discover that consulting is the perfect fit, but you'll probably find that some elements fit better than others and that, with some creative thinking, you can design a consulting service that rewards both you and your clients. This chapter takes you deeper into the life of consulting and advising.

The World of Consultants

If your image of being a consultant is wearing custom business suits, eating at the finest restaurants, and having a limo at your beck and call, you're right—and wrong. Yes, a few top-level business consultants live in penthouses and fly around the world to offer advice-for-a-price. However, most consultants live more modestly. Some drive Cadillacs, but many drive Chevys. They are consultants because they love problem solving. They sincerely want to help others find solutions. The money is vital to continuing their career, but it doesn't define what they do.

If your goal is to become rich as a consultant, you must reach the top of your field. This is no easy feat; many are already overcrowded with people trying to become rich. If you instead choose a field that fits your personal and professional goals and skills, you may not become monetarily wealthy, but you will find riches and independence that no employee can enjoy.

ESSENTIAL

Attend a conference or seminar for professional consultants in your field or a related field. You will be able to meet with working consultants in meetings, at meals, and in the elevator. Be ready with a few succinct questions that will help you understand what you're getting into. Other people often love to help if you make them feel important.

Your Life as a Consultant

What can you expect your life to be like if you decide to become a professional consultant? That depends. If you're a square peg trying to fit into a round hole, you will be uncomfortable. If you don't enjoy solving problems and using your skills to help people, you will probably be miserable. If you're looking for a way to get rich quick, try another line of work. But if you enjoy helping other people, have good communication skills, experience and/or training in your field, and the need to be an independent businessperson, offering consulting services may be a rewarding way to make a living.

In addition, operating a successful consulting service can help you develop the lifestyle you desire. If you enjoy traveling, consulting can pay you for doing it. If you'd prefer to work from home, consulting can fund a home office. If you enjoy meeting new people, consulting can make you both well known and popular.

Most important, a well-managed consulting service can help you find financial security and a sense of significance that few other professions offer.

Typical Business Day for a Consultant

There are no typical consultants, so there are really no typical days for a consultant. That's what makes it fun. One successful investment consultant in California works during New York Stock Exchange hours, quitting about 2 P.M. Pacific Time each afternoon, an hour after the market closes. She is then ready to greet her three children as they come in from school. An export consultant who specializes in Pacific Rim countries works late at night when Japanese, Korean, Chinese, and Taiwanese businesses are open. A successful home decorating consultant prefers to work weekends and only by appointment.

ESSENTIAL

Want to know what a consultant does all day? Go to work for her. Get any job you can so that you can observe business operations. Be a receptionist, a trainee, or even a janitor. You should not try to take clients or proprietary information, but you can learn much by observing how the consultant works and what she does.

Most important to a consultant is time. Getting the most value from each minute is important, especially when someone is paying you $1 to $5 for each of those minutes. Depending on the type of consulting, appointment schedules may be kept and closely followed. Besides tools of the trade, the two most important tools for most consultants are an appointment calendar and a priority list. A successful consultant in nearly any trade will refer to these tools many times a day. Chapter 14 will show you how to work by priority.

Developing Expertise

Consultants are experts. Where will you get the expertise needed for your chosen consulting business? From education, training, experience, and observation. Applying these components will help you develop valuable skills. Documenting these skills will help you develop your credentials. Developing expertise follows the same broad process whether you're a financial consultant or a dog trainer.

Education and Training

Education is the process of building knowledge. Training is the process of building a skill. Both are necessary to all consultants. However, some consulting fields are primarily knowledge-based (financial consultant) while others are skill-based (dog trainer). Once you have selected your field of consulting, it will be your first job to ensure that you have exemplary education and training in this field. You may already have it, but you may need to go get it.

FACT

Many community colleges and adult schools offer certification programs that can help you build your credentials. Ask career counselors at local schools for education and training recommendations in your selected field. Speak with the program instructor before you decide to begin the course. Community colleges and adult schools are an excellent place to learn more.

For example, if you want to be a dog trainer for the movies, you'll need to ensure that your knowledge of movie production is comprehensive. You'll also need to develop skills you can use to motivate dogs to do specific tricks. Before you begin your consulting business you must identify the education and training required for success in your field and make sure you get it.

Experience and Observation

People learn from experience (what they do) and observation (what they see). In the dog training example, you can use prior experience in training your family dogs to do tricks. If you don't have this experience, you can begin to develop it now. Observing how other trainers work and the results they get also will help you develop your expertise.

Financial consultants also use experience and observation in developing expertise. They must have experience in financial analysis as well as in scrutinizing the analysis of others.

Your Skills

A skill is an application of knowledge in performing an action. Communication is a skill. So is analyzing a financial statement or teaching a dog to jump over a barrier on command. You have many skills, some of which directly relate to a consulting profession. As you define your consulting business over the following chapters, identify the skills that are required. Make a list. Think as a client of the service you hope to provide. What skills would be most helpful?

ESSENTIAL

In developing expertise, work backward. That is, define the credentials you need and the skills required for those credentials, then list the necessary education, training, experience, and observations to develop those skills. Finally, determine how you can gain the credentials or experience you need and come up with a plan for doing so.

Your Credentials

A professional dog trainer may have certification from an animal behavior college or program. A physical fitness trainer should have a degree in physical education or certification from a well-known physical training facility.

If you're not sure of the most valuable credentials in your chosen field, look to your competitors. They may list their educational and professional credentials, which can help you determine what credentials your business should have to succeed.

Developing Resources

In addition to what you know, your consulting business will use what others know. You will go to other experts for information or advice. You may also refer to technical or reference books, government reports, or other data. Chapter 5 goes deeper into this topic. For now, take a brief look at your need to develop data and human resources for your consulting business.

Data Resources

Many consultants rely on data as the raw material that helps them help others. For example, investment consultants need to keep up to date on the latest investment data and watch for data trends. They subscribe to numerous data services that assist them in developing sound advice for clients. Physical fitness consultants draw data from the client: height, weight, health, physical conditioning levels, etc. They compare this personal data with fitness data from experts to develop personalized fitness plans and goals.

FACT

Governments are a treasure house of data. Thousands of statistics are available at the U.S. Census Bureau (*www.census.gov*), Bureau of Labor Statistics (*www.bls.gov*), and the Small Business Administration (*www .sba.gov*), to name a few. Canadian statistics are available online *at http://canada.gc.ca*. State and municipal governments, too, can supply data for many consulting services. Follow state links at *www.usa.gov*.

As you design your consulting service, consider the types of data you will require and begin developing sources for accurate data. You will use this data to develop information that will be useful—and valuable—to your clients.

Human Resources

Investment consultants don't rely solely on their own knowledge. They also have contacts within the industry who help them gather, analyze, and communicate valuable information. Dog trainers do the same thing. Many consultants, especially those new to the field, find and use a mentor who can advise them on topics in which they are less familiar.

Begin identifying potential mentors in your field. They are well-respected consultants or topical resources who can answer tougher questions for you. Yes, you may have to pay them for advice, but you'll learn to ask cost-effective questions and produce profit on the answers.

Developing Contacts

Consulting is a people business. You will get data and information from resources, process it, and sell resulting knowledge and wisdom to clients. You will deal with people every day. Start developing contacts and relationships now.

QUESTION

Where can I find useful business contacts locally?
Begin with your local chamber of commerce, an association of local business people. Also contact professional service groups such as Kiwanis, Soroptomists, Lions, and Toastmasters. Their meetings are typically listed in local newspapers and are open to the public.

Who are these people? They are your resources or input contacts and your clients or output contacts. Both groups are vital to your consulting business's success.

Input Contacts

Who will supply the input data to your consulting process? These will be the data and human resources described previously. They include experts, associations, publications, marketing reports, specialized tool sources, and other raw materials for your service. You probably already know who some of them are. Start listing them in an address book, notebook, or computer contact file.

For example, a movie dog trainer would begin gathering contact information on other trainers and training methods, sources of intelligent and easily trained dogs, veterinarians, groomers, and dog food vendors. A career counselor would develop a library of career books, training materials, and statistics on various careers.

Output Contacts

Who are your consulting process's outputs? Your clients. They are the people who will receive and pay for the services that you provide. Use your address book, notebook, or computer contact file to begin listing and gathering data on them. These may be people for whom you've provided similar services or people you believe fit your typical client profile.

A financial consultant who specializes in assisting retirees with their investments will identify people over a defined age who have a specific net worth. Chapter 12 offers more details on marketing to potential clients. For now, define and begin finding people who will purchase your output, your consulting services.

Adding Value

As you can see, consultants are paid to gather input (data, information) and produce output (knowledge, wisdom). That's their process. It's the same broad process whether the consultant is an immigration consultant or a voice trainer. So why don't prospective clients simply gather the education and data to do the job themselves?

Many do. For simpler problems, many people do the research and make their own decision without outside help. Others ask trusted advisors who don't charge a fee, such as a reputable salesperson. Still others simply ignore the problem. Many people can solve their own problems without help, though not efficiently nor completely.

That's where consultants come in. That's you. Your service will be to help others clearly define specific problems and offer well-considered solutions that are valuable. You are adding value. The greater the value you add, the more successful you will be and the greater will be your rewards.

For example, senior citizens can take the time and effort to learn how to invest their money without paid consultants. Millions of them do it every day. Why do they need an investment advisor? It will be your job to help them understand why. For example:

- You can increase returns by knowing when to invest, based on experience.
- You can help clients find little-known investment opportunities.
- You can help reduce taxation with your unique knowledge of tax shelters.
- Your fees are based on results.
- Your specialized training reduces the risks of investment loss.

The list can go on. Each of these points adds value to your service over clients doing it themselves. People don't mind paying for services if the perceived value is greater than the price.

The Consulting Process

Chapter 1 introduced the concept of a consulting process. It was outlined as:

- Diagnose
- Design
- Implement
- Measure

In some consulting fields, the process can be more complex than that. The complexity you select depends on the complexity and value of the services you will sell. For dog training, this four-step process is sufficient. For investment consulting, the process is more developed—and the outcome more critical. Many professional consultants use the following seven-step process as they produce solutions for their clients:

- Needs analysis
- Project definition
- Gather information
- Gap analysis

- Develop recommendations
- Implementation
- Review

Let's take a closer look at these steps.

There is no one perfect way to process problems into solutions and prospects into clients. Feel free to modify this suggested—and proven—process to fit your own requirements and methods. You may even have multiple processes, depending on the complexity of the problem or the needs of different client groups.

Needs Analysis

What's the problem? What does the client need? These are critical questions to begin your consulting process. Until you know what the need is, you won't be able to offer a solution.

How do you analyze needs? By listening! As you develop your consulting business concept, you will also develop a list of core questions to ask prospects and clients to analyze their needs. For example:

- **Senior Investment Counselor:** How much do you have invested now? Where? What are the results?
- **Movie Dog Trainer:** What is the scene about? What do you want the dog to do?

All of your clients have a problem for which they need a solution. You must know what that problem is and what the client's needs are. Finding out requires active listening.

Project Definition

As you interview your client, you'll discover there are many problems. If they have a common source, you may be able to help resolve more than one. However, you must first define the core problem. It can be the biggest problem, the source problem, or some other condition. It will be your initial task to help the client define the project. Otherwise, how will you know when you have achieved the needed results? For example:

- **Senior Investment Counselor:** You need to develop an annuity in the next five years that offers a return of $2,000 a month.
- **Movie Dog Trainer:** You want a scruffy dog to walk into the scene, pick up a set of car keys, and run off stage left.

Clearly defining the problem is the first step toward producing a valuable solution.

Gather Information

To produce a solution, you'll need more information. This information may be in the form of additional facts, the results of interviews, or your own observations. You'll need both quantitative (numbers) and qualitative (views, opinions) information before you develop a viable solution.

Many questions will occur to you as you consider the client's defined problem. You may need to see the problem for yourself or you may need to measure the problem. This is research and it is a vital part of consulting, whether you're selling investment information to a senior, choreographing a specific action in a movie, or helping a client start an e-business.

Gap Analysis

Before a full solution can be offered, you must know where things stand now. For example, a senior investment counselor must know how much the client currently has invested.

Put another way, in order to help the client get from "here" to "there," you must first define "here." If the client's investment is currently not returning any income, the solution is different than if the investment now returns $1,000 a month, halfway to the $2,000 monthly goal. The movie dog trainer must analyze whether the selected pet performer knows a similar pickup trick or must be taught it. That's gap analysis.

Develop Recommendations

Based on your knowledge and wisdom—in combination with the data and information you've discovered—you are now ready to offer one or more recommended solutions. This is what the client is paying for: your carefully considered solution. In the coming chapters, you'll learn how to make that presentation in the most useful form. For now, know that you will first review the agreed problem with the client, outline what you know and what you have learned about the solution, then present the solution as one of value.

Implementation

In some consulting situations, you will also be the implementer. You will manage the senior's investment portfolio or be on the movie set to direct the dog through the scene. In other projects, you will pass your recommendations on to your client or to a third party for implementation. In each case, you will need to develop specific recommendations on how to implement your solution. "Invest more money" is not a solution for your senior client. You will either need to implement a specific plan or document it so that the client can. Implementation is also called solution management.

Review

Feedback is a vital part of all processes. In industry, processes (such as producing soap) are controlled by measuring the output against what is expected (a setpoint or benchmark) and adjusting the input accordingly. To ensure that your consulting process is valuable to your client—and future clients—you must review and analyze the results. You must get feedback from your client.

If you are implementing the solution, feedback is easier to measure. You know the desired results and you measure the actual results against them. Did the senior meet his monthly income goal? Did the movie dog give a satisfactory performance in one take or did it take ten? You need to know so you can make future advice more valuable.

You also need feedback on the client's perceptions. Are they happy? Will they use your services again? Will they recommend you to others? This post-project review is vital to your consulting business' future success.

Minimizing Risk

Mark Twain noted, "There are two times in a man's life when he should not speculate: when he can't afford it, and when he can."

Certainly, there are many risks involved in starting and running your own business, no matter what type of business it is. But you can minimize these risks by understanding what you're getting into and knowing how to get out of it if you must. Never enter a room without an exit. Chapter 19 will help you to discover those exits as well as help you to keep from using them.

QUESTION

How can I minimize risk?
Start slow and learn from every error. A $100 mistake can net you a $1,000 education if you carefully analyze and learn from it. What went wrong? What should have happened? What will you do next time? Also, analyze and learn from other people's mistakes. It's cheaper!

Investing Time and Money

A major risk to starting your consulting service is that you will lose your investment of time and money. How can you minimize these risks? Some consultants start their service at home in their spare time while working another job. This structure presents a number of challenges, but they can be overcome. The business can depend on an answering service or a relative to handle phone inquiries. In fact, depending on the needs of clients, a consulting service can turn this limitation to an advantage by offering evening and weekend appointments that competitors do not.

Selecting a Location

The most successful consulting services are those that operate from a professional office near their clients. As a new consultant, you may be tempted to locate in a lower-rent area to reduce financial risk. Don't! You'll actually be increasing your financial risk because a poor location will yield a higher percentage of income going to rent. For example, a high-rent office may cost $1,500 a month but bring you $15,000 a month in business, costing 10 percent of income, whereas an $800-a-month office may only bring you $4,000 in business each month, costing 20 percent of income. The cheaper route can actually increase your risk.

The best way to minimize risks is to understand what they are and prepare for those from which you cannot recover. You'll want business insurance. You'll want sufficient operating capital to get you through the first six to twelve months of your business. You'll want only minimal office supplies. You'll want to come up with alternative services to ensure you have income. You'll want to make sure that any leases you sign can be renegotiated if your business doesn't work out. As suggested earlier, make sure you have sufficient exits before you enter.

ESSENTIAL

An alternative to high rent is shared rent. That is, you may be able to sublease a desk or office from another business. This can be especially effective if the landlord offers a related but noncompeting service with which you can share clients.

The Market for Consulting Services

One of the most important things that consultants do is market their services. Chapter 12 will extensively cover the many ways you can market your business or consumer consulting service. For now, let's look at marketing in general and help you see that marketing is both vital and fun.

The purpose of marketing is simply to bring products and clients together. To do this, you will first determine who your client is. For example, the client of a printing consultant is any business that uses printing services: larger businesses that produce documents, literature, forms, or packaging materials. If the specialization is packaging, clients are manufacturers who must package their product for the consumer.

By first defining your client you can then define your market. If you plan to advise people on selecting appropriate pets from an animal shelter, you will define two markets:

- People who consider the animal shelter as a source of pets but don't know how to make the best selection.
- People who have not previously considered an animal shelter as a source of good pets.

CHAPTER 3

Consulting Requirements

Starting a consulting business sounds like fun, doesn't it? Ingenuity. Independence. Income. It can be one of the most rewarding jobs you'll ever have. So what are the requirements for getting into this field? They obviously vary depending on what advice you offer, but there are many commonalities, including making sure the job fits you. This chapter will guide you in your decision.

Your Personal Goals

What will you need to start and operate a successful consulting service? Certainly you will need your own special knowledge, skills, talent, some money, and some clients. But just as necessary is a personal desire to help others. This is important if you are an employee; it is vital if you are the owner.

As a consumer, you can easily read the attitudes of people who serve you. You know when someone is helping you because it's their job or because they enjoy doing their job. And clients usually respond by supporting and recommending those who help solve problems and make them feel important. Businesses appreciate clients' attention—and they get it.

Before you decide whether operating a consulting service is for you, you must know who you are. What do you feel most comfortable doing? Under what conditions do you enjoy working with people? Under what conditions do you prefer to avoid people? What are your personal goals? What are your financial goals? How much risk do you feel comfortable taking? Most important, is a consulting service a good fit in your life or will it cause more problems than it cures? Self-analysis can be difficult, but it is the only way of ensuring that this or any other goal will bring you the results you want in your life.

Analyzing Yourself

Maybe by this stage in your life you've developed a list of long-term personal goals. Most people have not. It isn't mandatory that you develop a long list of your life's goals before you start a consulting service or other business, but it will increase your chances of personal and financial success if you know what you want from the future.

How can you get started on this list of personal goals? Take some time away from your current work, find a quiet and restful location, and ask yourself questions that will help you determine what you enjoy doing. If you'd like, write them down so you can add to them or refer to them later. This is a good exercise in self-awareness that anyone can benefit from. Here are the questions:

- What is it you want from your life?
- Do you have specific goals?

- What plans do you have for the next year of your life?
- Is there anything that people often compliment you about? A talent, hobby, or skill?
- Is there some work or task you would do even if you weren't paid?
- Is there some cause or mission that drives you?
- Is there some opportunity that strikes you as worthwhile?

Setting Goals

A goal is an objective. It is somewhere you want to be or something you want to have or do. It can be the goal of owning your own consulting service, the option of working at home, or the objective of amassing $1 million in assets within 10 years to fund your retirement. Whatever they are, they are your personal goals and they reflect who you are and what you want from your life.

Take some time to write down your personal goals, what you want to accomplish with your life. Financial goals are covered later in this chapter. For now, define what you want to do with your life if you had an adequate and guaranteed income.

Your Personal Values

Values are tools that will take you toward your personal goals. Values are standards or qualities that you've established to help you make daily decisions. Those people who succeed in any business have some common personal values. Let's look at those values together to determine your strengths and opportunities.

Self-Awareness

The process of starting and operating any business is difficult. It will require that you constantly test yourself, maintaining what works and changing what doesn't. But that's what many people love about being a business owner: the endless challenges. It makes them aware of their characteristics and requires that they continue to grow.

Hard Work

The great thing about being an independent businessperson is that you get to select which twelve hours of the day you're going to work! As your consulting business grows, you'll spend at least six hours a day producing your service and another two to eight hours marketing and administrating it. If your consulting service is full-time, don't expect to work just a forty-hour week—at least at first.

Discipline

Discipline is the power behind hard work. You can know exactly what needs to be done and still not do it. Self-discipline forces you to act. Having goals that are meaningful to you will increase your self-discipline.

Independence

Great business owners often make poor employees. They're too independent. That's all right. They cannot, however, be stubborn. Business owners must maintain a balance between independence and open-mindedness to succeed.

ESSENTIAL

If your consulting business will involve a spouse or partner, involve her in your business analysis. Interview her for her viewpoint on your personal values and risk tolerance. Ask if she would like to participate in your business and, if so, how. Remember that you will rely on life partners to cooperate in your business decision, even if they don't actively participate. Work together.

Self-Confidence

It takes a lot of self-confidence to start a business. It takes a lot more to make it successful. But self-confidence isn't ego. It's a belief in your unique skills founded on past success. You know you can successfully operate a consulting service because you have the skills—not just the desire—to do so.

Adaptability

Life is chaos. No matter how much you plan, conditions and events change. Products change. Markets change. You will change. A successful business owner must adapt to these changes. Without change, life becomes very dull.

Judgment

To succeed in business, you must make good decisions every day. Wisdom requires knowledge. You must be able to gather complete and accurate facts and make the best decision you can from those facts. You will not be right every time, but you will be right most of the time. This is good judgment.

Stress Tolerance

Stress has been defined as "the confusion created when one's mind overrides the body's desire to clobber some yo-yo who desperately deserves it." Humor can help reduce stress. Stress is a part of everyday life, especially in business. Learning to live with stress without taking it personally can help you succeed in business.

ESSENTIAL

A good place to begin measuring your stress tolerance is in your current employment or responsibilities. Be aware that the stress level of an employer is typically higher than that of an employee. If you're stressed out now, wait until you're the boss. If stress is a problem, find ways to relax your underlying nature and reduce your self-inflicted stress.

Need to Achieve

Success is the achievement of something you go after. It may be the completion of a project, the start of a business, or the learning of a new skill. This need is a driving force within successful business owners that helps give them the energy to reach their goal.

Your personal values will influence daily decisions you make as a professional consultant. Take the time now to consider and analyze your personal values so the consulting business you build will fit you.

Your Financial Goals

As much as you may love helping people, you must also have financial goals. Without a fair salary and profit, you won't be able to help people for very long. To be successful, all goals—including financial ones—must be appropriate, specific, and attainable.

Appropriate

What is an appropriate financial goal for your consulting service? One that funds your other goals. If your business goal is to open a new consulting service office each year for three years, your financial goal must be one that will fund such an ambitious goal. If your business goal is to build a successful consulting service so you can sell it in ten years and retire, your financial goal must match the expected selling price of your business. If your business goal is to make a good salary as well as a fair return on your investment, you must first determine what a good salary and a fair return mean to you.

Specific

There's a popular T-shirt slogan that says: "When I was young, I always wanted to be somebody. I should have been more specific."

Generic goals don't work. They aren't sufficiently clear to help in daily decisions. To be valuable, a goal must be specific:

- An annual net income, after taxes, of at least $75,000.
- An award as the best physical fitness trainer in Smith County.
- Sufficient profit to hire an assistant within six months.
- Contact twelve new prospects each day for the first month.

Make sure your financial and personal goals are specific. Your business plan (see Chapter 7) will be a document of specific goals.

Attainable

One more point to make about goals: They must be attainable. To be useful, they must be realistic. Having a goal of making $1 million a year in income is certainly specific, but for most consultants, it is not attainable. It isn't realistic. Instead, develop goals that are a moderate stretch but can be reached. Give yourself a challenge rather than an impossibility.

One successful tax consulting service owner established a financial goal of developing annual sales of $200,000 within three years in order to take on a partner who could offer other financial services. He then wanted to spend two more years developing the single location—working the bugs out— before selling the business to the partner for enough to pay off his mortgage and do some traveling. His goals were specific and attainable. Yours should be, too.

Risk Tolerance

Business is legalized gambling. When you start a business you're gambling that you will succeed. You're also facing the risk that you will fail and have personal and financial losses. How much does this risk bother you? How much risk can you tolerate?

Everyone's risk tolerance level is different. Some people cannot afford to lose a dime. Of course, as they say in Las Vegas: "One who can't afford to lose, can't afford to gamble." Others say: "I started with nothing. Anything I get is gain." Still others determine potential losses and say: "It's worth the gamble, but I'm going to do whatever I can to improve the odds."

To minimize your business risks, you must understand them and their consequences. Chapter 19 will guide you in managing risk once your business is established. However, you need to consider consulting business risks before you invest time and money into starting your business.

Understanding Risk

As you plan for a new or growing business, you know you're taking some kind of a risk, but what does that mean exactly? And how can you keep the risk to a minimum? Your investors (if you have any) want to know the answers—and so should you.

Risk is the likelihood of loss or injury. In business, risk is the possibility of loss of value. Understandably, you don't want to risk everything you have on a business venture that may not return the invested value plus a reward for accepting the risk. The chances of losing money in an insured savings account, for example, are infinitesimal, so the reward is a small rate of interest. The stock market offers greater potential gains—and losses—than savings because the risk is greater.

FACT

Operating any business is about managing risk. You need to understand the value of what you are investing, consider the potential gains and losses, and make a decision. You will do so as you invest time and money in the daily operation of your venture. Hundreds of business decisions require that you understand the risks involved.

Value

The greater the value of something, the greater the loss if you lose it. People buy health insurance to reduce the risk of major financial loss in the case of catastrophic illness. Other insurance services work on the same principle: someone accepts a portion of the risk of loss in exchange for something of value—your insurance premiums.

QUESTION

How can I calculate probability and risk?
There are numerous software programs that can guide you in estimating business risk. They range from simple risk management to mathematical and statistical probabilities. Use your favorite search engine for searches like *probability calculator, business risk calculator,* and similar terms. Be aware that some are designed for engineering and actuarial probabilities rather than business.

Your business will require an investment of money and time (value) that may be in jeopardy or be exposed to possible loss. You don't want to lose these things of value, so you do what you can to reduce risk to an acceptable limit. You act more conservatively in your transactions or buy insurance as needed. Whenever you make decisions regarding things of value in your business or your life, you (hopefully) consider the risk.

How do you calculate risk? There are complex formulas used by engineers, accountants, and actuaries, but most are based on a simple formula:

$$R = P \times C$$

Translated: *Risk is calculated as the Probability of an event multiplied by the Consequence of it occurring*. To calculate business risk, you need to understand probabilities and consequences.

Probability

Probability is the likelihood that something has happened or will happen. For example, what is the probability that your new business will celebrate its fifth anniversary? What is the probability that the service you provide will be profitable? These are important questions to your business's success. How can you answer them?

In some fields, probability is easy to calculate. Mathematics, for example, deals with probability in firm numbers that don't really change. Smart gamblers live by probability tables in making bets. Statisticians use probability based on historical data. In business, probability is more complicated to calculate because there are often factors that are more difficult to measure, such as the probability of your business still operating in five years. However, there is sufficient historical data to offer a degree of accuracy in calculating probability.

You will use probability in many ways in your business plan and its operation. As you do, seek the most reliable sources of proven or historical data, such as business research resources. Your business plan and activities depend upon the accuracy of these estimates of probability.

Consequence

Consequence is the result of an action. If the result of your business venture's success for five years is that you will have a million dollars in the bank, you will use this fact and the probability of it happening to determine the risk.

In business, quantifying consequences can be difficult and you must rely on an estimate or judgment of approximate value. As with probability, you must consider all resources and use the most reliable ones. The accuracy of your risk calculation depends on how precise your consequence is stated. Estimates are defensible guesses.

Risks of Gambling

Las Vegas is financed by people who don't understand risk. They pay billions of dollars each year to casinos on bad risks. They often make emotional decisions rather than logical ones. "I feel lucky," they say. Luck, as professional gamblers know, has nothing to do with feelings. The pros know that if the odds (probability) and payoff (consequence) are within an acceptable range of risk, the bet is "smart."

Starting and growing a consulting business is a gamble. You may win or you may lose. The smart bet is to understand the risk, accurately determine probabilities and consequences, and then make your decisions based on facts rather than feelings. Yes, there is an element of luck (unknown circumstances) in all enterprises, but those who depend on luck to succeed usually discover how unlucky business can be. Before you begin your venture, understand the risks and rewards as well as your tolerance for risk.

Licensing Requirements

Do you need a business license to be a consultant? Probably. In fact, you may need more than one, depending on what field you're in. How can you find out what licenses are needed? Contact governmental offices and professional organizations.

Local Business Licenses

Once you've determined exactly where your consulting office will be located, you will need to check with local and state governments to see what licenses are required. "Local" may mean your town, township, community, city, county, or regional government. Most require some type of business license application and fee. They want to have a record of your business in case there are complaints from clients or neighbors. Of course, they also want the business license fee.

In addition, most licensing bodies require that you pay some form of tax on your income or your assets. Income taxes will be covered in Chapter 10, which covers keeping good records.

Local Zoning

Most local governments have zoning laws that your business must comply with. The government doesn't want a noisy or high-traffic business setting up in a residential zone. Some zoning laws prohibit any home-based businesses, though many communities look the other way if there are no traffic or noise issues.

To find out about local business zoning requirements, contact your local government office. Make sure your business will comply before deciding to set it up. Many local governments have a one-stop office where businesses can find out about local licensing, zoning, and regulations. Check your local telephone book for appropriate offices.

Professional Licenses

Some types of businesses, especially those in financial fields, require professional licenses. You can find out about these from trade associations in your field. In addition, contact the Small Business Administration (*www .sba.gov*) regarding licenses and permits. In Canada, contact Canada Business Services for Entrepreneurs (*http://canadabusiness.ca*).

Certifications

A certification is an earned credential. For example, the Business Marketing Association (*www.marketing.org*) offers a certified business communicator designation to applicants who meet training and experience requirements and pass a comprehensive test. Other trades have similar certificates available.

Certificates aren't required for most consulting businesses, but they do add credibility to your qualifications. Once you've defined your consulting business, seek out certifications that can help clients recognize your qualifications.

Tools and Equipment for Consulting

Even the simplest consulting business requires tools and equipment. These can include office furniture, office supplies, a telephone system, a computer system, and probably an Internet connection. Many consulting services also require specialty equipment for activity (exercise equipment) or testing (diagnostic equipment).

FACT

The Internal Revenue Service (*www.irs.gov*) allows you to deduct legitimate expenses for your home office. For more information, read Tax Topic 509 on its website. To calculate deductions, you will file Form 8829 (*Expenses for Business Use of Your Home*) with your federal taxes.

Office Furniture

Whether you establish your office in a professional office building or in a spare bedroom, you'll need office furniture. If you will meet with clients in your office, you'll want office furniture that impresses them. Some professional office buildings rent fully furnished offices and even include shared secretarial and receptionist service. Alternately, you can lease office furniture and equipment as needed.

Home offices without client visitors are easier to furnish. A desk can be as simple as a pair of two-drawer file cabinets with a plywood top. Shelving and seating don't have to be fancy, just functional. Before you start your consulting service, you'll need to decide where your office will be and how to best furnish it.

Office Supplies

Office supplies include pens, pencils, paper, file folders, paper clips, and stationery. Most businesses use them. Fortunately, you can easily select office supplies at a local stationery store, office supply franchise store (Staples, OfficeDepot) or online (*www.quill.com, www .reliable.com*). You also can pick them up at a general merchandise store (Walmart, Costco). For now, know that you will need them and estimate how much you will use in a typical month so you can budget for the ongoing expense.

Telephone System

Your consulting service will require a telephone system. Its complexity and cost depend on what you will be doing, how you will interact with clients, and how large your budget is. Many new consultants start with a single cell phone that they take everywhere. If they are office-bound, consultants may prefer a wired or wireless telephone.

Technology has made telephone systems with more features at lower costs. For about $100, you can have a wireless two-line, two-phone system with call waiting, call forwarding, intercom, and a digital answering system. In addition, long-distance service is competitive, so you can keep the costs down for toll-free inbound calls, high-volume outbound calls, and international calls.

ESSENTIAL

Don't forget faxes. Though many consulting businesses have replaced fax machines with e-mail attachments, many clients may still require communication via fax. You may need a dedicated telephone for faxes; sometimes you can share it with a backup voice line. In addition, DSL (digital subscriber line) phone service can often be used for both voice and fax on the same line.

Computer System

Most consulting services could not survive in the modern world without computers and software. Computers have revolutionized business by processing and sharing data at phenomenal speeds. Old businesses shoveled data; new businesses use computers as data bulldozers.

When selecting your consulting business's computer system, answer these questions:

- What software do I need to do my job most efficiently?
- What computer hardware (computer, monitor, printer) does this software require?
- How large a computer system do I need?

This book cannot tell you all of the software programs you will need. However, most businesses require a word processor, spreadsheet program, presentation program, and database program. These common software programs often are bundled together and can interact with each other. You can easily import a spreadsheet or presentation into the word processor to produce a client proposal.

FACT

Microsoft Office is a suite of computer software commonly used in business. It includes Word (word processor), Excel (spreadsheet), PowerPoint (presentation) and other programs. In addition, you can use OpenOffice, a suite of similar and compatible programs: Writer (word processor), Calc (spreadsheet), Impress (presentation) and others. Best of all, OpenOffice is free! Visit *www.openoffice.org* for specifics.

Internet Connection

Consultants rely on the latest information in their field. That means using the Internet for the latest news, statistics, opportunities, and instantaneous communication with clients.

Electronic connection to the Internet is available in a variety of ways. Many businesses use a connection through their telephone company with high-speed (called broadband) connections such as DSL or T1. Others access the Internet through a cable company service, the same people that deliver cable TV. In areas where DSL/T1 or cable connections are not available, businesses use satellite Internet service. There are benefits and limitations to each. Depending on what services you need (fast or unlimited uploading of files, for example), you may choose one over another. In all cases, sign the shortest commitment contract you can so that you can upgrade or reduce costs as your business grows.

Protecting Primary Resources

You will be selling qualified advice to those who can profit from it. To develop good advice, you will need to keep up on the latest information within your chosen fields. This means buying books, subscribing to magazines, and interviewing experts.

Of course, this book can't advise you on all of the primary information resources for your specialty. However, you are probably aware of most of them already. If not, reading books and subscribing to primary trade journals in the specific field will give you many of them. Membership in related trade associations will bring you the rest of them.

Depending on your specialty, you can take advantage of the thousands of free experts on almost any topic available through the federal government. To find them, begin at the primary federal government information website, *www.usa.gov*. Also contact the Small Business Administration (*www.sba.gov*) and agencies within your specialized fields.

Be aware that your primary resources are among your trade secrets. If clients and competitors knew exactly how you did your consulting magic, they may work directly with those resources and not you. Once your business is established, even your support employees should not know or have full access to your primary resources. You've spent much time and effort finding and developing them. Don't give them away to anyone. Instead, process their data into valuable information that clients will buy.

Now that you've considered the many requirements of a consulting service, it's time to begin setting it up. Chapter 4 will start you on the road to setting up your successful consulting business.

Setting Up Your Consulting Service

Setting up any new business can be exciting. It also can be fraught with danger. Because consulting businesses don't require as much start-up capital as other ventures, the risks are lower. However, you still are risking money and time and you want to do it right. This chapter guides you through the selection of a business name, structuring your business, calculating financial requirements, setting up your office, and other critical components of success.

Naming Your Business

What shall you name your consulting business? Is the name important? How can you make sure that competitors don't steal your name? These are legitimate questions that require an answer before you proceed. The following are recommendations from professional consultants who have successfully named their businesses.

Selecting a Name

Depending on the type of consulting services you offer, your business name can be your own name, a variation of your name, or a unique new name. For example:

- Bob Jones, Consultant
- Jones Consulting Services
- X-pert Services

Which business name is better? The answer depends on the image you are trying to project to prospects and clients. Using your own name is practical if your name has defined value. That is, if you have already developed a recognized name in your field, you can make the most of its value. If your name is not as well known or your business is more formal, consider using your surname—or even a made-up surname—as a component of your business name. Finally, if you are considering developing a unique brand that isn't tied to your name, pick a name that communicates better to the client. Remember that the name of your business is for the benefit of your prospects and clients, not you.

Protecting Your Name

Businesses with a name of their own are required to file for a fictitious business name permit. Jones Consulting Services is not the owner's name, it's the business name. To conduct business, Bob Jones must file for a fictitious business name (also known as a DBA—doing business as) with the body that governs businesses in the area in which it is located. The filing is required before the business can be set up and the bank will require it before it will open a business account in that name.

Your business name must be recorded if it is anything except your personal name. For example:

- Bob Jones, Consultant (DBA not required)
- Jones Consulting Services (DBA required)
- X-pert Services (DBA required)

Laws regarding fictitious business names vary by state and municipality. Check with local business authorities to determine your requirements.

Branding Your Name

Branding is developing a recognizable image or symbol that represents its owner. Cattle are branded to indicate ownership. Products are branded to make them easier to identify. Coke, Ford, and CNN all are brand names.

FACT

If your business has a unique name that you would like to protect, you can file for a registered trademark. You will probably need the services of a trademark attorney to do so. For further information, contact the United States Patent and Trademark Office (*http://uspto.gov*), a component of the U.S. Department of Commerce.

Brands are important because they make selection easier for clients, which builds business. For example, you can look for the McDonald's brand in Peoria or Paris and expect a consistent product. Consumers believe that the brand means fast food of a consistent quality and value. You may or may not choose McDonald's, but, if you do, you know what to expect. That consistent brand image has earned McDonald's trillions of dollars.

No matter how small your new business, you should remember that you are building a brand. You eventually want people to hire or rehire you because they believe your services offer value for the investment. Chapter 12, on marketing your services, will cover branding in greater detail.

Structuring Your Business

The first businesses had a simple structure: one owner for one business. Then more money was needed and partnerships emerged. Liability became an issue and corporations were developed. Today, business owners have a variety of structures that can be adapted to the needs and complexities of their venture.

Your small business requires a structure. Which one? The answer depends on many factors, as well as state laws. The factors include investment options, liability, and taxation. Your business plan (see Chapter 7) will define the business structure even before you select a management team. The following is a summary of the most popular configurations. They include sole proprietorship, partnership, limited liability company, S Corporation, and C Corporation.

ALERT

The easiest time to set up the most appropriate business structure is in the planning stage. Once the business is established, it is more difficult to change it. Review your options and seek professional advice from a business attorney and/or accountant. An hour or two of consulting can save you time and money. Maybe your tax consultant will trade services with you.

Sole Proprietorship

A proprietor is a business structure with a single owner. The exception is that some states allow a category called sole proprietor (husband and wife) comprised of a married couple. The sole proprietor does business in his/her/their name and pays personal rather than corporate income taxes.

A sole proprietorship is relatively easy to set up in just a few days. The profits from the business are treated as the owner's personal income, just as if they were wages. The owner(s) will pay federal and state income tax as well as federal self-employment tax. As an employee, you have half of required Social Security and Medicare taxes deducted from your wages; your employer pays the other half. As a sole proprietor, you must pay both sides of these taxes, currently more than 15 percent of your business profits.

The majority of new businesses started each year begin as sole proprietorships. Some eventually take other business structures to attract capital or reduce owner liability. Others retain this structure as they are passed on. At any time, a business can reorganize under a new structure, though it typically occurs when the business wants to move to a new stage in its development.

Partnership

Some businesses require additional knowledge or capital to begin or grow. A partnership is a business structure with two or more individuals as owners. Each partner's contribution to the business is defined and they agree on how the resulting profits will be split. The specific terms are included in a partnership agreement.

ALERT

Beware of companies that offer to incorporate your business for a small fee. Corporate attorneys charge $1,000 or more to handle incorporation for simple businesses. Those that are more complex or have numerous stock levels will cost much more. Discuss your incorporation needs with an experienced business attorney and ask for ways to minimize costs. Most offer pricing options.

For taxes and liability, partners are treated like separate individuals. If the agreement says Partner A gets two-thirds of the profits, that partner will probably be responsible for paying two-thirds of the taxes. It also outlines who has what management responsibilities.

Some partnerships are limited. That is, one or more partners are limited in their rights or responsibilities. It's called a limited partnership. Partners may be limited in what authority they have in the daily operations or in the business liability they accept. A partner without these limits is called a general partner. Your attorney or accountant can help you establish the most appropriate business structure for your new or growing venture.

Limited Liability Company

A limited liability company (LLC) is a hybrid. In some situations, owners are treated as individuals and, in other conditions, as investors in a corporation. The structure is defined in an operating agreement. The LLC business can be managed by an owner-manager or a hired manager.

LLCs are established for two reasons: liability and taxation. The structure is set up to define what will happen if the business loses lots of money. Can creditors come after individual owners? Do they have limited liability? As with other complex business structures, consult with professional advisors to determine which is the most appropriate for your venture.

S Corporation

A corporation is a separate legal unit. It is not the owners; it is, within the law, its own entity. The corporation can be owned by individuals or other corporations, called stockholders. The corporation operates within the law under its own by-laws. Ownership shares are transferable. If an owner dies, the shares are sold or transferred and the corporation lives on. The liability of shareholders is limited, typically to their investment.

An S Corporation (S Corp) is a modified corporate structure based on Subchapter S in Chapter 1 of the Internal Revenue Code (IRC). S Corps are different in that the profits made by the corporation are passed on to the shareholders who must pay taxes on them as individuals. The S Corp does not pay taxes on income; it passes the obligation on.

To become an S Corp, the business must be a domestic corporation or a limited liability company with fewer than 100 shareholders. There must only be one class of stock and the corporation's profits and losses must be passed on to shareholders proportionately. Setting up an S Corp requires professional assistance, but it isn't as difficult as establishing a full corporation. S Corps are especially popular structures for consulting businesses and partnerships that want to grow beyond two or three partners. If you are setting up an S corp, it's a good idea to seek legal counsel.

C Corporation

A C Corporation (C Corp) is a full corporate structure based on Subchapter C in Chapter 1 of the IRC. Unlike S Corps, the C Corp must pay income taxes. The profits or dividends passed on to shareholders are then taxed as income. So-called double taxation is the primary reason many smaller businesses prefer other business structure forms.

The primary advantages to C Corps are that shareholders have limited liability and they are more flexible in ownership. It can have more stockholders than an S Corp and have numerous classes or levels of stock. The New York Stock Exchange (NYSE) and other stock exchanges primarily trade in C Corp stocks. These are termed publicly traded stocks; anyone can buy them and invest in these corporations.

FACT

A share of stock represents a share of ownership in a corporation. It is a share in the equity or value of that corporation. A shareholder or stockholder is an individual or business entity (including another corporation) that owns at least one equity share. In most corporations, a shareholder can participate in corporate elections. If publicly traded, the shares can be bought and sold to others through a stock exchange.

Other options include incorporating in a state other than the one where your business operations are. For example, you can incorporate in Delaware or Nevada. The advantage to a Delaware corporation is that the state's laws benefit larger businesses. More than half of all publicly traded corporations on the NYSE are incorporated in Delaware. Nevada incorporations offer similar benefits to privately held and smaller corporations. Establishing a C Corp is complex and requires professional advice. As you design your business, understand the opportunities and limitations of each structure.

Calculating Financial Requirements

How much money will you need to build a profitable consulting service? To estimate start-up costs, you will need to make your best guess of how much it will cost to set up your office for the day you open the front door to your first client. This includes the cost of preparing and equipping your office, getting required licenses and professional memberships, getting the phone hooked up, and funding your initial advertising.

Estimating Operating Costs

Estimating operating costs can be more difficult because it requires that you estimate your living expenses. Most people who have been employees spend as much as they make; they're not sure exactly what they need to live on. However, by starting with your current net (after taxes) salary, you can roughly calculate whether you require more or less to live on. If you operate your business as a sole proprietor, your income taxes and self-employment (social security) tax will be paid by the business.

Other operating costs are those expenses that you will pay each month to keep the doors open (fixed or overhead expenses) as well as those that increase as sales increase (variable expenses). Business start-up experts suggest that a new consultant should calculate start-up requirements as:

- one year of living expenses
- 10 percent contingency
- six months of office expenses

From this, the new consultant can deduct:

- cash and securities on hand
- accounts receivable
- contracted but unbilled business
- credit line access

For example, if you need $60,000 to live on for the next year, add $6,000 as contingency. If office expenses are estimated at $2,000 a month, add in $12,000 to cover the first six months. If $4,000 is needed for a computer and office furniture, the initial capital requirements are $82,000. If you have $20,000 in cash, $5,000 in money owed to you, and $30,000 in consulting contracts, you still need $27,000. A credit line of at least $27,000 or a loan for the same amount will theoretically give you sufficient money to start and operate your consulting business through the first year.

Finding Start-up Money

Where can you get the money you need to start your business? A survey of small businesses found that 73 percent were funded by the owners and their families, 13 percent by outside investors, 8 percent by banks, and 6 percent by alliances with other businesses. However, the survey reported that the businesses that were owner-financed had the highest failure rate.

QUESTION

Where can I get the money to start my consulting service?
In addition to self-funding, outside investors, banks, and alliances, many fund their business by earning a large consulting contract. Their business grows around a primary client for whom they offer reduced rates for a long-term contract. With timely billing, they can meet expenses and build a reputation that will earn additional clients and success.

Choosing Your Office

Where should your office be? At home? In the business district? Near your competitors' offices? The answer isn't up to you—it's up to your clients.

ALERT

Home business experts recommend that if you do choose to establish a home office, set aside a dedicated area and treat it as if it were ten miles away. Close the door during nonbusiness hours and turn off your computer. Otherwise, you may allow your business to manage your time instead of the other way around.

Home Office

One of the business advantages that technology offers is the ability to work virtually from anywhere in the world. You can simultaneously talk on the phone to suppliers in Indonesia, e-mail clients in Toronto, and text your assistant in Denver—and you can do it all dressed in your pajamas. Many consultants get into this field and even select their specialty based on whether they can work from a home office.

The downside of working from a home office is learning to separate home and office. It requires that you not only set aside a specific area for an office, but also that you separate your life into work and no-work times. Otherwise, you'll be responding to business e-mail when you should be relaxing or enjoying family relationships.

Business Office

Many consultants compromise by renting a small office that is near their home and/or their primary client's business office. This helps separate home and business while reducing potential commute time. Where could you rent a business office?

- Near your clients' offices
- Near a restaurant where you can easily lunch with prospects
- Near an airport (if you fly frequently)
- In a professional building that shares support staff

Another option is an SBA incubator. The Small Business Administration (*www.sba.gov*) encourages the development of new businesses. Some regional offices have Small Business Development Centers (SBDCs) that offer small offices and even support staff to start-up businesses that meet specific criteria. Contact your regional SBA office (listed in your local telephone book) for additional information.

Near Competitors

Remember that your consulting business's location should be selected for the convenience of your clients and prospects, not simply your commute. If your business is just starting up, the most convenient place for your clients may be near their current consulting service's location. Move in next door.

A small office in the same building as that of a major competitor may catch the eye of prospects. It also adds credentials to your business. "Yes, we're next door to J.P. Smart Consulting in the Yoko Building." Additionally, use signs to attract attention to your office.

No Office

Some successful consulting services don't actually have an office. Personal consultants, especially, have the option of working at their client's location or a neutral location. They can manage communications with a portable laptop computer that they use wherever they are.

If your specialty allows you to not have a physical office, you still will want a mailing address. You can use a mailing service or your home address. A professional mailing address is preferred, especially if there's a chance that prospects or clients may show up unannounced. Many professional office buildings offer mail drop services at a low fee.

Setting Your Hours

Which half of the day will you work at your new consulting business? And why is the answer important? Because clients and prospects who want to contact you should be able to reach you quickly. That's why you should set your consulting hours based on your clients' needs rather than your own.

For example, personal fitness trainers often work evenings and weekends. Stock market consultants are available when the stock exchange is open as well as before and after. If they consult on the Nikkei and other foreign markets, their hours must fit those of their clients as well as the marketplace. You need to define your business hours, including the days, hours, and holidays you will be available and when you will be on call.

Days

"Days of business" means different things in various businesses. Many businesses operate Monday through Friday, though some are Monday through Saturday or even Tuesday through Friday. Other businesses operate Friday-Saturday-Sunday. Whatever your prospects and clients work should be your minimum.

International businesses sometimes have different weekends than those in North America. For example, businesses in many Christian countries are closed on Sunday. In Jewish countries, their holy day is Saturday, and in Islamic countries, many don't conduct business on Fridays. If your consulting business is international, you must respect your clients' preferences.

Hours

Your consulting service's hours, again, depend on when clients want you to work. Establish your own working hours to reflect the needs of those who need your services. Tax advisors often work long hours from January through April, cutting hours back in the summer. Others must be available to clients until late evening or on weekends.

If you're not sure what hours your prospective clients prefer, ask them. Also find out what hours your competitors are open for business. If you find that competitors are not serving their clients all the hours the client wants, you may have an opportunity to make your services available and pick up business.

Holidays

Some consulting services can close during clients' holidays and others must be available during them. For example, a banking advisor typically doesn't have to serve clients on banking holidays. However, a dog trainer may need to work holidays when clients have free time from their jobs.

On Call

Some consultants are on call 24/7. A client calls and you must answer. If that's what your clients need and you've decided that you can provide 24/7 service, then those are your hours. Many time-critical service businesses require that their consultants be available on-call. If an automated teller machine breaks or a client has a medical emergency, the appropriate consultant must be ready to take action. If these are your clients, be ready to give them the service they need—and are paying for.

Advanced Time Management

How can the consulting service business owner ensure her time is well managed? First, by organizing work space so that important papers don't get lost and unimportant papers do. You can also make a rule that you will avoid handling papers more than once. If you pick up a piece of paper, make a decision regarding it right then.

ESSENTIAL

A time management planning system can help you get the most out of your day. Specifically designed systems give you a handy place to record appointments, daily to-do lists, special projects, and contact information. If you prefer to manage time using computers, there are numerous contact management and scheduling programs that will help you manage your time.

Set up a regular work schedule. Whatever it is, try to stick to it. If you manage your time well, you will be able to. If you have one time of the day that seems more productive for you than others, plan your most important functions around it.

Using Time Efficiently

What about travel and waiting time? Take work with you in a briefcase or purchase a laptop computer that you can use to stay productive every minute. As your time management skills improve you'll learn how to do more than one thing at a time. You could be making job notes or talking with a key employee or gathering information on an upcoming project while you're waiting to talk with a client.

Meetings seem to be one of the biggest time-wasters there are. But you can change this by thoroughly preparing for all of your meetings. To be productive, meetings must have a purpose or an agenda and a time limit. Even if you didn't call the meeting, if you see that it has no focus or structure you can step in and say, "I have another appointment in an hour. What topics do we have to cover?" and come up with an agenda that way.

Reduce Stress

Time and stress are closely related. The lack of time to do what you need to do often increases personal stress. How do you manage both? The following are ideas from a successful consultant.

- Plan your time and establish priorities on a daily "to do" list.
- Decide what your prime time is and do your most important or difficult tasks then.
- Set business hours, specific times when you're at work and times when you turn on the answering machine because you're on duty but off call. You, your clients, and your family will appreciate knowing your set routine, even though you know that for special events or emergencies you can break that schedule.
- Confirm your appointments one-half day before the appointment—in the afternoon for next morning or morning for that afternoon. It will save you time, and your clients will appreciate the consideration.
- If you're working from home, give your business as much of a separate and distinct identity as possible. Although you might save a few dollars by using the dining room table as a desk and a cardboard box as a file cabinet, the stress and strain of operating without proper space and supplies will take its toll.
- Have a separate room or area for your business, with a separate entrance if clients visit. Consider sound-proofing so your family won't be bothered by your noise and vice versa. In addition to the psychological and physical comfort of having a separate room for your home office, the IRS requires it in order for you to make a legitimate claim for tax deductions.

Keep all of these tips in mind as you make plans for your business.

CHAPTER 5

Resources for Consultants

A resource is a person, product, or service that can help you reach your objectives. Resources for your consulting service include education and training, your own experiences, trade associations, conventions, seminars, training courses, publications, and governmental offices. Together they can increase your working knowledge of consulting services and business as well as help you understand how to work efficiently and profitably.

Analyzing Your Knowledge

What do you know? Consulting is a knowledge business and information is your inventory. Whatever consulting field you select, you must have extensive knowledge—even be considered an expert. That's what your clients want and that's what they pay for. They may ask for advice on how to build a bridge or to win more often at bridge. If you're a consultant in one of these fields, you must know the answer.

Analyzing your knowledge means documenting your education and training relevant to your field, defining your experience and what you have learned, and translating your knowledge into terms the client can understand.

Your Education and Training

You will hear the question often: Where did you get your training in this field? It's a fair question. No one will entrust their life savings to a financial consultant whose primary credential is graduation from bartending school. Nor will someone buy advice on starting an online business if the "consultant" has no training in technology or business.

As you define and refine your own consulting service concept, list your education and training in various fields. Most modern workers have more than one resume. They have training in two or even three fields or specialties. List your education and training by topics as if you were writing a resume for a consulting job. Include high school courses, college courses, graduate school education, external degrees, seminars, conferences, and adult education classes you've completed. Then write a short summary of what you learned from the training. Did you expand your knowledge of a topic, develop new skills, or both?

Your Experience

Knowing isn't the same as doing. You need experience, participation in and learning from situations and events. For example, experience in managing real estate transactions can be valuable if you are selling your knowledge in this field. Clients will want to know that you not only have real estate education and training, but also have practical experience. Most important, they want to be assured that you have gained valuable knowledge from this experience. Write a summary of what you have learned from your experiences related to the consulting fields you are considering. If you plan to be an etiquette consultant, list situations and events where you have successfully applied your knowledge of cultural etiquette.

QUESTION

What experience-developing options do I have?
Find opportunities that are related to your field. If you want to be a tax consultant, volunteer for the AARP senior tax assistance program (*www.aarp.org*) and help elderly filers. Alternately, apply for an internship in a trade or organization that will look good on your resume.

You also can learn by observation. You don't always have to directly participate in situations to gain knowledge from them. You can watch and learn. For example, you don't have to be a child to observe what children need to be happy. You can carefully study them and learn from your observations.

- Which of your own decisions have been successful and which have not?
- Was there any specific advice or resources that seemed to work best?
- If you have hired consultants in the past, what did you look for in them?
- Did you have a problem for which you would have paid well for a solution?
- Is there some advice you have received from others that you feel has been invaluable to you?
- List five or six elements that, in your experience, must be included in an effective consulting service.

Many people become consultants because they have used consultants in a field and have been dissatisfied with the results. They think, "I can do better than that!" Your experience in selecting, hiring, and using consultants is invaluable as you define what you want to do and how you wish to do it. Take time to review your own experiences with consulting services. Consider what advice you have received as well as what advice you would have liked to receive.

In any business, success requires empathy and empathy requires experience. The more you understand about your client, the better you will be able to serve her.

ESSENTIAL

Consulting is an exchange. You have the knowledge and wisdom on a specific topic. Your client has the money. You exchange what you know, in the form of sharing information or designing a solution, and in return your client gives you money. The transaction must have sufficient value to both parties.

Vertical Translation

Consultants are like teachers; they translate their knowledge into facts and concepts. Teachers simplify the complexities of a topic, such as history, into bite-size specifics, such as the place and dates of an important event. They then build on those facts with additional facts. Eventually, the student "knows" about the conditions of the event as if he were there. The student has knowledge. This process is vertical translation, converting complex knowledge into simpler knowledge and communicating it to others a step at a time.

Your job as a consultant will include vertical translation or the education of clients. You will share your knowledge with them, teaching as much as they can absorb about a topic.

Expanding Your Credentials

As you develop your list of consulting credentials, you may see holes. Your specialty may require a specific degree or a professional certification that you don't have. If so, it's time to beef up your consulting resume. You'll add more education and more experience.

More Education

Many people get a formal education in one field, then move to a related or even dissimilar field for their career. For example, an arts major may wind up working in the computer field. If your new consulting field requires a specific level of education, you may have to get it.

ALERT

Not all educational institutions are fully accredited. Some will sell you a degree on easy terms, but the degree is worthless if it isn't accepted by other learning institutions, employers, or knowledgeable clients. Talk with colleges and professional educators in your field to help you choose accredited education and training sources.

To expand your formal education or training, first define exactly what credentials are required in your field. It may be a specific degree, such as an AS or MBA. Or you may need technical certification, such as the Computer Technology Industry Association (CompTIA) A+ certification program (*http://certification.comptia.org*). Then find a reputable program that can help you earn that credential. By expanding your credentials, you can potentially earn more as a consultant.

More Experience

Knowledge also can come from experience. Your consulting field may not require a college degree, but it will require that you have worked in your chosen field for many years—and learned valuable lessons.

If your field is experience-based, make sure that your consulting resume includes that experience. If not, begin to develop it now. For example, if you want to be a retail consultant and have worked in the retail trade as a manager but never as a clerk, get a job as a clerk to see the business from that perspective. You won't have to work very long to recognize challenges and opportunities that add to your experience and knowledge.

Knowledge Resources

Knowledge is power. It also is the source of income for consultants. The more you know—the more client problems you can solve with your knowledge—the more you will earn. Your education, training, and experience form the base on which you will build your inventory of knowledge. In addition, you will use trade associations, conventions and seminars, books, magazines and trade journals, and other valuable resources. Nearly all can be accessed through one of the most powerful tools for consultants: the Internet.

The Internet

The Internet has not only changed business over the past decade, it also has dramatically changed education and experience. The Internet is a global system of *inter*connected computer *net*works. Data is exchanged between the computers using a data language called Internet Protocol. Each digital message includes its destination address, just like letters in the postal system. The messages are distributed to the appropriate computer by using its address. The messages may be information, files, instructions, or other data. When you open up a new web page in your computer's browser program, it sends a request for data, accepts it from the Internet, and displays it on your computer screen.

Because the Internet Protocol and other codes are standardized worldwide, your computer can communicate with other computers anywhere in the world. You can exchange e-mail with friends in France or download programs from Dubai. The Internet is a tool that most consultants cannot do without.

How do consultants use the Internet? The most obvious uses are electronic mail (e-mail), file transfer, and graphic display. HyperText Markup Language (HTML) is used to display text and graphics on computer screens. Financial consultants can watch stock market activity in real time, personal trainers can communicate with clients via e-mail, and salary administrators can do research on the latest employment trends. Nearly all consultants can benefit from the Internet. It's a vital resource.

Trade Associations for Consultants

A trade association is a group of businesses that agree to share information regarding their trade among themselves. Plumbers have them, car makers have them—and so do consultants. A comprehensive listing of trade and consumer associations is available at most public libraries under the title *Encyclopedia of Associations*, published by Gale Research/Cengage Learning (*http://gale.cengage.com*). You also can find associations using online search engines.

There are associations for bridal consultants, acoustical consultants, merger and acquisition consultants, professional writing consultants, computer consultants, airport consultants, insurance management consultants, and many others.

A few of the trade associations for business consultants include:

- American Management Association (*www.amanet.org*)
- Association of Management Consulting Firms (*http://amcf.org*)
- Association of Professional Consultants (*http://consultapc.org*)
- Institute of Management Consultants (*www.imcusa.org*)

In addition, most specialties have their own associations, such as:

- National Exercise & Sports Trainers Association (*http://nestacertified.com*)
- American Association of Political Consultants (*http://theaapc.org*)
- Association of Image Consultants International (*http://aici.org*)
- Golf Consultants Association (*http://golfconsultants.org.uk*)

There are thousands more associations of consultants. Use an Internet search engine to find them: "YOUR FIELD consulting association" and variations. You also can identify trade associations in your field by reading the literature or websites of your competitors to determine what associations they belong to.

Conventions and Seminars for Consultants

Many professional associations and marketing groups sponsor annual conventions of members and professionals. Workshops, guest speakers, and roundtables are organized to encourage consultants from across the country to share information, techniques, and ideas. Associations that sponsor conventions include Association of Management Consulting Firms and American Association of Professional Consultants.

Books for Consultants

There is a wide shelf of books written to help consultants ply their trade. Besides the one you're reading, they include:

- *How to Make it Big as a Consultant* by William A. Cohen (AMACOM)
- *Million Dollar Consulting: The Professional's Guide to Growing a Practice* by Alan Weiss (McGraw-Hill)
- *Start and Run a Profitable Consulting Business* by Douglas A. Gray (Self-Counsel Press)
- *The Consultant's Calling: Bringing Who You Are to What You Do* by Geoffrey M. Beliman (Jossey-Bass Inc.)
- *The Independent Consultant's Q & A Book* by Lawrence Tuller (Adams Media)

You can find other books on consulting at bookstores and on the Internet.

Magazines and Trade Journals

It pays to stay up-to-date with the latest in trends and news. The following are a few of the many magazines and journals for consultants.

- Consulting Magazine (*http://consultingmag.com*)
- Journal of Legal Nurse Consulting (*www.aalnc.org*)
- Consultant News (*http://consultant-news.com*)
- Magazine for Independent Professionals (*http://1099.com*)

There are hundreds of other professional magazines for consultants. In addition, consultants should subscribe to the primary journals in their trade. If you're a dog training consultant, make sure you get all the dog magazines. If you consult on interior decorating, subscribe to the primary magazines in this field, both those for consumers and those for professional designers. You need to know what is happening in your trade.

Consulting Service Opportunities

A business opportunity is an arrangement by which someone who has found success in a specific business teaches you how to do the same. A business opportunity is different from a franchise because the requirements for offering a franchise, and the related fees, are much higher than they are for an opportunity. Depending on the opportunity, you may be licensed to use their name in your advertisement. A supplier will furnish you with a product that you can then resell to your clients.

Franchises

Franchising is a form of licensing by which the owner (the franchisor) of a product or service distributes through affiliated dealers (the franchisees). The franchise license is typically for a specific geographical area. The product or service is marketed by a brand name (McDonalds, Chevrolet), and the franchisor controls the way it is marketed. The franchisor requires consistency among the franchisees: standardized products or services, trademarks, uniform symbols, equipment, and storefronts. The franchisor typically offers assistance in organizing, training, merchandising, and management. In exchange, the franchisor receives initial franchise fees and an ongoing fee based on sales levels.

There is a wide variety of franchises available for those who want to sell advice to others. They include wedding consulting, financial and investment planning, shipping consultants, stock sales, building inspection, small business consulting, accounting services, and many more franchise opportunities.

Franchise Opportunities

One useful source of information on available franchises is the International Franchise Association (*http://franchise.org*). The IFA's *Franchise Opportunities Guide* is a comprehensive listing of franchisors by industry and business category. *Franchising Opportunities* is their bi-monthly magazine. Their newsletter, Franchising World, includes information on developing trends in franchising. Other sources include *Entrepreneur, Income Opportunities*, and other magazines available on most newsstands.

Small Business Administration Resources

Founded more than forty years ago, the U.S. Small Business Administration, or SBA, (*http://sba.gov*) has offices in 100 cities across the United States and a charter to help small businesses start and grow. The SBA offers counseling and booklets on business topics, and administers a small business loan guarantee program. To find your area's SBA office, check the white pages of metropolitan telephone books in your region under "United States Government, Small Business Administration."

Answer Desk

The SBA also operates the Small Business Answer Desk, a toll-free response line (800-827-5722) that answers questions about SBA services. The e-mail address is *answerdesk@sba.gov*. In addition, the SBA sponsors the 13,000 Service Corps of Retired Executives (SCORE) volunteers, Active Corps of Executives (ACE) volunteers, Business Development Centers, and Technology Access Centers listed online at *http://sba.gov*.

SCORE (*www.score.org*) is a national nonprofit association with the goal of helping small businesses. SCORE is sponsored by the SBA and offices are usually in or near the local SBA office. SCORE members, who are retired men and women, and ACE members, who are still active in their own business, donate their time and experience to counseling individuals regarding small business.

Publications

The SBA offers numerous publications, services, and videos for starting and managing small businesses. Publications are available on products/ideas/inventions, financial management, management and planning, marketing, crime prevention, personnel management, and other topics. The booklets can be purchased at SBA offices; from SBA Publications, P.O. Box 30, Denver, CO 80201; or for free online at *http://sba.gov*. Ask first for SBA Form 115A, *The Small Business Directory*, which lists available publications and includes an order form.

SBDC

The 700 Small Business Development Centers (SBDCs) are regional centers funded by the SBA and managed in conjunction with regional colleges. An SBDC offers free and confidential counseling for small business owners and managers, new businesses, home-based businesses, and people with ideas concerning retail, service, wholesale, manufacturing, and farm businesses. SBDCs sponsor seminars on business topics, assist in developing business and marketing plans, inform entrepreneurs of employer requirements, and teach cash flow budgeting and management. SBDCs also gather information sources, assist in locating business resources, and make referrals.

FACT

The SBA offers monthly web chats, online seminars, and discussions on topics that are important to small businesses. Topics include preparing for disaster, doing business with the federal government, managing business credit, and year-end tax savings. Transcripts are available. For more information, visit *http://sba.gov/tools*.

SBI

Small Business Institutes are partnerships between the SBA and nearly 500 colleges offering counseling services to area businesses. SBIs conduct market research, develop business and marketing plans, and help small businesses work out manufacturing problems. Contact your regional SBA office to find out if a local college has such a program. You could get free or low-cost assistance from the college's business faculty and students.

Tax Information Resources

The U.S. Treasury Department's Internal Revenue Service offers numerous Small Business Tax Education Program videos through their regional offices. Topics include depreciation, business use of your home, employment taxes, excise taxes, starting a business, sole proprietorships, partnerships, self-employed retirement plans, Sub-Chapter S corporations, and federal tax deposits.

Home Business Taxes

If you're considering using a portion of your home as a business office, request *Business Use of Your Home* (Publication 587) from the Internal

Revenue Service (*www.irs.gov*). It's free and will help you determine if your business qualifies for this option as well as how to take advantage of it to lower your taxes.

Car Expenses

Depending on how much you use your business vehicle for personal use, you can either list all costs of operating the vehicle as an expense or you can deduct a standard mileage rate as an expense when you file income taxes. For more information, request *Business Use of a Car* (Publication 917) from the Internal Revenue Service (*www.irs.gov*). There's no charge for this publication.

Other Deductible Expenses

What business expenses are deductible? There's a long list. The best answer is found in a free publication offered by the Internal Revenue Service, *Business Expenses* (Publication 535) available at any IRS office or online at *www.irs.gov*. You can choose to deduct a limited amount of what you spend to acquire certain tangible property for use in your business instead of treating the amount as a capital expense.

CHAPTER 6

Identifying Your Clients

Your consulting service will profit from offering expert advice and solutions to clients that need them. If you don't identify potential clients who will benefit from your solutions, you will not succeed. As you consider and select the type of consulting services you will provide, it is vital that you also identify clients who will benefit from them. This chapter will help you find them.

Who Are Your Clients?

To identify who your prospective clients are, you first need to decide what you are selling. The previous chapters offered numerous ideas, outlined the job of consulting and its requirements, showed you how to set up a consulting service, and offered professional resources. It's now time to define your consulting service and those who will best benefit from your knowledge and advice.

Define Your Service

What are you proposing to sell? Chapter 1 offered a list of more than 150 broad consulting fields and each has numerous specialties within it. In addition, each specialty can be approached differently. You can specialize in instruction or advice. For example, as a party consultant, you can offer classes in hosting a holiday party or you can coordinate all aspects of a corporate party—or both.

To help you define your consulting service, the following list includes some example definitions:

- Assist shopping mall developers with land-use planning.
- Help struggling college students learn how to study more effectively.
- Consult with homeowners who are considering major remodeling projects.
- Help employers read and understand applicant body language.
- Offer problem resolution classes to couples preparing for marriage.
- Offer plans and advice to large landowners on renewable forestry options.
- Advise families on cost-effective vacations in foreign countries.

There are thousands of other consulting service concepts available. Each can be implemented in various ways depending on the consultant and the clients. For every problem-solver there is a problem that others want solved.

Find Prospects

Once you have defined what services you will offer, identifying prospective clients is much easier. For example, if your specialty is helping employers read and understand applicant body language, your prospects, certainly, are employers. More specifically, they are employers who are making critical hires and need all the information they can gather on candidates. Some prospects will want their human resource staff to attend a seminar on reading candidate body language. Others will want you to participate in critical hiring interviews and offer readings and advice.

You're defining your prospects: Employers who need information or advice on hiring candidate body language. You can be more specific, focusing on employers in the financial and banking industries, in retail management, or in other fields. These are the people who will pay you for your knowledge and advice. In Chapter 7, you will learn more about writing a business plan, which will help you research and summarize your prospective clients.

What Do They Need?

Defining what you offer and to whom helps you focus on your prospective clients. Why should they buy any services from you? Because they need them. Part of your job in finding prospective clients is to help them recognize their legitimate need.

Prospective clients need solutions to specific problems. Your consulting business should be designed to offer and, if necessary, implement those solutions. Whether your clients want to build a retirement nest egg or lose twenty pounds by the holidays, the consultant's job is to identify and resolve a client's need.

Take a look at the high traffic in a shopping mall. Not everyone who shops buys. There are many reasons for this, including the fact that there is no current perceived need. In addition, the prospect may not have the authority or the money to buy. For example, a husband may love the new model television but, by agreement, won't buy until he and his wife are mutually committed to the purchase of a specific television.

What authority is required to make a purchase? The authority to decide on and pay for a selection. It may be implied authority: a young woman orders a hamburger. Or it may be deferred authority: a family lets Junior decide where they will have lunch. Or it could be cooperative authority: the couple must agree on a lunch location. Market research and analysis may not tell you much about the buying authority of your clients. You will need to do your own research with individuals to better understand how buyers buy.

How can you determine what level of buying authority a client has? Ask. Some of the questions that can help you discover buying authority include:

- Is there anyone else who needs this information before a purchase can be made?
- Does your manager/partner/lender need to help with this decision?
- Would you like to discuss this purchase with anyone else before making a decision?

Similar questions, based on what you are selling and to whom, can help you identify buying authority and direct your selling efforts appropriately.

ESSENTIAL

Whether you are selling your services to a person or to a corporation, you are actually selling to an individual. That individual may represent the need of hundreds or even thousands of other people, but your client is still an individual. Treat prospective clients as individual people who have specific and valuable problems and your consulting service will surpass that of your competitors.

In addition, you need to understand how people other than individual clients participate in the buying decision. Some are initiators who make the suggestion but don't make the purchase: I think those shoes would look lovely on you. Others are influencers: If you don't buy those shoes right now, I will. Still others are permitters: Buy those shoes if you like them. As you study individual clients, you will learn what authority they have and need to make buying decisions. Knowing how and why prospective clients may buy from you will help you in identifying and selling to them.

Types of Businesses

Defining and finding clients requires that you understand what business, if any, they are in. You can then determine better what type of business you are in. It's easier than you think.

First, you will decide whether your business will sell your consulting services to consumers (the general public) or to other businesses. Selling to consumers, such as retail stores and personal service, is called business-to-consumers and abbreviated B2C. If your clients are other businesses, you will operate a business-to-business (B2B) venture. There's also business-to-government (B2G) selling, but it's similar to B2B.

ESSENTIAL

Your business can't be all things to all people. All businesses, especially consulting services, must find a specialty—a niche market—in which they can be a major resource. Even the largest consulting firms in the world specialize. Find yours, then clearly identify your prospective clients.

Second, you can categorize your business as offering products, services, or both. A consultant offers a service and a training business sells a combination of products and services. You also must determine whether your clients are businesses, consumers, or the government.

Third, you can categorize your client's business by what level in the marketing process it functions in. For example, a toy store is retail, a company that sells toys to toy stores is a wholesaler, and a business that makes toys is a manufacturer. Some businesses import or distribute toys, offering them to wholesalers or directly to retailers.

Fourth, your clients' business can be categorized by size. Depending on the industry, a small business is one with fewer than 100 employees, a medium-sized business has up to 500 employees, and a large business has more. In the European Union, businesses often are smaller and these category numbers are halved.

Finding Clients

Chapter 12 deals with marketing, which will also tell you where to find groups of clients. It may identify them by zip code, income levels, commuting hours, or hair color. However, these are still groups and not individual clients. To plan your business, you must know your clients as individuals. Where should you look?

Find Suspects

Let's define client categories. A suspect is a person who may be a candidate for the services you plan to offer. A prospect is one who you have clearly identified as a potential client; to become a client, you only need to help the person identify and value problems that need solutions. A client is someone to whom you have sold a service or product and potentially can sell more. Business is a process. The process of consulting requires that you identify suspects, qualify them as prospects, and sell them on becoming clients.

Armed with your consulting business definition, you now can define who your suspects are—people who may be candidates for your services. The questions you'll need to answer include:

- Who are they?
- What do they do for a living?
- Where do they work?
- What common identities do they have? Are they members in a specific club, neighbors who share common interests, or attendees at the same annual convention?

Once suspects are identified, you can begin the process of learning more about them and how to help them identify common problems that you can solve. If your service is to help individuals select appropriate pets from local animal shelters, you can use advertising and influencers to convert suspects into prospects.

Finding Influencers

Again, not everyone who shops buys. However, many who make the decision to buy do so with the help of initiators, influencers, and permitters. Who are they? Interview prospective clients to find out.

- Do you typically buy consulting services by yourself or with others?
- When you buy consulting services, does someone help you make the decision?
- Did anyone suggest that you buy this service?
- Have you suggested to others that they buy a similar service?

In addition, many types of transactions have influencers that you may not recognize as such. For example, someone may buy a brand of toothpaste or a car because an influential person buys it. Celebrity endorsements are popular for this reason. In many communities, there are local influencers who are respected for their knowledge and authority, It may be the local mayor or city official, a member of the clergy, or a minor celebrity. In developing your consulting business, finding and interviewing these influencers can help you build your venture with minimal effort. An endorsement of your consulting business can influence lenders and investors.

QUESTION

How can I find local influencers?
Interview the editor or publisher of your local newspaper, asking for referrals to other influential individuals. If there is a primary business in town that you hope to get as a client, get an early commitment so that your business and marketing plans can mention this fact. Ask the chamber of commerce manager and other association executives for guidance and referrals to local influencers.

Asking Clients

There are two primary methods of determining what clients want: ask them and watch them. Of course, before your business opens its doors, you don't have clients to ask or observe. An existing business that wants to grow does. Start-up companies, however, can study a competitor's clients to determine what they want. You can even become a client of your primary competitors.

If you do get the opportunity to interview future clients on their choices and desires, make your interviews measurable. Standardize the questions you ask. For example, "What do you like about Acme Relocation Service?" is an open-ended opinion question that can take the interview off into a dozen different directions. However, "Do you ever purchase relocation advice?" is a quantifiable question answered with either yes or no.

The key to getting good market data from client interviews is to ask a few important and quantifiable questions. Define what you want to know before you write your questions and start asking them. For example, if your survey goal is to determine whether your wedding consultancy should offer a line of designer wedding dresses, your interview questions could be:

- What brands of wedding dresses do you like the best?
- Have you seen ads for Dreamland Dresses?
- Dreamland Dresses are priced 25 percent below comparable designer wedding dresses. Does this price difference appeal to you?
- If our wedding service carried Dreamland Dresses, would you consider purchasing them?
- What do you think about designer dresses versus budget dresses?

That last question, obviously, can't be answered by yes or no. It's an open-ended question designed to get the interviewee to talk more. Not all survey questions should require closed, multiple-choice responses. Sometimes you can learn more of what the client wants with an open-ended question than with a dozen closed questions. They're just not as easy to quantify and most interviewers save them for the last questions.

Frequently, market analysis turns up hidden and unmet needs that offer a better direction to businesses. The better you understand your buyers, the more you will sell.

Quantifying Responses

By standardizing your client survey and primarily using closed questions, you can soon develop a relatively accurate report on the survey topic. How many prospective clients should you interview? The more you get, the more accurate your survey will be. The higher the price of what you will be selling, the more surveys you should take. If they are short and uncomplicated surveys, you can give one in less than a minute.

Survey says: "Among 105 clients interviewed, 78 percent have heard of Dreamland Dresses, Dreamland is preferred two-to-one over Chantel brand, and, if available from my wedding service at a lower price, they would consider buying them. Overall, interviewees prefer budget wedding dresses that look identical to designer dresses, and Dreamland is the favorite of the majority." That is the type of actionable data that your wedding service can use as you add profitable product lines to your consulting business.

Features and Benefits

Whatever your business sells is more than a service or a product. It is a solution to a problem that your clients have. The problem may be finding a safe place to care for their children during the workday, eating a healthy and delicious meal where it is convenient to them, or reducing the cost of manufacturing equipment by purchasing it from a reputable importer. All consumers are seeking solutions to specific problems. All businesses are established to help consumers solve problems. Consultants, especially, are in the problem-solving business.

How do consumers discover these solutions? Through businesses explaining the features and benefits of their products and services. A feature is a characteristic. Typically, it's a primary or even unique feature. It's a characteristic that buyers are seeking or should be seeking as they make a purchase. More important, a benefit is the reason they seek the feature. It is what the product or service offers to the buyer. Both of these topics—features and benefits—will be described in greater detail in coming chapters as you develop your business concept and match it to clients. For now, consider the topics as they relate to your consulting business's description of services and products offered.

Service Features

Services aren't tangible, but they still have features. For example, a time management consultant offers a service that features proven methods and results. The business owners and employees know how to help others manage their time better. That's the service feature.

Businesses typically offer more than one feature. Service businesses, for example, understand what their clients require and offer a variety of services, each with numerous features. A time management consultant may also offer training classes featuring concise guides that summarize what is learned in the class. This is a secondary service feature. Include a comprehensive list of service features in your consulting business plan (see Chapter 7).

Service Benefits

Clients want to know: What's in it for me? What's the benefit? Your consulting business plan should summarize the benefits that clients will receive for primary and secondary services. What do your clients want and how will they benefit from it?

In addition, if your consulting business has investors, your plan should think of them as clients and answer the same question: What's in it for me? How will the investors benefit from investing in your business opportunity?

QUESTION

What's the difference between a product and a service?
A product is tangible. You can touch it. A service is intangible. Oral advice offered to a client is an intangible service. A written report for a client is a service provided as a document product. Even though some consulting services offer tangible products, they are secondary to the service. Consulting is considered a service business in which some products are produced and/or sold.

Product Features

Many consulting businesses eventually sell products as well as services. For example, a seminar is a service product, as are training aids. The products sold by any business have features or characteristics. A seminar has a convenient location and valuable agenda, a computer printer uses low-cost ink cartridges, a car has unique styling. The specific products your business sells will have explicit features. Your business, too, will have characteristics that make it better or unique. Your business plan must not assume that readers will already know what features your products and business have. You must tell them.

Product Benefits

Do your potential clients really care about the primary features of your business? They should. In fact, that's why you even mention the features—to indicate the benefits. Clients of Acme Communication Services don't need to go anywhere else when looking for marketing communications (marcom) advice. The primary benefit is ease of shopping.

Benefits must be described in terms the client understands. You can find all typical marcom advice and services at Acme. That's the benefit. Your investors want to know what features and benefits your business expects to develop. Your marketing strategy (see Chapter 12) will expand on product and business features and benefits.

One important benefit your business can offer is listening intently to your clients and taking action on what you hear from them. Clients want to know that your business is interested in satisfying their needs and wants. By interviewing clients and using surveys, you can continue to be aware of what clients are thinking and how to keep them coming back to your business.

A major step in starting your consulting service is defining your business and identifying your prospective clients. This chapter was a major step in that process. The following chapter will guide you in documenting your ideas for a successful business by writing your business plan.

CHAPTER 7

Writing Your Business Plan

Businesses large and small benefit from defining their start up and operation in a document called a business plan. Your business plan offers an opportunity to describe your ideas and to explain how your consulting business will make a profit. It will both guide you in management and help any investors understand your vision. This chapter will help you produce a business plan for your consulting service.

Executive Summary

A business plan's executive summary is a concise digest of all components. Though it is first in most business plans, it often is written last. Once you're done with all of the other components, you'll return to it and make needed changes to ensure consistency and accuracy. Or better, you will use it as you develop your business plan, pulling it out and revising it as needed. When you reach your ultimate destination, a complete and thorough business plan, your executive summary will be ready to serve as its map.

Components

What are the typical components of a business plan? The answer depends on the specifics of the plan. However, as most business plans include the same types of information, some generalizations can be made. For example, most business plan executive summaries include:

- Concept
- Background
- Mission statement
- Marketing
- Keys to success
- Capital requirements

The order of these components will be dictated by the type of business. Fortunately, it is easy to reorder components of your business plan and your executive summary as it grows.

Concept

A concept is an idea. You think your community could use an exotic pet trainer and an idea is conceived: Why don't *you* train exotic pets? It is the core question of your business idea. It is a summary of your question rephrased: Is an exotic pet training service a viable business opportunity for me? These questions will lead to others, each requiring an answer before a decision can be made. Your business plan is a document written to convince yourself and possibly others that such a business concept is viable. If it isn't, the business plan won't get finished.

Mission Statement

A mission is a purpose. A mission statement is a written declaration of a purpose. In your business plan, it briefly explains the function of your business. It can be a single sentence or a paragraph. It should use concrete rather than abstract words. Your business's mission statement should be unique and not describe any other business. It should be focused on the opportunity and tell readers specifically what your business is about.

ALERT

A concise mission statement is the most important component of your business plan. As your business grows, new opportunities will arise. Your business's mission statement will help you focus on the reasons you got into the business and help keep you on track. If a business is unsuccessful or less than successful, an imprecise mission statement is often the cause.

The Rest of the Executive Summary

The other three components of an executive summary (marketing, keys to success, and capital requirements) are summarized from other components of your business plan.

Present Situation and Objectives

Writing a business plan is analogous to building a house. First, you need an overall plan. That's your first draft of the executive summary. Then you need a foundation, built on solid ground, that outlines and supports your business. That's your section called Present Situation and Objectives. Some business plan books and software programs call this by other names, but the function is the same: To start and support business construction. It expands your plan with more details that will be further expanded in subsequent sections of your business plan.

The first component of defining the present situation (also called "opportunities") is analyzing the marketplace for what you plan to sell. Your executive summary mentions the market; here's where you discuss it in further detail. What you say about the market depends on the purpose of your business plan and your level of research. For example, if you're writing a start-up plan, your analysis will primarily be as a knowledgeable outsider who has done the research and maybe even worked in a similar field, but not operated this type of business. If you're writing a growth plan, you have experience in the market and can build upon it with new research and insights. Perspective is key.

Market Environment

Even if you have experience in the marketplace in which you plan to build your business, you'll need to do additional research. The following are some typical market environment statements:

- The market for travel consultants in the Pacific Northwest is rapidly growing.
- The local marketplace for tax advisors is small, but it is expected to grow later this year because of legislative changes in how businesses are taxed.
- The local market for strategic planners is saturated, but there is a shortage of planners who are bilingual.
- The market for website optimizers is poised to grow by 25 percent in the coming year according to a recent Wall Street Journal article.

A concise definition of the market environment for what you expect to sell can help you begin to expand your business plan and help you focus on opportunities.

Market Opportunities

An opportunity is a favorable juncture of circumstances. A new technology can offer you an opportunity to develop a proven business concept in a new way. Your business concept and market environment can be combined to help you select from among numerous opportunities.

Consider the many combinations of what you already know and what clients need. At that juncture, opportunities abound.

To take advantage of them, you must understand the circumstances and effectively use good timing. What do you know about the current business circumstances for the service(s) that you're planning to sell? What do you know and what can you discover?

Timing is everything, especially in business. If you knew what stocks would go up tomorrow or when your lucky numbers would be selected in the lottery, you could become rich. Many fortunes have been made—and lost—by the timing of events.

ESSENTIAL

Timing is the ability to select the moment to do something for optimum effect. Open your consulting business when there is a great need and you will thrive. Open it a month after a major competitor opens with more services and lower fees and your business probably will expire. As you plan your business's present situation, consider its timing.

Objectives

"If you don't know where you're going, how will you know when you get there?"

Too many new businesses have only one simple objective: to make a profit. Yes, but how? One of the primary functions of your business plan is to make you think about and document the business's objectives or goals.

Most businesses have more than one goal. In fact, they often have many complementary goals that must work together to satisfy the overall objective of making a profit. If business design goals are met but financial goals aren't, the business will not succeed. These goals will be expanded upon as your plan develops. Before you invest more time and money in your business concept, however, you should clearly define them. They describe where your business is going.

Business goals answer the question: *How* do you expect to make a profit? Your response will be something like: Acme Consulting will profit by offering practical solutions to common career problems faced by military retirees. You will then break down that statement into specific and attainable goals and subgoals.

Service Description

What is it that you're selling? Investment services? Beauty services? Home inspection services? None of the above. Nor any other product or service! If you think of your business as a problem-solving venture, you will be more in tune with what clients want. It will help you in understanding how to best offer services to your clients.

A service is work performed for another. The services your business provides to clients must solve specifically defined problems. That's how your clients look at your business. As you develop your business plan, consider what problems your services will solve for potential clients, but state your plan in terms of the solution. Later, in your market analysis, you will expand on these definitions with an analysis of exactly who needs your business services and how to reach them.

Market Analysis

There have been marketplaces around the world for thousands of years. A marketplace is an actual or virtual area where goods and services are exchanged, typically for coin of the realm. Santa Fe has a marketplace, as does Baghdad. eBay is a virtual marketplace. At each, sellers present their wares—oranges, falafel, classic comic books—to buyers. If the buyer and seller agree on the price, a sale is made and products or services transfer hands.

Your business operates within one or more marketplaces, depending on the type of business. A reunion-planning service will operate within a geographic area that is convenient to those who will use the service. An Internet business sells to the world—or at least as much of the world as the product or service can be delivered to.

The following questions need to be answered in a market analysis:

- What is your business's marketplace? Is it limited physically?
- Is there a virtual marketplace for what you sell? Are you able to compete within it?

Your Marketplace

Before you begin selling any product or service, you must understand the marketplace in which you will be operating. Who will be buying from you? How do they buy your type of product or service? Can you make buying easier or more convenient for them?

Selecting an appropriate business from the available opportunities is critical to the success of your enterprise. In addition, choosing your marketplace is important. One location may be more convenient to your residence, but not to the majority of your potential clients. To serve your clients, you must be where they want to buy. Physical locations for businesses must be selected based on buyers' preferences.

Market Limits

All marketplaces have limits, even online markets. The limits may be linguistic, geographic, monetary, cultural, or governmental. Before developing your consulting business, you must consider its limitations.

Market limits may also be dictated by your finances. For example, your consulting service would fit perfectly in the new professional business center going in, but initial profits just won't allow you to afford the rent. However, your business's long-term plans may include a move to the mall in three to five years. If so, explain that to your investors in the market analysis section of your business plan.

Virtual Marketing

Billions of dollars in products and services are traded over the Internet every year. Online selling has made world marketers out of small, specialized businesses. For a relatively small investment, a business can join the millions of online sellers.

Therein lies the problem. There are millions of online sellers, all competing in the new virtual economy. Unless your product or service is unique and you understand the verities of online marketing, your virtual business will remain unfound by your target clients. However, if you do have unique products or services and learn to market on the Internet, it is a relatively low-cost method of setting up a profitable business.

Before you analyze your business's potential market, you must first identify that marketplace. Is it local or world-wide? Is it limited by franchise agreements or start-up costs? Is it limited by the client's language or knowledge? Is it defined by the available distribution systems?

ALERT

Use the Internet as a way to help your prospective clients understand who you are and what you do. Produce a website that is a virtual brochure for your consulting services. Show visitors that you not only understand the problems they face, but also that you can offer them viable and proven solutions.

Clients

Established consulting businesses have it easier. If they have a proven service and an ideal location, many clients will find them. Of course, they will strive to attract more clients, but their target market knows where they are and what they sell.

ESSENTIAL

You can use market analysis services to help identify your potential clients. Many are listed in metropolitan telephone books under "marketing services." Find ones that specialize in the type of clients that you are looking for: business executives, software companies, musicians, lenders, families, etc. They can save you a lot of time in finding and reaching prospects.

New businesses often don't have this opportunity. They must identify individual clients and strive to attract and serve them. Consulting businesses that are trying to grow into new markets have similar challenges. What's the solution? New and growing businesses must identify individual clients by first determining who they are, what they want, how they prefer to buy, and what authority they have in the buying process.

Who Are Your Clients?

You've identified your marketplace and defined the groups of people who will buy from you, but who are the individuals? Are they like you? Do they have similar needs and problems? Consider them individuals with whom you have commonality. Look to friends, acquaintances, business contacts, and other individuals to help you put the faces of real people in your business plan's marketing strategy.

What Do Your Clients Want?

Interview people who you expect to be your typical clients. What are the problems that your products or services solve for individual clients? Match their need with your offering. It will help you personalize your business to individuals if you give clients a face and a name. You can better visualize who they are as people rather than as a member of the left-handed widget market segment. In addition to the obvious opportunities to increase profits, selling to individual clients rather than market groups offers personal satisfaction for what you do.

How Do They Prefer to Buy?

Basic marketing studies won't tell you much about how individual clients prefer to buy. That requires your first-hand knowledge as well as your observation skills. A deeper understanding of how the people you will serve actually buy will enhance your business plan. How can you find out these preferences? By asking individuals. Question topics include:

- What facts do you need to make an informed buying decision?
- What buying authority do you have?
- How do you prefer to make your purchases?
- When do you prefer to buy?
- How important is service after the sale to you?
- What other conditions are helpful in your buying process?

To go beyond what your competitors do for clients, go beyond the questions they ask. Find out from individual clients how they prefer to buy.

Competition

Free enterprise is a double-edged sword. It gives you the right to build a business—and your competitors the right to take it away. That's the nature of business. Your job as a new business owner is to identify your competition and develop a plan for responding to their threats. Once your business is successful, you will continue to face the challenges of competitors. You need to have an action plan for competition and your investors need to know what it is.

ALERT

Many new businesses simply ignore their competitors. They don't identify, analyze, and attempt to defeat their competition. Then they wonder what happened to all of their clients. To be successful in business, you must know who your competitors are and what they are up to.

Competitors are two or more organisms vying for the same resource. Two runners striving for first place are competitors. So are five hungry puppies at feeding time. If they all want the same thing, they are competitors.

So who are your business's competitors? Any other businesses (organisms) contending for the same clients (resources) as your business. Actually, the definition is even broader than that. Any person or business who may get one of your client's dollars instead of you is a competitor. If your clients must decide whether to buy something from you or anything from someone else, you are in competition. The resource in this case is the dollar.

As you develop your business plan, begin a list of all potential competitors to your business concept. Once the list is complete you will analyze it and eliminate those who are less significant.

Analyzing Competition

Every business or organism that may get a client's money instead of you is a competitor. However, many of these competitors aren't significant bullies. You won't have to worry about them stealing your lunch money. Even so, you need to consider who they are and what impact they have on your business plan.

Products and Services

To be competitors, businesses must offer products and/or services that offer clients a similar solution to a specific problem. In the example of a tax service, the client has many options. If your tax service will focus on busy middle-income families within a local area, you can begin analyzing and eliminating some of the businesses on your long list. Few prospective clients in this market will get their tax advice from a book or a free service for senior tax filers.

Pricing

In further analysis, you may discover that some competitors price their products or services significantly higher than your pricing structure. For example, a certified public accountant may charge two or three times what your tax service charges for the same preparation and filing. In addition, most middle-income families won't trust volunteer tax preparers to do the work.

Client Service

Two competitors in the tax example depend on technology for service: the online tax preparation service and the software program. These can be significant competitors to your business, depending on how comfortable your prospective clients are with using technology to prepare and file their taxes.

You can do your own competitive analysis. The best place to start is by becoming a client of your primary competitors. Find out, from the client's viewpoint, how they provide their services, what they charge, and how well they perform. Doing so can help you understand what opportunities your consulting service can provide to clients.

Make sure your business plan includes an analysis of significant competitors. By identifying and scrutinizing them, you will not only discover what they are doing to succeed, but you will also be able to plan ways of beating them in the race for clients.

Marketing Strategy

Every endeavor has a strategy for winning. Want to win at Scrabble? Texas Hold 'em? Stock car racing? Politics? Business? You need a strategy, a plan toward a goal. The word comes from the Greek term for "generalship," the guy who develops and carries out military plans. It suggests that the endeavor is a battle that must be well planned and executed for success.

Your business is a battle. You will be fighting for fiscal territory with the help of economic weapons and soldiers in service. You will win a few and lose a few battles, but your goal will be to win the business "war" and live to fight another day. To develop an accurate comprehensive plan, you must ask and answer some fundamental questions about your business.

What Business Are You In?

The question seems so simple that many entrepreneurs don't bother answering it—then they have problems as they lose their business focus. As your plan is developed and you get new data, your business focus may change slightly or significantly. In any case, you must update and verify your business definition.

Large corporations call this defining the "core business." AT&T sells communication. That's its core business. You should not expect AT&T to begin selling cars or mutual funds. The people who run the company clearly understand and focus on the core business. So should you.

Make sure you understand and clearly define your core business as succinctly as possible. What is it your business uniquely does to earn a profit?

What Market Segment Do You Want to Reach?

No business can sell to everyone. The marketplace is limited by geography, economics, product selection, service availability, competitive, and other restricting factors. So each business must define the market segment that it can best reach. It may be a local market or a niche online market or one that is defined by the income of clients. In each case, these segmentations must be clearly defined so a comprehensive plan can be strategized.

Pricing and Profitability

Many businesses believe that pricing is the most critical component of their new venture. It isn't. It is one of many. Without a clear identification of clients and competitors, pricing can be erroneously set and either repel clients or attract competitors.

A price is the amount or conditions required to consummate a transaction. If the price for a tube of toothpaste is $2.99, that's what you must pay to make it yours. If the price for a new car is $25,000 plus your old car, that's what it will cost you to complete the transaction. Some purchases have additional conditions, such as approval of a law, lender, or other authority. You cannot purchase alcohol, for example, unless you are of the legal age in your state.

It is critical that your business plan includes specifics on how you will price your services. Yes, your investors, if any, want to know your pricing structure; however, you also need to analyze and document it. Without appropriate pricing, your business may not be profitable. You need to establish pricing guidelines, make certain they are competitive, and make pricing easy to implement and easy to adjust if needed to meet changing business conditions.

Margins and Discounts

A margin is the measurement of a difference. In business, you'll be using price margins, gross margins, profit margins, and other margins. Pricing is the task of establishing a price difference between what you pay and what you charge for products and services. Gross margins and markups have an impact on pricing and profitability.

A gross margin is the amount of income left after paying for the goods sold. If your business sells $1,000 in services that cost you $600 to produce, the gross profit or margin is $400. It's more useful to calculate gross margin as a percentage of revenue. Simply deduct costs from sales, divide the result by sales, and convert it into a percent. Divide the gross margin of $400 by the sales of $1,000 to get 0.4, then state it as a percentage: 40 percent. In the example, the gross margin is 40 percent.

Costs

The price at which you sell your service has a big impact on your business's profitability. However, it isn't the only factor. Costs are critical, too. A cost is what you pay for something. It could be the employee costs required to provide a specific service or the wholesale cost products you will sell with your services.

In business, costs are typically segmented based on whether they are fixed or variable. A fixed cost is one that doesn't change in proportion to business activity. A retailer or manufacturer, for example, must pay rent, utility bills, and salaries regardless of whether sales levels are high or low. Fixed costs typically are not included in the costs of goods sold. A variable cost is one that does change in proportion to business activity. Typical variable costs for a business include the cost of goods sold, materials, and production costs.

Financial Statements

The goal of your new or growing business is to bring in more money than you pay out. The difference is the profit. It is vital as you plan your consulting business to establish a trustworthy system that tracks and manages income, expenses, and profits. The tracking system includes various financial statements, including the income statement, balance sheet, and cash flow statements.

Income Statement

An income statement is a financial document that shows how gross income (income before expenses) is converted into net income (income after expenses). Gross income or revenue is sometimes called the top line and net income (before taxes, etc.) is the bottom line. Because the statement considers profits and losses, it also is referred to as a profit and loss (P&L) statement.

ALERT

Some entrepreneurs and accountants refer to an income statement as an operating statement or an earnings report. There are slight differences between these reports, but the terms often are used interchangeably. For consistency, use the most accepted: income statement.

Balance Sheet

In the world of finance, a balance sheet is a summary of assets, liabilities, and equity. If you've applied for a personal loan, the application included a simplified balance sheet structure:

- What do you own (assets)?
- What do you owe (liabilities)?
- What is your net worth (assets minus liabilities)?

Your business will have a more developed balance sheet than you personally do. It will include more detail and require more verification. Your business's investors want to know exactly what they are getting into—and they'll want assurance that you know, too.

A balance sheet is also called a statement of financial position. It is a snapshot of your business on a specific date. It may be the first day of operation, the beginning of the third year, or on the date that you sell your business. It's called a balance sheet because the financial components on one side (assets) must equal the financial components on the other (liabilities and equity). Equity is also known as capital, net worth, ownership equity, and other terms.

QUESTION

Where did the term *balance sheet* come from?
The term "balance sheet" is based on double-entry recordkeeping that always makes two entries for every transaction or event. The purchase of a building (asset) is offset by a reduction in cash and credit (liabilities). The difference is your business's equity in the building. The two entries must balance each other.

Cash Flow Statement

Cash flow is the tracking of actual income and expenses as cash or other liquid assets. In earlier times, cash flow statements were called statement of change in financial position and flow of funds statement. These titles help describe their purpose as records of where the money is coming from, where it is going, and when. Another way of looking at income and expenses is:

- Income = sources of cash
- Expense = uses of cash

Obviously, you cannot use more cash than you receive. Only the federal government can print more money.

Once you've written—and rewritten—your business plan, remember to update the executive summary. Finally, set it aside for awhile, then reread it with a fresh eye to make sure it clearly answers your primary question: How can I make a profit as a consultant?

CHAPTER 8

Getting Help

No business successfully operates alone. Your consulting service is no exception. To provide your services, you will need the services of others, including an accountant, attorney, and insurance professional. You may also need help from a banker or other lender, a partner, or investors in a corporation. This chapter shows you how new consulting services like yours get help.

Hiring an Accountant

Many new consulting services fail because of poor financial management. Sometimes the best decision a new business owner makes is to hire the services of a public accounting firm. An accountant can design record-keeping systems, set up ways to maintain records, analyze financial information, and help you relate that information to profitability.

Financial Data

Daily bits of information will flow into your consulting services business. As you serve clients, you will generate information about sales, cash, supplies, purchase expenses, payroll, accounts payable, and, if credit is offered to clients, accounts receivable.

To capture theses facts and figures, a system is necessary. If you don't feel comfortable setting up and managing such a system, don't be shy about hiring an accounting service. An accountant can help you design one to record the information you need so you can control finances and make profitable decisions.

The Accountant's Job

Once a system of records has been set up, the question is: Who should keep the books? The accounting service that has set up the books may keep them. However, if you have a general understanding of record keeping you can do them yourself and save money. Use your accountant for rechecking and analyzing your records. Once your business has grown, you may want to hire someone to keep your records and perform other office functions. In addition to record keeping, an accountant can advise you on financial management, providing you with cash flow requirements, budget forecasts, borrowing, business organization, and tax information.

Data Analysis

By analyzing cash flow requirements, an accountant can help you work out the amount of cash needed to operate your firm during a specific period—for example, three months, six months, or the next year. She considers how much cash you will need to carry client accounts receivable, to buy equipment and supplies, to pay bills, and to repay loans. In addition, an accountant can determine how much cash will come from collection of accounts receivable and how much will have to be borrowed or pulled from an existing line of credit. While working out the cash requirements, your accountant may notice and call your attention to danger spots, such as accounts that are past due.

FACT

Most accountants can oversee your recordkeeping electronically. You make transaction entries in one of the primary financial software programs, such as QuickBooks, and submit it weekly or monthly to your accountant, who reviews it and makes any correcting entries. If this sounds like a good option for your consulting service, discuss it with your accountant.

If you're applying for a loan, your accountant can assemble financial information—for example, a profit-and-loss or income statement and a balance sheet. The purpose of such data is to show the lender the financial position of your business and its ability to repay the loan. Using this information, your accountant can advise you on whether you need a short-term or long-term loan. If you have never borrowed before, your accountant may help you by introducing you to a lender who knows and respects the accountant's reputation. This alone may be worth the cost of hiring an accountant.

Taxation Help

Taxes are another area in which an accountant can contribute advice and assistance. Normally, a record-keeping system that provides the information you need for making profitable decisions will suffice for tax purposes. However, if you purchase equipment that requires special depreciation, have employees who handle cash or require payroll taxes, or have extensive bad debts, a good accountant can help you identify the problem, suggest a method of keeping better records, and help you minimize your tax obligation by writing off bad debts as a business expense. Accounting firms will also get your federal and state withholding numbers for you, instruct you on where and when to file tax returns, prepare tax returns, and do general tax planning for your small business.

ALERT

Get referrals for accountants from trusted friends, business associates, professional associations, and other business services. Discuss fees in advance and draw up a written agreement about how you will work together. Your accountant should alert you to potential danger areas and advise you on how to handle growth spurts, how to best plan for slow business times, and how to financially mature and protect your business future from unnecessary risks.

Hiring an Attorney

Most attorneys specialize in one field or another: criminal cases, divorce and family matters, taxation, business law, etc. To find an attorney who is familiar with a business of your size and trade, ask for a referral from a business colleague, your banker, your accountant, your local chamber of commerce, or other business services in your area. Many local bar associations run an attorney referral and information service; check your local telephone book's Yellow Pages under "Attorneys' Referral & Information Services." Some referral services give you only names and phone numbers; others actually give information on experience and fees to help you match your needs to the attorney's background and charges.

The Attorney's Job

An attorney can help you decide what the most advantageous business structure is for you. He can also help you with zoning, licensing problems, unpaid bills, contracts and agreements, employment laws, copyright questions, trademarks, and some tax problems.

Because there is always the possibility of a lawsuit, claim, or other legal action against your business, it is wise to have an attorney who is already familiar with your business lined up before a crisis arises. An attorney with experience serving consulting businesses can also advise you on federal, state, and local laws, programs, and agencies to help you prepare for or prevent potential problems.

Attorney-Client Relationship

Let your attorney know that you expect to be informed of all developments and consulted before any decisions are made on your behalf. You may also want to receive copies of all documents, letters, and memos written and received regarding your project. If this isn't practical, you should at least have the opportunity to read such correspondence at your attorney's office.

Hiring an Insurance Professional

A good insurance agent is as valuable to your success as any other professional consultant. An experienced and trustworthy insurance agent can both reduce your exposure to risk and keep your insurance costs to a minimum.

Finding an Insurance Agent

Ask other consultants and business services to recommend a qualified insurance agent. Search for one who primarily serves the business community rather than families or individuals. They will better understand your problems and concerns.

Ask prospective agents for advice on a specific problem. Don't tell them what you think the solution is. Their responses can help you determine who is better at cost-effective problem solving for business risks.

Independent Agents

The agent is the insurance industry's primary client representative. Typically, the independent agent is a small business owner and manager. By using this distribution system, insurance companies are represented by agents who receive a commission for selling the companies' products and services. An independent agent usually represents more than one insurance company.

Legal Defense Provision

Liability insurance coverage, particularly for property damage and bodily injury, usually includes legal defense at no additional charge when the policyholder is named in a lawsuit that involves a claim covered by the policy. Litigation is costly, whether the claimant's suit is valid or frivolous. The legal defense provision can greatly reduce the cost of a suit for you. Make sure you discuss this provision—and its cost—with your insurance agent.

Finding a Partner

Sometimes, the best source of help for your consulting service is offered by a working or financial partner. The Uniform Partnership Act (UPA), adopted by many states, defines a partnership as "an association of two or more persons to carry on as co-owners of a business for profit." How the partnership is structured, the powers and limitations of each partner, and their participation in the business are written into a document called the articles of partnership. The articles or descriptions can be written by the partners, found in a legal form from a stationery store, or written by an attorney. Obviously, using an attorney is the best option because it will ensure that the document is binding and reduce disputes that typically come up once the business is growing.

Articles of Partnership

Your firm's articles of partnership should include:

- The name, location, length, and purpose of the partnership
- The type of partnership
- A definition of the partners' individual contributions
- An agreement on how business expenses will be handled
- An outline of the authority of each partner
- A summary of the accounting methods that will be used
- A definition of how profits and losses will be distributed among the partners
- The salaries and capital draws for each partner

- An agreement of how the partnership will be modified or terminated, including dissolution of the partnership by death or disability of a member or by the decision of partners to disband
- A description of how the members will arbitrate and settle disputes as well as change terms of the partnership agreement

Partnerships are easier and less costly to form than corporations. In most states, all that's really needed is the articles of partnership.

QUESTION

How can I find out more about how partnerships are formed and taxed?
The Federal Internal Revenue Service (*www.irs.gov*) provides publication 541, titled *Partnerships*, that offers information on formation, termination, distributions, and taxation. It is periodically revised to keep it up to date; the most recent version can be found on the IRS website.

Help with Capital

A partnership can typically raise capital more easily than a sole proprietorship. This is because there are more people whose assets can be combined as equity for the loan. Lenders will look at the credit ratings of each partner, so make sure your business partners have good credit. Partnerships are frequently more flexible in the decision-making process than a corporation, but less flexible than a proprietorship.

Like proprietorships, partnerships offer relative freedom from government control and special taxation. A partnership doesn't pay income tax. Rather, all profits and losses flow through the partnership to the individual partners, who pay income and other taxes as if they were sole proprietors.

Downside of Partnerships

Of course, there are some minuses to partnerships. At least one partner will be a general partner and will assume unlimited liability for the business.

A general partner should get sufficient insurance coverage to reduce the risk from physical loss or personal injury, but the general partner is still liable.

A partnership is as stable or as unstable as its members. Elimination of any partner often means automatic dissolution of the partnership. However, the business can continue to operate if the agreement includes provisions for the right of survivorship and possible creation of a new partnership. Partnership insurance can assist surviving partners in purchasing the equity of a deceased partner.

ALERT

A partnership is similar to a marriage. It requires common goals, shared responsibilities, communication, and trust. Make sure the partner you select for your consulting business shares your goals, has defined responsibilities and authority, and maintains a line of communication.

Though a partnership has less difficulty in getting financing than a sole proprietorship, the fragile nature of partnerships sometimes makes it difficult to get long-term financing. The best source, as discussed earlier, is using the combined equity of the partners from assets they own as individuals. In fact, many partnerships are started because an active partner needs equity or financing that she cannot get without a partner with more assets or better credit.

Depending upon how the partnership agreement is drawn up, any partner may be able to bind all of the partners to financial obligations. Make sure your articles of partnership accurately reflects your intent regarding how partners can or cannot obligate the partnership. Also consider the advantages and disadvantages of structuring your partnership as a limited liability company.

A major drawback to partnerships is the difficulty faced when arranging the departure of a partner. Buying out the partner's interest may be difficult unless terms have been specifically worked out in the partnership agreement.

Get Legal Advice

As you can see, there are numerous pluses and minuses to partnerships. Many of the disadvantages can be addressed in your articles of partnership.

This is why it is recommended that you use an attorney experienced in such agreements as you construct your partnership. The cost is usually less than the value.

Limited Liability Company

Similar to a partnership, a limited liability company (LLC) is taxed only once on its profits. A C corporation is taxed twice. Unlike a partnership, an LLC protects partners by limiting their personal liability for actions of the company. An LLC offers liability protections similar to those of a corporation. In addition, LLCs have fewer restrictions on shareholders and allow the transfer of shares more easily than a corporation. Finally, profits are reported on personal rather than corporate tax returns.

ALERT

State laws governing LLCs are based on the Uniform Limited Liability Company Act (ULLCA) developed in 1995 and subsequently revised. The latest versions can be accessed online at the University of Pennsylvania Law School at *http://law.upenn.edu*. Also, check with your state attorney general for more information.

LLC Structure

LLCs must be privately held companies. While restructuring a C corporation into an LLC can be difficult and costly, changing your business form from an LLC to a C corporation is quite easy. One major drawback to LLCs is that their limitation of liability has not been extensively tested in the court system, as has that of corporations. If you decide to establish an LLC, make sure you have an attorney who has experience with this structure and who can advise you based on liability and tax issues in your state.

Setting up an LLC

About forty states recognize limited liability companies as a legal business structure. They have been popular in other countries for many years.

In establishing an LLC, you will need to file articles of organization and an operating agreement with state authorities.

Starting a Corporation

Businesses, as they grow, often become corporations (technically called C corporations), identified by an extension to their name: Corp., Inc., or, in Canada, Ltd. A corporation is usually formed by the authority of a state government. The steps to forming a corporation begin with writing incorporation papers and issuing capital stock. Then, approval must be obtained from the secretary of state in the state in which the corporation is being formed. Only then can the corporation act as a legal entity separate from those who own its stock.

Corporate Advantage

The primary advantage to incorporation is that it limits the stockholders' liability to their investments. If you buy $1,000 of stock in a corporation and it fails, you can only lose up to the $1,000 investment. The corporation's creditors cannot come back to you demanding more money. The exception is when you put up some of your own assets as collateral for the corporation.

Ownership of a corporation is a transferable asset. As mentioned earlier, the New York Stock Exchange and other exchanges make a big business out of transferring stock, or partial ownership, in corporations from one investor to another. If your consulting services business is a corporation, you can sell partial ownership or stock in it within certain limits. In fact, this is how many corporations get money to grow. A corporation can also issue long-term bonds to gain the cash required to purchase assets or build the business.

Corporate Structure

Your corporation has a separate and legal existence. Your corporation is not you or anybody else. It is itself. For example, in the case of illness, death, or other cause for loss of a corporate officer or owner, the corporation continues to exist and can do business.

The corporation can also delegate authority to hired managers, although they are often one and the same. Thus you become an employee of the corporation.

ESSENTIAL

The primary reason to establish a corporation over an LLC is funding. As your consulting business grows, if you cannot get sufficient limited partners to fund growth, consider the advantages—and disadvantages—of incorporating in order to get more capital.

Corporations have disadvantages, too. The corporation's state charter may limit the type of business it does to a specific industry or service. However, other states allow broad charters that permit corporations to operate in any legal enterprise.

Corporations face more governmental regulations on all levels—local, state, and federal. That means your business will spend more time and money fulfilling these requirements as a corporation than it would as a proprietorship or a partnership. If your corporate manager is not also a stockholder, he will have less incentive to be efficient than he would if he had a share in your business.

Incorporation Costs

As you can imagine, a corporation is more expensive to form than other types of business. Even if you don't use an attorney, there are forms and fees that will quickly add up. However, an attorney is a good investment when incorporating your consulting services business.

Corporate Taxation

Finally, corporations allow the federal and some state governments to tax income twice: once as a corporate net income and once as it's received by the individual stockholders in the form of salary or dividends. A Sub-Chapter S corporation allows small businesses to tax the business as if it were a sole proprietorship or partnership (no corporate income tax) and pass the tax liability on to the individual stockholders. There are about 2 million

Sub-Chapter S corporations in the United States. Recent changes in the law may make it easier to get financing for a Sub-S. Talk with an attorney or accountant about this option.

Finding Funding

A recent survey of small businesses reported that 23 percent had lines of credit, 7 percent had financial leases, 14 percent had mortgage loans, 12 percent had equipment loans, and 25 percent had vehicle loans. When considering funding your consulting service, you have many options besides self-funding.

Loan Qualification

The ability to get a loan when you need it is as necessary to the operation of your business as having the right equipment. Before a bank or any other lending agency will lend you money, the loan officer must feel satisfied with the answers to these five questions:

1. **What sort of person are you, the prospective borrower?** In most cases, the character of the borrower comes first. Next is your ability to manage your business.
2. **What are you going to do with the money?** The answer to this question will determine the type of loan and the duration.
3. **When and how do you plan to pay it back?** Your lender's judgment of your business ability and the type of loan will be a deciding factor in the answer to this question.
4. **Is the cushion in the loan large enough?** In other words, does the amount requested make suitable allowance for unexpected developments? The lender decides this question on the basis of your financial statement, which sets forth the condition of your business, and on the collateral pledged.
5. **What's the outlook for business in general and for your business in particular?**

When you set out to borrow money for your firm, it is important to know the kind of money you need from a bank or other lending institution. Let's discuss loans and other types of credit.

Loan Types

There are numerous types of loans available, all with their own unique name depending on the lender.

Signature Loan

A signature loan holds nothing in collateral except your promise to pay the lender back on terms with which you both agree. If your monetary needs are small, you only need the loan for a short time, your credit rating is excellent, and you're willing to pay a premium interest rate because you're not using physical collateral, a signature or character loan is an easy way to borrow money in a hurry.

FACT

Many small service businesses are initially funded with a home equity line of credit (HELOC) from which the owner can draw cash as needed. However, if the business has financial problems, home ownership may be in jeopardy. Discuss this option with your accountant and banker before proceeding.

Credit Cards

Many a small business has found at least some of its funding in the owner's personal credit card. Computers, printers, books, office supplies, office overhead, and other costs can be covered with your personal credit card. However, interest rates on credit cards are extremely high—sometimes double what you might pay on a collateral loan. But credit cards can offer you quick cash when you need it. If this is an option for you, talk to your credit card representative about raising your credit limit. Keep in mind that it will be much easier to do so while you're employed by someone else.

Line of Credit

A line of credit is similar to a loan except you don't borrow the money all at once. You get a credit limit, say $100,000, that you can tap any time you need money for business purposes. The most common is the revolving line of credit that you can draw from when business is off and pay back when business is good, providing you don't exceed your limit. A line of credit is an excellent way for a consulting service to work through the ups and downs of seasonal business. With some restrictions, a line of credit can be established using a portion of your home equity as collateral. Using a secured equity earns you a lower interest rate.

FACT

For information on business credit, visit the Federal Trade Commission (*www.ftc.gov*) online website for their document, *Getting Business Credit*. It offers guidelines for business credit applications as well as advice on how to file a complaint against lenders for unfair business practices.

Cosigner Loan

A cosigner loan should be one of the most popular loans for small businesses, but many business people never consider it. Simply, you find a cosigner or a co-maker with good credit or assets who will guarantee the loan with you. If you have a potential investor who believes in your business but doesn't want to put up the cash you need, ask her to cosign for a loan with you. Your chances of getting the loan are much better. Some cosigners will require that you pay them a fee of 1 to 4 percent of the balance or a flat fee; others will do it out of friendship or the hope of future business from you. In any case, consider this as an excellent source of capital for your new consulting service.

Equipment Leases

If you're purchasing equipment, computers, or other assets for your business, the supplier may loan or lease the equipment to you. This often requires about 25 percent down, so be ready to come up with some cash of your own.

Collateral Loan

A collateral loan is one in which some type of asset is put up as collateral; if you don't make payments you will lose the asset. The lender wants to make sure the value of the asset exceeds that of the loan and will usually lend 50 to 75 percent of asset value. A new consulting service owner often does not have sufficient collateral—real estate or equipment—to secure a collateral loan unless an owner uses personal assets such as a home.

Passbook Loan

Sometimes you can get a loan by assigning a savings account to the bank. In such cases, the bank gets an assignment from you and keeps your passbook. If you assign an account in another bank as collateral, the lending bank asks the other bank to mark its records to show that the account is held as collateral.

Life Insurance Loan

Another kind of collateral is life insurance. Banks will lend up to the cash value of a life insurance policy. You have to assign the policy to the bank. If the policy is on the life of an executive of a small corporation, corporate resolutions must be made authorizing the assignment. Most insurance companies allow you to sign the policy back to the original beneficiary when the assignment to the bank ends. Some people like to use life insurance as collateral rather than borrow directly from insurance companies. One reason is that a bank loan is often more convenient to get and may often carry a lower interest rate.

CHAPTER 9

Managing Costs

Starting a consulting service is only part of your goal. To succeed, you must manage its daily operation. You must control operating costs; stay within your budget; manage assets, liabilities, and net worth; and manage taxes. This chapter covers these and other responsibilities of your consulting service's daily operations as suggested by successful business owners. It will help you understand and focus on the nuts and bolts of your business as you keep your eyes on the broader purpose of your venture: to help others as you help yourself.

Estimating Your Operating Costs

Managing your consulting services business requires that you manage your business budget so you can continue to provide service, support, and employment to others as well as a profit to yourself. When you first start your business, you establish a preliminary budget. Now that your business is operating, you must establish an operating budget. The difference is that a preliminary budget is what you think your income and expenses will be; an operating budget is the actual income and expenses.

Your Budget

A budget is a forecast of all cash sources and cash expenditures. It most commonly covers a twelve-month period. At the end of the year, the projected income and expenses in the budget are compared to the actual performance as recorded in the financial statement.

A budget can greatly enhance your chances of success by helping you estimate future needs and plan profits, spending, and overall cash flow. A budget allows you to detect problems before they occur and to alter your plans to prevent those problems.

In business, budgets help you determine how much money you have and how you will use it. They will also help you decide whether you have enough money to achieve your financial goals. As part of your business plan, a budget can help convince a loan officer that you know your business and have anticipated its needs.

ALERT

Not sure what your consulting business budget should look like? Ask your competitors. That is, use your membership in trade associations to discover what similar consultants have established for their operating budgets. Compare by size—for example, get expense percentages for consultants of approximately the same income level as yours. Ask your trade association for financial guidelines.

A budget will indicate the cash required for necessary labor and materials, the day-to-day operating costs, the revenue needed to support business operations, and expected profit. If your budget indicates that you need more revenue than you can earn, you can adjust your plans by:

- **Reducing expenditures** (hiring independent contractors or part-time employees instead of full-time employees, purchasing less expensive furniture, eliminating an extra telephone line)
- **Expanding sales** (offering additional services, conducting an aggressive marketing campaign, hiring a salesperson)
- **Lowering your salary** or profit expectations

By gathering and managing data on your income and expenses you can better decide what actions you need to take to keep your consulting service profitable. You're the boss.

Budget Components

There are three main elements to a budget: sales revenue, total costs, and profit.

Consulting services often have higher variable costs than fixed costs. That is because, once overhead is paid, expenses like research and travel fluctuate with income. Smart consultants closely track variable expenses so they don't get out of hand and cut into profits.

Sales are the cornerstone of a budget. It is crucial to estimate anticipated sales as accurately as possible. Base estimates on actual past sales figures. Once you target sales, you can calculate the related expenses necessary to achieve your goals.

Total costs include fixed and variable costs. Estimating costs is complicated because you must identify which costs will change—and by how much—and which costs will remain unchanged as sales increase. You must also consider inflation and rising prices.

Variable costs are those that vary directly with sales. Paper and printer toner expenses are examples of variable costs for your consulting services business. Fixed costs are those that don't change regardless of sales volume.

Rent is considered a fixed cost, as are salaries. Semi-variable costs, such as telephone expenses, have both variable and fixed components. Part of the expense is fixed (telephone line charges), and part is variable (long-distance charges).

The Bottom Line

Profit should be large enough to make a return on cash investment and your labor. Your investment is the money you put into the firm at start-up and the profit you have left in the firm (retained earnings) from prior years. If you can receive 10 percent interest on $25,000 by investing outside of your business, then you should expect a similar return when investing $25,000 in equipment and other assets within the business. In targeting profits, you also want to be sure you're receiving a fair return on your labor. Your weekly paycheck should reflect what you could be earning elsewhere as an employee.

Budgeting Operating Costs

As you develop your budget, you'll be working with the budget equation. The basic budget equation is:

Sales = Total Costs + Profit

This equation shows that every sales dollar you receive is made up partly of a recovery of your costs and partly of profit. Another way to express the basic budgeting equation is:

Sales – Total Costs = Profit

This equation shows that, after reimbursing yourself for the cost of producing your service, the remaining part of the sales dollar is profit. For example, if you expect $1,000 for a specific job and you know that it will cost $900 to market and perform this service, your profit will be $100. Depending on the form of your business (proprietorship, partnership, or corporation), you may keep profits in your business, called retained earnings, or pass them on to investors: yourself, your partners, your shareholders.

Calculations

In calculating an operating budget, you will often make estimates based on past sales and cost figures. You will need to adjust these figures to reflect price increases, inflation, and other factors. For example, during the past three years, a consultant spent an average of $5,000 on advertising costs per year. For the coming year, she expects an advertising cost increase of 10 percent (0.10). To calculate next year's advertising costs, she multiplies the average annual advertising costs by the percentage price increase ($5,000 × 0.10 = $500) and adds that amount to the original annual cost (5,000 + $500 = $5,500). A shortcut method is to multiply the original advertising cost by one plus the rate of increase ($5,000 × 1.10 = $5,500).

QUESTION

How can I track my operating budget?
Systems like QuickBooks (*http://quickbooks.intuit.com*) and Peachtree (*www.peachtree.com*) include budgeting tools that not only help establish your business budget, but also can help you track actual income and expenses against your budget to help you manage both.

If your consulting services business is a new venture and has no past financial records, rely on your own experience and knowledge of the industry to estimate demand for and costs of your service. Your accountant or trade association may also be able to help you develop realistic estimates.

Budget Creation

Before you create an operating budget, you must answer three questions:

- How much net profit do you realistically want your business to generate during the calendar year?
- How much will it cost to produce that profit?
- How much sales revenue is necessary to support both profit and cost requirements?

To answer these questions, consider expected sales and all costs, either direct or indirect, associated with your consulting services. To make the safest estimates when budgeting, many companies overestimate expenses and underestimate sales revenue.

Start constructing your budget with either a forecast of sales or a forecast of profits. For practical purposes, most small businesses start with a forecast of profits. In other words, decide what profit you realistically want to make and then list the expenses you will incur to make that profit.

Managing the Value of Your Business

The financial value or net worth of your business is calculated on its total assets and liabilities. Your business's balance sheet (which will be covered in Chapter 10) tracks the value of your business.

Assets

Assets include not only cash, inventory, land, building, equipment, furniture, and the like, but also money due from individuals or other businesses (known as accounts or notes receivable). Each of these assets requires your constant management. You must track each asset's value and make adjustments as needed to increase its value.

ESSENTIAL

Accounting software packages can help you record and manage your consulting business's assets, liabilities, and net worth. Choose a package that fits the needs of your service business and is compatible with your accountant's system.

Liabilities

Liabilities are funds acquired for a business through loans or the sale of property or services to the business on credit. Creditors do not acquire ownership in your business, but promissory notes to be paid at a designated future date (known as accounts or notes payable).

Managing liabilities requires that you know what you owe, to whom, under what terms, and when it is due. You will constantly review these liabilities to ensure that they are paid when due with sufficient cash assets.

Net Worth

Net worth (or shareholders' equity or capital) is money put into a business by its owners or left in it as retained earnings for use by the business in acquiring assets. For sole proprietorships, this is the value of your business to you. If your business is a partnership, an LLC, or a corporation, the net worth is the value of your business less that distributed to partners, investors, and/or shareholders.

Valuation Formula

The formula for this structure is:

Assets = Liabilities + Net Worth

That is, the total funds invested in assets of the business is equal to the funds supplied to the business by its creditors plus the funds supplied to the business by its owners. If a business owes more money to creditors than it possesses in value of assets owned and retained earnings, the net worth or owner's equity of the business will be a negative number.

Assets – Liabilities = Net Worth

In addition to managing the services that your consulting service provides, it will be your job to manage the assets and liabilities that indicate its financial value.

Reducing Operating Costs

It doesn't matter what your billings are. The only thing that matters is how much you keep.

Every dollar saved in overhead is a dollar on the bottom line of net profit—and a dollar less borrowed. The object of reducing costs in your consulting services business is to increase profits. Increasing profits through cost reduction must be based on the concept of an organized, planned program. Unless adequate records are maintained through an efficient and accurate accounting system, there can be no basis for analyzing costs.

Cost Reduction

Cost reduction is not simply attempting to slash any and all expenses without order. The owner-manager must understand the nature of expenses and how expenses interrelate with sales, overhead, gross profits, and net profits. Nor does cost reduction mean only the reduction of specific expenses. You can achieve greater profits through more efficient use of your expense dollar. Some of the ways you do this are by increasing the average sale per client, by getting a larger return for your promotion and sales dollar, and by improving your internal methods and procedures.

As an example, one telecommunications consultant was quite pleased when, in a single year, sales went from $60,000 to $200,000. However, at the end of the year, records showed that net profit the prior year, with lower sales, was actually higher. Why? Because the expenses of doing business grew at a rate faster than the income.

Your goal should be to pay the right price for prosperity. Determining that price for your operation goes beyond knowing what your expenses are. Reducing expenses to increase profit requires that you get the most efficient use of your expense dollars.

Employee Savings

Checking job records, you might determine that one of your employees is significantly less efficient than other employees performing the same tasks. You can then reduce expenses by increasing this employee's efficiency through training. By watching this employee perform his job, you can determine where the inefficiencies are and help him overcome them. If you do this with consideration for your employee, he will appreciate your attention, and so will your profit line.

Necessary Expenses

Sometimes you cannot cut an expense item. But you can get more from it and thus increase your profits. In analyzing your expenses, you should use percentages rather than actual dollar amounts. For example, if you increase sales and keep the dollar amount of an expense the same, you have decreased that expense as a percentage of income. When you decrease your cost percentage, you increase your percentage of profit.

ESSENTIAL

Business management means managing any components that have an impact on profitability. That's just about everything. You will track and manage costs, income, assets and liabilities, and employees. The better you do at managing these components, the more profitable your consulting service will be.

On the other hand, if your sales volume remains the same, you can increase the percentage of profit by reducing a specific item of expense. Your goal, of course, is to simultaneously decrease specific expenses and increase their productive worth.

Before you can determine whether cutting expenses will increase profits, you need information about your operation. This information can be obtained only if you adequately use record-keeping and financial management systems, as covered in Chapter 10.

Managing Taxes

Like it or not, the government is your business partner. And, as your partner, it receives a portion of your profits—even before you do. However, government can also help you make a profit through the Small Business Administration, Department of Commerce, state corporate divisions, and numerous other business services. Remember, the government is your *partner* in your consulting business.

Types of Taxes

The owner-manager of a small business plays two roles in managing taxes. In one role, you're a debtor. In the other, you may be an agent or tax collector. It's important that you understand your obligations as a business owner.

As a debtor, you're liable for various taxes and you pay them as part of your business obligations. For example, each year, you owe federal income taxes, which you pay out of the earning of your business. Other tax debts include state income taxes and real estate taxes.

As an agent, you collect various taxes and pass the funds on to the appropriate government agency. If you have employees, you deduct federal income, social security insurance, or FICA taxes, and, in some states, you collect state income taxes from the wages of your employees. If your state requires sales tax on your consulting business, you will collect it from your clients and periodically send it on to the state as required by law.

FACT

Paying taxes is a necessity. Some of what you get for your taxes is assistance in finding ways to legitimately avoid taxes. Don't pay more than you absolutely need to. Use the services of the Internal Revenue Service (*www.irs.gov*) to minimize your income tax obligations.

Income Tax

If you are a sole proprietor, you pay your income tax just like any other individual citizen. Your income, expenses, and profit or loss are calculated on Schedule C, which is filed with your annual Form 1040. A partnership files its own tax forms and passes the profits on to the partners for filing on their personal income tax forms. A corporation files on IRS Form 1120 or short form 1120A. Sub-chapter S corporations file on IRS Form 1120S. Self-employment tax—social security insurance for the self-employed—is reported on your IRS 1040 form using Schedule SE.

Individual proprietors and partners are required by law to put the federal income tax and self-employment tax liability on a pay-as-you-go basis. That is, you file a Declaration of Estimated Tax (Form 1040 ES) on or before

April 15, then make payments on April 15, June 15, September 15, and January 15.

Income tax returns from a corporation are due on the fifteenth day of the third month following the end of its taxable year, which may or may not coincide with the calendar year. To find out more about your tax obligations, contact your regional IRS office or visit its website for the following publications, as appropriate:

- Tax Guide for Small Business (Publication 334)
- Guide to Free Tax Services (Publication 910)
- Your Federal Income Tax (Publication 17)
- Employer's Tax Guide (Circular E)
- Taxpayers Starting a Business (Publication 583)
- Self-Employment Tax (Publication 533)
- Retirement Plans for the Self-Employed (Publication 560)
- Tax Withholding and Estimated Tax (Publication 505)
- Business Use of Your Home (Publication 587)

In addition, there are a number of federal forms you'll need for good record keeping and accurate taxation:

- Application for Employer Identification Number (Form SS-4) if you have employees
- Tax Calendars (Publication 509)
- Employer's Annual Unemployment Tax Return (Form 940)
- Employer's Quarterly Federal Tax Return (Form 941)
- Employee's Withholding Allowance Certificate (W-4) for each employee
- Employer's Wage and Tax Statement (W-2) for each employee
- Reconciliation/Transmittal of Income and Tax Statements (W-3)
- Instructions for Forms 1120 and 1120A for corporate taxes

Managing costs means establishing a profitable budget and sticking to it. This process requires accurate recordkeeping, the topic of the next chapter.

CHAPTER 10

Keeping Good Records

To make a profit with your consulting service, you must know what your income and expenses are. This means keeping good financial records. You must have an easy-to-use and accurate recordkeeping system in place and know how to use it. You also must understand the dynamics of your business's income and expenses. Your success depends on it.

Your Recordkeeping Systems

Why keep records? There are many reasons. For the individual just starting a consulting services business, an adequate recordkeeping system increases the chances of survival. Established consulting services can also enhance their chances of staying in business and earning increasing profits with a good recordkeeping system.

Keeping accurate and up-to-date business records is, for some people, the most difficult and uninteresting aspect of operating a business. If this area of business management is one that you believe will be hard for you, plan now how you will handle this task. Don't wait until tax time or until you're totally confused. Take a course at a local community college or hire an accountant to advise you on setting up and maintaining your recordkeeping system. Another option is to trade your specialized consulting services with a professional accountant client.

Benefits of Good Records

Here are some of the questions that good business records can answer:

- How much business am I doing?
- How much credit am I extending?
- How are my collections?
- What are my losses from credit sales?
- Who owes me money? Who is delinquent?
- Should I continue extending credit to delinquent accounts?
- How much cash do I have on hand?
- How much cash do I have in the bank?
- Does this amount agree with what records tell me I should have, or is there a shortage?
- How much have I invested in supplies?
- How often do I turn over my supplies inventory?
- How much do I owe my suppliers and other creditors?
- How much gross profit or margin did I earn?
- What were my expenses? What's my weekly payroll?

- Do I have adequate payroll records to meet the requirements of workers' compensation insurance, unemployment compensation insurance, and withholding taxes?
- How much net profit did I earn?
- How much income tax will I owe?
- Are my sales, expenses, profits, and capital showing improvements or did I do better last year than this year?
- How do I stand compared with two periods ago?
- Is my business's position about the same, improving, or deteriorating?
- On what services am I making a profit, breaking even, or losing money?
- Am I taking full advantage of cash discounts for prompt payments?
- Are the discounts I get from suppliers as great as those I give to my clients?
- How do the financial facts of my consulting business compare with those of similar businesses?

The primary function of a good recordkeeping system is to be able to manage profits and taxes. That means easily and accurately tracking income and expenses. Your system can be computerized with numerous accounting programs or it can be a simple journal and ledger—whatever it takes to effectively manage business profits and pay accurate taxes.

Designing a Good System

Your records will be used to prepare tax returns, make business decisions, and apply for loans. Set aside a special time each day to update your records. It will pay off in the long run; you'll get more deductions and fewer headaches. A good recordkeeping system should be:

- Simple to use
- Easy to understand
- Reliable
- Accurate
- Consistent
- Timely

Several published systems and software systems provide simplified records, usually in a single record book. These systems cover the primary records required for all businesses; some are modified specifically for the consulting services business. Check your local office supply store, your trade association, or trade journals for more information on specialized record books.

Simply, your records should tell you these three facts:

- How much cash you owe
- How much cash is owed to you
- How much cash you have on hand

Journals and Records

To keep track of everything, you should have these basic journals:

- A sales journal shows the business transaction, date, for whom it was performed, and the amount of the invoice.
- A cash receipts register shows the amount of money received, from whom, and for what.
- A cash disbursements register or check register shows each check disbursed, the date of the disbursement, number of the check, to whom it was made out, the amount of money disbursed, and for what purpose.
- A general journal for noncash transactions and those involving the owner's equity in the business.

In addition, here are other records you will need in your business:

- Accounts receivable is the record of accounts for which you haven't been fully paid.
- Accounts payable is the record of accounts for which you will have to pay money because you have purchased a product or service but haven't paid for it all.
- Inventory record is a record of your firm's investment in paper, envelopes, books, videos, and other items you intend to resell.

- Equipment is a record of your firm's investment in equipment that you will use in providing your service and will not normally resell.
- Payroll is a record of the wages of employees and their deductions for income, FICA, and other taxes as well as other payroll deductions.

Some businesses combine all of these journals into a single journal. In fact, there are many good one-write systems that allow you to make a single entry for each transaction. You can also use computer software such as Quicken, Quick-Books, Microsoft Money, or Manage Your Money to track income and expenses in a checkbook format. More extensive accounting software programs include Peachtree Accounting and M.Y.O.B. (Mind Your Own Business).

FACT

Many small and medium businesses use QuickBooks as their primary accounting system. However, many smaller businesses don't require the level of detail that QuickBooks and similar systems offer. In fact, they can be overkill for a simple business. If you don't need a full double-entry bookkeeping system, consider one of the checkbook systems, such as Quicken (*www.quicken.com*).

Cash versus Accrual

One of the questions about recordkeeping your consulting service must answer is: cash or accrual? It pertains to how you will record income and expenses. A cash system records a transaction when the cash is received or disbursed. An accrual system records a transaction when it is accrued or when it is delivered. For example, if you sell your services to a client, you can record the transaction when you receive payment (cash) or when it is earned (accrual).

Most small businesses operate on the cash system. However, if your consulting service often doesn't get paid for services right away because of long-term contracts, you may want to consider accrual accounting. There are advantages and disadvantages to both methods. However, it can be difficult to switch your accounting system from one to the other, so it is better to select one method and stick with it. Ask your accountant to advise you on the best method for your consulting business's needs and structure.

ESSENTIAL

When you report your business income and expenses for taxation, you will identify whether your business tracks on a cash or accrual basis. If you change your accounting method from that of a prior taxable year, you will need to report it to the IRS on Form 3115. Contact your local Internal Revenue office or go online (*www.irs.gov*) for instructions.

Single versus Double Entry

There are two ways to record transactions in your business: with a single entry or with a double entry. The primary advantage to single-entry record keeping is that it is easy. As the name implies, you make a single entry that records the source of each income or destination of each expense. Each entry is either a plus or a minus to the amount of cash that you have. Receipt of a check on an outstanding account is a plus. Payment of a supplies order is a minus.

Choosing

As long as you have a limited number of transactions, single-entry accounting is adequate. But as your consulting service grows in complexity, you will want a check-and-balance system that ensures that records are accurate. Double-entry accounting requires that you make two offsetting entries that balance each other. A check received on an outstanding account is a debit to cash and a credit to accounts receivable. Payment for a supplies order is a debit to supplies and a credit to cash.

Debits and Credits

Every account has two sides: a left or debit side and a right or credit side. The posted (recorded) debits must always equal the posted credits. Some types of accounts are called debit accounts because their balance is typically a debit. Asset accounts (cash, accounts receivable) are debit accounts. Liability accounts (accounts payable, notes payable) usually carry a credit balance. Income carries a credit balance while expenses carry a debit balance. Everything else within double-entry bookkeeping is based on the previously mentioned rules.

If at the end of the month the debits don't equal the credits, check for debits erroneously posted as credits, credits erroneously posted as debits, transposition of numbers (123 to 132), and incorrect math. Double-entry systems make errors easier to find than single-entry systems, so double entry is often the best choice for complex businesses.

Double Entries

Here are some examples of common double entries:

- Cash income = debit cash and credit income
- Credit or accrued income = debit accounts receivable and credit income
- Cash expense = debit expense account and credit cash
- Credit or accrued expense = debit expense account and credit accounts payable
- Prepaid expense = debit prepaid expenses and credit cash

If you choose one of the accounting software programs, double entries will be automatic. However, you still need to understand the basics of double-entry recordkeeping. Fortunately, most of these programs include tutorials that can help you learn what you need to know.

Invoicing

Most of your clients will not pay you cash when you perform your services. Instead, they will want to receive an invoice. An invoice is a list of goods or services, usually specifying the price and terms of sale. Keeping track of payment on service invoices will be an important part of your recordkeeping system.

Invoice Types

There are two types of invoices commonly used by consulting services: itemized and nonitemized. Some of your clients will prefer one over another. An itemized invoice includes a list of what is being charged for, including services, hours of service, and a list of specific expenses that require reimbursement by the client. A nonitemized invoice is simply a short description of the service and the price. If you've agreed on a single fee for a short-term engagement, you and the client may agree on a nonitemized invoice.

ESSENTIAL

Invoice management software is available in stand-alone programs or in conjunction with popular accounting packages. They are designed to automate the invoicing process and track invoices that have been sent out. Many also can accept and process credit or debit card payment for invoiced services. If your consulting service relies extensively on invoices, consider an integrated invoice management program with your accounting software.

Invoice Components

All invoices that you provide to clients for services rendered should include the following components:

- Your business name
- Unique invoice number (for tracking)
- Client name and contact information
- Invoice date
- Purchase order number (if needed by the client)
- Service summary
- Fee calculation
- Reimbursable expenses (if any)
- Tax requirements (tax calculation, federal ID number, or Goods and Service Tax calculation)
- Total amount payable

- Terms of payment
- Where to send payment

Invoice Tracking

Invoices record the amount of money with terms that clients owe you. Payment will be received some day, so invoices are considered accounts receivable. (If someone sends you an invoice for services, it is categorized as an account payable, an account you will pay.)

It is vital to the success of your consulting business that you not only send out invoices to clients, but that you also track them. Most accounting software programs include modules to track and manage invoices. In fact, many offer an automated invoicing system to help you prepare invoices as well. You provide a service—you should be paid for it. Your invoice tracking system is the key to making sure that you have the income needed to cover expenses.

Managing Equipment Records

Office and related equipment must be tracked and managed. Keep an accurate and up-to-date list of permanent equipment used in your consulting services business. Be especially careful to keep track of equipment that is useful for a year or longer and is of appreciable value. Equipment records should show the date the item was purchased, the name of the seller, a description of item, the check number of payment(s), and the amount of purchase including tax. If you own a number of items, keep a separate list for vehicles, computers and printers, and office furniture and fixtures. From these records you will develop a depreciation worksheet and provide supporting information for fixed asset accounts.

ESSENTIAL

Remember, a calendar year is twelve consecutive months beginning January 1 and ending December 31. A fiscal year is twelve consecutive months ending on the last day of any month other than December. A short tax year is less than twelve months because your firm was not in business a full year or you have changed your tax year.

A charge to expenses should be made to cover depreciation of all fixed assets except land. Fixed assets are any item you purchase to use in your business for a year or longer. Examples are buildings, vehicles, equipment, furniture, and office fixtures. Smaller businesses will usually change depreciation at the end of their fiscal year, but if your business grows and you have major fixed assets, you or your accountant may decide to calculate depreciation monthly.

Managing Petty Cash

Most business expenses will be paid by business check, credit card, debit card, or electronic funds transfer (EFT), or they will be placed on account with the seller. However, small expenses that will be paid by an employee or with cash require reimbursement. Because the amount is typically small, the fund from which the reimbursement comes is usually known as petty cash.

A petty cash fund should be set up to be used for payments of small amounts not covered by invoices. A check should be drawn for, say, $200. The check is cashed and the money placed in a box or drawer. When small cash payments are made for such items as postage, shipping, or supplies, the items are listed on a printed form or even a slip of paper. When the fund is nearly exhausted, the items are summarized and a check is drawn to cover the exact amount spent. The check is cashed and the fund replenished. At all times, the cash in the drawer plus the listed expenditures should equal the established amount of the petty cash fund.

It can sometimes be difficult for owner-managers not to mingle their business and personal money. Some keep a separate notebook in their purse or pocket to record business expenses paid from personal funds. They then report these transactions to their accountant or accounting system and draw business funds to replace them. Others use separate business and personal debit cards to ensure that accurate records are maintained.

Online Banking

Online banking has been around for more than thirty years. However, most of it was inter-bank transactions. One bank transferred money electronically to another. Clients couldn't do it. The Internet has changed this dramatically in the banking client's favor.

Most banks and other financial institutions now offer secure connections to accounts by clients. With online banking, you can check account balances, verify deposits, transfer money between accounts, pay bills, and access lines of credit. Best of all, you can do it from the convenience of your desktop, laptop, or Blackberry from anywhere in the world.

To use online banking, you first must have an account with a bank that offers this service. Most do. In fact, many are very helpful in helping you set up a secure online banking account that you can manage from your computer. They even have client service personnel dedicated to helping you with online transactions.

Online Security

The reason online banking is viable is because security tools and common sense make the transactions secure. Your banker can explain how their security system works. Most use a two-step security process that may require that you not only know your account name and password, but also register your computer electronically. If the system doesn't recognize your computer, you will be asked additional security questions (mother's maiden name, birth city, favorite pet, etc.).

ALERT

Visit *http://security.yahoo.com* or *www.microsoft.com/protect* for clear explanations of Internet security systems. Articles cover identity theft, spyware, viruses, and security tips for new users. Billions of dollars in online transactions are safely conducted every day using proven security systems and common sense.

Obviously, banks want your trust. Transaction security systems are established to earn and maintain that trust. You must also use common sense when banking online. However, once you learn how your bank's system works and have secure tools, you will be able to better manage your business with online banking.

Convenience

Online banking is more convenient than teller banking. For example, you can establish direct deposits with your clients so that they can electronically pay your invoices without having to write and mail a check. The money is automatically and securely transferred from their account to yours.

In addition, you can establish automated bill-paying services with your suppliers. Once a month, your office supply company e-mails you an electronic invoice for all purchases, and you approve payment and indicate a payment date. The money is then transferred from your bank account to the supplier's account on the indicated date. No stamps necessary.

If you have employees, you can pay them electronically on the designated payday. Their wages or salary, less deductions, are automatically transferred to their banking account. Payroll taxes are electronically sent to the appropriate agency.

Accounting Software

Online banking is made even easier because most popular accounting software programs can be used to transfer funds to and from your bank. The software is developed using banking data standards that make the flow easier and more accurate. For example, QuickBooks can access a Bank of America business checking account to transfer funds and update your accounting records.

You can learn more about online banking from your banker. Some offices offer introductory classes. Others have online instruction that makes the process easier. Remember that it is up to you to protect your security passwords and not give them to anyone who may abuse your bank account. With that caveat, online banking can make good records easier to manage.

CHAPTER 11

Pricing Your Services

Establishing value pricing for your services is an important step in starting a successful consulting business. To do so, you must understand pricing components, the various types of pricing, and margins and discounts. You also need to compare pricing to value. Then you can develop a rate sheet and use it in writing proposals and contracts. Smart pricing is an important step toward profitability.

Service Pricing Basics

To understand the basics of service pricing, first consider the three Cs of pricing:

- Cost
- Competition
- Client

Cost Pricing

How much does my service cost me to furnish? Once you've established your start-up costs and your monthly operating costs, you'll have a good idea of how much your service will cost you to furnish to your clients. But there's one more important factor that you need: your amount of available time.

Business Consultants

Business consultants typically require about a quarter of their time to market their services and another quarter to keep themselves informed on the latest information in their field (read magazines and books, attend seminars, interview leaders). So they're down to about eighty billable hours per month, unless they continue working after normal hours. If the operating or overhead costs total $8,000 a month, for example, that amount is divided by 80 billable hours to come up with an hourly fee of $100. Depending on their specialty, demand for their service, and other factors, business consultants charge $80 to $300 or more per hour. Business consultants who work on larger projects often establish a per-diem fee that covers their costs for a seven-hour to ten-hour day.

Consumer Consultants

Consumer consultants often spend less time marketing and learning than business consultants. Many consumer consultants can bill up to three-quarters of their time, about 120 hours a month. If the operating or overhead costs total $6,000 a month, that amount is divided by 120 billable hours to come up with an hourly fee of $50. Depending on what they do and for whom they do it, consumer consultants charge between $40 and $120 an hour. However, because the public prefers to pay for results rather than time, consumer consultants often set prices based on an undisclosed hourly rate. A career consultant, for example, will offer a career placement package for $495 that is based on six hours of counseling at $80 an hour and about $15 worth of materials. Service pricing based on costs will be covered in greater detail later in this chapter.

Competitive Pricing

How much are your competitors charging? A few telephone calls should get you this information. Of course, you must make sure you're comparing apples with apples. Your competitor may not have your level of skill in this area, or she may have more. Your competitor may also include costs for some specialized resources that you don't have. To determine your competitor's hourly rate rather than product price, ask her, "If I preferred to pay you by the hour, how much would you charge?"

FACT

How can you find your competitors? Find a copy of *Consultants and Consulting Organizations Directory* published by Gale Research (*www.gale.cengage.com*) at larger public, college, or business school libraries. It lists more than 26,000 individual and firm consultants by name, location, services, and other factors. If your business is primarily local, check your telephone book first.

Why should you care what your competitors charge? Because your clients will probably get bids from them also. You don't necessarily have to match or beat their bids, but you do need to know what competitors' rates are so that you can help the client make a fair comparison.

Service pricing based on competitors will be covered in greater detail later in this chapter.

Client Pricing

How much do the clients expect to pay? Remember that the question isn't how much *will* clients pay, it's how much do they *expect* to pay? The difference is expectations. You may get some clients for your service to pay an excessive fee for a while, but they'll soon move to other sources. What you want to find out is what they think your service is actually worth to them. Most understand that, if they pay you too little, you will soon be out of business and won't be able to help them in the future. They may not admit to it, but they know it.

How can you know how much the client expects to pay for your skills? Ask a few of them. They may tell you what they're used to paying, what they think is a fair price, or maybe what they wish they were paying. Take them all into consideration. Ask the question of them and let them take a few minutes to explain why they think so. You'll get some valuable insight into what clients expect from you as well as what you should expect from them.

Again, make sure you're comparing similar skills and similar fees. For example, a client may expect more skills than you can offer.

Calculating Service Costs

The price at which you sell your services (and products) has a great impact on your business's profitability. However, it isn't the only factor. Costs are critical, too. A cost is what you pay for something. Depending on the type of business, it could be the wholesale cost of products you sell at retail, the employee costs required to provide a specific service, or the cost of raw materials used in manufacturing.

Cost typically includes more than just the purchase price. For example, a retailer will buy products at cost, then have the products shipped to the store and prepared for sale by an employee. All of these are costs. In selling services, any product costs may be minimal or nonexistent. The preparation of the service is the primary cost of goods sold.

In business, costs are typically segmented based on whether they are fixed or variable. The following further explains calculating business costs.

Fixed Costs

A fixed cost is one that doesn't change in proportion to business activity. A service provider, retailer, or manufacturer, for example, must pay rent, utility bills, and some salaries regardless of whether sales levels are high or low. Fixed costs are not typically included in the costs of goods sold.

Fixed costs for a consultant include office overhead. Consider that your business has fixed costs that will impact your profitability and pricing.

Variable Costs

A variable cost is one that does change in proportion to business activity. Typical variable costs for a business include the cost of goods sold, materials, and production costs. A consultant has variable costs that may include resources required for research. A manufacturer who buys parts only does so as they are needed to make things, hence it is a variable cost and considered part of the costs of goods sold.

Defining variable costs can be tricky for some businesses. The office needs electricity for some lights and security whether or not there are employees present; that's a direct expense. However, Monday morning arrives and the computers are turned on for work; that electricity is a variable expense. Smaller companies don't differentiate, but large companies do. Your consulting service, too, will have some costs that vary directly with services and others that vary only slightly. Tracking both can help you establish your pricing.

Value Pricing

Now you know what your time costs you, what your competitors charge for their time and skills, and what clients expect to pay for your service. So which figure is right? All and none. What you want is a price that will drive away about 10 percent of your prospects as too high and another 10 percent as too low.

Selling Value

Here's a technique that will make your business more profitable, put your business above your competitors, and keep your clients happy: sell value not price. How can a fancy restaurant charge five times as much as the diner next door for the exact same ingredients? They sell value. Call it ambiance or image or snobbery or nonprice considerations or whatever. The fancy restaurant makes the client's purchase an event rather than just a transaction. The fancy restaurant treats the client like an individual rather than a number, gives extra service, uses finer dinnerware, and prepares the food to look more appetizing.

You'll see the same technique—selling value rather than price—in any competitive business where one firm wants to stand out above the others. Chevys are sold on price, Cadillacs are sold on value—and both are built by General Motors. Value says that, whether the price is large or small, you will get your money's worth.

The Value of Consulting

So how does a consultant sell value? By establishing pricing based on results rather than time worked. For example, a marketing consultant may charge a percentage of the client's marketing budget to review, manage, and audit it. A financial consultant could charge a percentage of return on investments rather than an hourly fee. Attorneys often base their fees in civil cases on a percentage of recovery. They may earn 25, 35, or even 50 percent of the recovery—or nothing if they lose. Depending on your specialization, consider setting your fees based on value. This is an effective way of countering competitors who want to compare hourly rates.

FACT

Price is the cost of something. Value is the worth of something. Make sure your consulting service offers value to the client that is greater than the price. And make sure that your prospects and customers fully understand the value *before* you present the price.

Imagine going to the grocery store and seeing a can of tomato sauce that was discolored and dented. You'd probably pass it by for one that looked neat, fresh, and undamaged. Yet the contents of each can may be exactly the same quality. Appearance does make a difference, especially in the consulting services business. For just a few dollars more, your business can develop a clean, professional appearance that will tell prospects and clients that you offer quality. Keep your office neat and orderly. Dress professionally. Use quality papers.

Why is your service worth something?

- **You're knowledgeable.** You know about your specialty and how to perform a valuable service.
- **You're efficient.** You know how to work smart to get the job done in less time.
- **You're honest.** You will not knowingly mislead your client or charge for services not performed.
- **You're helpful.** You want to solve the client's problem and not just perform a job.
- **You're fair.** You charge a reasonable fee for an important service.
- **You're accessible.** You respond to questions, answer telephone calls, and follow up with clients.

Successful consulting services don't shun the question of pricing or apologize for high rates. They look forward to the question so that they can explain why their service is worth more than that of other consultants. They sell—and deliver—value.

Pricing Analysis

It is critical that you fully develop appropriate pricing. Without it, your business may not be profitable. You need to establish pricing guidelines and make certain they are competitive. Your pricing system should be easy to implement and easy to adjust to meet changing business conditions.

Business schools teach the four P's of marketing: product, promotion, price, and place (location). Three of the four are expenses; only price generates revenue. Pricing can be critical to the success of any business, though the most successful ones focus on value-added service so that price is less an issue.

How can you establish an effective pricing policy for your business? You must consider all the consequences of pricing to your business success. In the early history of business, keystone pricing was done at all levels because it was easy to calculate. It simply doubles the price you paid. For example, a shopkeeper would set a retail price that is double the wholesale price. A wholesaler would double the manufacturer's price. Easy pricing. However, as business—and competition—has become more sophisticated, so has pricing. The following are some of the most common methods of computing a selling price.

- Break-even point
- Cost-plus pricing
- Rate-of-return pricing
- Demand pricing

Each has its own advantages and disadvantages. Depending on the type of business you are starting or growing, one may be more common than others.

Break-Even Point

Break-even point means that the income covers the expenses. It's easier to understand break-even point in retail than in a service business. For example, if a retail store has to sell 120 widgets to cover the wholesale and overhead costs of a 400-widget order, that's the break-even point. Its profit will begin when it sells the 121st widget. Break-even calculations are more common to retail stores that buy large wholesale lots, such as dollar or bargain stores, though a break-even analysis can be calculated for any product or service. Consultant services can also use break-even pricing, identifying the day of the fiscal year when all annual expenses are paid and all future income is profit.

Cost-Plus Pricing

Cost-plus pricing is more common among smaller businesses. Products or services are priced at a predetermined percentage above the direct costs to achieve an expected gross margin. To understand this method, some terms need to be defined.

The gross margin is the relationship of the profit to the cost. A widget with a wholesale cost of $6 is sold at a retail price of $10. Calculate: $(10-6) \div 10 = 40\%$, the gross margin.

The markup is the relationship of the profit to the selling price. It's the percentage added to the cost to get the retail price. Consider another widget with a retail price of $5 and a wholesale cost of $2. Calculate: $(5-2) \div 2 = 150\%$, the markup.

Should your business use gross margin or markup? They are two ways of looking at cost-plus pricing. Many businesses prefer using markup. It's easier to calculate. For example, if the wholesale cost is $4 and the markup is 100 percent, simply add 100 percent of the cost to the cost to get a retail price of $8. Margins and markups are explained in more detail later in this chapter.

ALERT

In the real world, most small businesses use a variety of gross margins and markups. Primary merchandise or services may have one gross margin or markup while an impulse product or service or one that has less local competition may have a higher gross margin or markup.

Rate-of-Return Pricing

A key element of business planning is calculating the return on investment (ROI). It's the ratio of the money gained or lost on an investment relative to the amount of money invested. For example, a $10,000 investment that earns a profit (or interest) of $1,000 has an ROI of 10 percent (1000 ÷ 10000 = 0.10). This is the number that all of your business investors—including you—are looking for. They will then compare it to ROIs for opportunities with comparable risks. If they can get a 10 percent ROI on a less risky investment (less chance of loss), they will invest there.

Your consulting business can set pricing by calculating a rate of return on your initial investment. As an example, let's use a rate of return of 12 percent. That means a $100,000 investment should pay back $12,000 a year or $1,000 a month in interest from the profit. The same method can be used to calculate a price as long as all other fixed and variable expenses, including payroll and your salary, are already factored in.

Most consulting services profit from the value of time rather than of physical assets, so ROI and rate-of-return pricing isn't as useful to them. However, they can use it as a double-check against other types of service pricing.

Demand Pricing

Airlines are notorious for demand or yield pricing. Buy the ticket well in advance and the price is lower than if you walk up to the counter on the day of the flight. Retailers, wholesalers, and service businesses can't use this method as easily unless they sell hot/cold merchandise. If your consulting business can offer the latest in-demand services, your price can be higher. When supply catches up and the market is saturated with people offering these services, prices will slide until they are unprofitable to offer and you drop them.

QUESTION

My business is seasonal. How can I establish profitable pricing?
Though your business operates seasonally, it probably will have overhead costs during the off-season. These costs must be factored into your overall costs so that your consulting business will still be viable when the next selling season arrives. As you establish prices, calculate annual overhead costs including any ongoing labor needed to keep the business in operation.

There are many other types of pricing methods. As you research and develop your own business you will find ones that are most popular for your venture. Remember that the key to pricing is profitability more than ease of use. That's why there are hand-held business calculators and software to do the figuring for you.

Competitive Pricing

Many businesses begin by simply pricing their products or services at levels below that of their competitors. That's okay, *if* your costs are lower or you are willing to make a lower profit in order to build your business. To establish competitive pricing, then, you must know what your competitors are paying to produce the services they sell. That isn't always easy. If you have been employed by your competitor or in a similar business, you may have some insight into that business's costs and pricing structure.

Smart businesses don't get trapped in the "I'll beat any competitor's price" trap. A competitor with deep pockets can drain your profits by setting up a few services that are offered at under cost—called loss leaders. Instead, sell your services based on perceived value.

Perceived Value

How much is a house worth? Whatever a buyer and a seller agree it is worth. On a specific day, the price may be $300,000. The perceived value a year later may be higher or lower, depending on market conditions that impact the buyer and seller. A seller may be in a hurry to get rid of the home or the buyer may see an investment opportunity that can lower the perceived value of the house.

Perception is a belief based on outside influences. Perceived value is what someone believes the worth of a product, service, or benefit is. Commodity products, such as toothpaste, are sold by price, though the manufacturer attempts to increase perceived value—our brand is better than their brand—through advertising. Services are priced based on the relative value of benefits to the buyer. If the service will save the buyer $1,000, the service price will be set at a fraction of that. An intelligent buyer won't pay $2,000 to save $1,000, for example. Be sure your consulting business considers the various ways that products and services are priced and establishes a pricing structure that offers long-term profitability.

Margins and Discounts

A margin is the measurement of a difference. In business, you'll be using price margins, gross margins, profit margins, and other margins. Pricing is the task of establishing a price difference between what you pay and what you charge for products and services. Gross margins and markups have an impact on pricing and profitability. A discount is a price reduction.

Margins

First, understand that margins are different depending on what type of business is being discussed. A retail business, for example, will use one level of margins or buy/sell differences, while wholesalers, manufacturers, and representatives use others. In addition, you must consider the approximate profit margins of your buyers as you establish prices. For example, a wholesaler selling to retailers must know what margins its clients use so that the wholesale price margins can remain competitive.

The gross margin can help you establish profitable prices. If it costs you $600 to produce a specific service and you want to establish a price that offers you a 40 percent gross margin you can divide the cost (600) by 1-minus-the-GM (1–.4 = .6) or $1,000.

Another common pricing term is markup, which is just another way of looking at gross margin. The difference is that it is a markup based on cost rather than sales. Services that cost $600 that you will sell at $1,000, as in the above example, will have a markup of 66.67 percent—the selling price is the cost times 1.6667. The "1" is the cost and the ".6667" is the markup.

Discounts

Pricing also involves discounts, a reduction from the standard price. If you offer a specific service at 10 percent off the regular price, that's the discount rate. The standard price is sometimes called the rate-sheet price, the one you've established for the value of your time. The effective or market price is the one the client actually pays.

Why would your business want to offer discounts to clients? Many reasons. The primary ones include:

- Increase short-term sales
- Reward valued clients
- Motivate clients to buy

Businesses of all types and sizes—from aircraft consultants to hot dog stands—use various discounts and allowances to increase profitability. They include:

- Discounts for noncredit payments
- Quantity discounts
- Functional discounts (for the buyer taking over some function of the transaction, such as implementation)
- Seasonal discounts
- Promotional discounts
- Membership discounts

Your rate sheet should outline any primary discounts and allowances that you will offer to clients and explain why and how the discounts will be applied. In addition, make sure that such discounts and allowances don't have a negative effect on profitability. To be cost effective, discounts must increase profits sufficiently to make up for potential losses.

ALERT

Discount policies should be in writing: "A 10 percent discount will be granted to any client who uses $1,500 of our services in a month. Each time a client reaches this amount, this discount will be automatically subtracted from the total cost of his next purchase/request for our services."

How can you determine what discounts and allowances will work for your business? Take a look at your competitors. What discounts do they offer clients and why? Also look at similar businesses for discount structures that you can profitably apply to your business. Just make sure they meet their intended purpose: to increase overall profitability.

Developing Your Rate Sheet

How can you develop a price list that is both profitable and competitive? By knowing what it costs to develop your service as well as how much your competitors charge for a similar service.

Establish Rates

First, you must establish standard rates for your primary services. For example, you may determine that your primary service, time management consulting, requires that you charge $82 an hour for your services. You find that your competitors are charging $70 an hour for the same service. What should you do?

If you want to undercut your competitor (and maybe start a price war), you can price the service at $65 and make a smaller profit. Or you can offer it at the same price as your competitor and offer something your competition doesn't offer, such as free access to some of your resources. Or you can compete by offering more individualized service, giving the perception of greater value. Clients want value.

Retainers

A retainer is a contract that says you will be available to a client for a specific number of consulting hours (or services) for a set fee, and will not consult for the client's competitor. Retainers are popular with business and professional services and are catching on with consumer consultants as well. Retainers offer security to both the client and the consultant. Establishing a standard rate sheet, offering various levels of service, offering specific discounts, and accepting retainers can help you make your consulting service profitable.

Proposals

A proposal is an offer to work with a client under specific terms and conditions. A proposal does not become a contract until both parties agree and either sign the proposal or sign a full contract written to expand on the proposal's terms.

ESSENTIAL

Many consulting trade associations offer suggested proposals that you can modify to your own needs. It's one of the many benefits of association membership. Most consultants have a few boilerplate or standardized proposals that they modify for specific client needs. They can make the proposal process much easier.

The following is a typical proposal for a business consultant. A contract must identify the parties involved, define the agreement of what is to be done, explain the details of payment, and be signed by all parties. You don't have to be an attorney to write a binding contract.

AAA Management Services
Building Business for Success
935 View Street
Yourtown, CA 98765
(567) 890-1234

Proposal for Consulting Services

On February 15, 2009, discussions were held between John Smith, owner of AAA Management Services, and Mary Johnson, owner of Johnson Studios, for the purpose of enhancing Johnson Studios' profitability in the coming year.

In response to these discussions, AAA Management Services proposes to assist Mary Johnson and other owners and employees of Johnson Studios in producing and analyzing accounting records, and making recommendations on increasing business profitability.

AAA Management Services' fee will be based on the number of actual hours incurred on Johnson Studios' behalf at a rate of $160 per hour. AAA Management Service agrees to submit weekly time reports every Monday for actual hours incurred during the previous week. Johnson Studios agrees to pay the invoices on presentation. Either party may cancel this agreement within seven (7) days written notice to the other party.

Johnson Studios further agrees to pay all authorized expenses when due.

For AAA Management Services   For Johnson Studios

_____   _____

Date: _____   Date: _____

Marketing Your Services

You may have the most advanced problem-solving resources and methods—but if potential clients don't know about them, your consulting service won't succeed. You must market your services! This chapter will guide you in further defining your prospective clients and turning them into clients. It will show you how to identify those who most need what you offer. It will share tips from successful consultants in many service fields who know how to reach their market and their potential.

Marketing 101

A market is simply the group of prospects who would most benefit from certain services. For a street vendor, the market is anyone nearby who may have a need for what is sold: hot dogs, flowers, knock-off watches. The market for your consulting service is made up of those who could potentially benefit from your service—a very broad definition that will apply to you and to your competitors. Defining your consulting service's market means determining the characteristics of those who would most benefit from your unique combination of knowledge, skills, and resources.

Consultant Marketing

To understand how you will market your consulting service, you must first understand what a consulting service is. Let's review: Consulting is a problem-solving business based on knowledge and relationships. Period. Without these elements, you don't have a business. Because there are dozens of types of consultants—and hundreds of potential markets—we will use broad examples. But you'll quickly get the idea and be able to apply it to your specialty.

For example, how would you define the market for a consultant who can only work evenings and weekends, but cannot have clients meet at her home? That's who you are to your prospects. A prospect for this service is someone who is currently working and cannot take time off work to come to an office. The fact that you do not have a regular office can be turned into a marketing advantage: you offer the convenience of meeting clients at their homes for the consultation. By defining your unique benefits, you can best define your prospects or market.

Focus

Let's say that the best opportunity for you and your skills is to specialize in consulting people on defensive driving techniques. In this example, who are your prospects? Your prospects are those who have had tickets or driving accidents. So how do you find prospects? First, you go where they go. You can typically purchase a list from the state department of motor vehicles or other resources. You limit the list to the geographic area you want to serve. Then you write to or call these people, offering your services.

Obviously, if you are a tax consultant, the way you approach your prospects will be somewhat different—yet the principles will be the same. You will first determine whether there is sufficient opportunity for you to build your business and whether potential competitors are already adequately serving this market. Then you will focus your attention and your marketing on those who can best use your services.

Prospects

Who are your prospects? They are the people who have been influenced by your advertising as well as those recommended to you by satisfied clients. They are former clients, newcomers to the area or field, clients who need immediate help, and your competitors' dissatisfied clients. They are people who have never before required help or advice as well as those who frequently use the services of a consultant or advisor.

Some start-up consulting services begin their businesses by serving clients who cannot be served by their current or former employer. By working with them, you reduce the amount of marketing you must do to develop clients. Most start-up consulting services then pay a marketing fee or a finder's fee to these sources. It's another reason to maintain a good relationship with all of your past and current employers.

Smart Marketing

Marketing is a science. It's not a perfect science where the answer to a question is always the same. It's a science based on data, information, knowledge, and wisdom. Data is easy to get and build into information. From this information comes knowledge and, eventually, wisdom. Wisdom is what makes your business profitable. Marketing builds your business.

The purpose of marketing is to get more clients. That's it. If you're new to business, the purpose is to get your first clients. If you've established a substantial business, the purpose is to keep the clients you have.

There are dozens of ways you can market your services to prospects and clients. They include the many forms of advertising, as well as literature, direct mail, and telephone marketing.

Defining Clients

Clients are vital to your business. That's obvious. The better quality of clients, the greater the success of your business. There are two ways of defining prospective clients or prospects: demographics and psychographics.

Demographics

Demographics is a study of statistics about people: where they live, how much they make, how they buy, what brands they like. Retailers use census information to build demographics that help them decide where to build a store. Consulting services can use demographics, too. They can learn who would use their services and, then, where to find them.

As an example, a consultant specializing in hotel operations must know more than the fact that prospects are a member of a specific trade association. The consultant must also know when hotel management needs the most help and how they typically find it. This information is available from experience, from industry studies, and from other experts in the trade.

Psychographics

Psychographics is the study of why people buy. You would think that most people buy for logical reasons. However, even in the business world, people often buy for emotional reasons and justify their decision with logical motives. Knowing why your clients buy will help you sell to them more effectively.

If you've built a solid reputation in your area as a consultant whose name means quality, you can sell that name. People want to go with a winner, so you will get some jobs just because people know you were involved. Learn what makes your clients buy and help them buy from you.

Market Research

Understanding your clients is so important that large corporations spend millions of dollars annually on market research. Although some formal research is important, a small business can usually avoid this expense. Typically, the owner or manager of a small consulting service knows the prospective clients personally. From this foundation, you can use a systemic effort to build your understanding of your clients.

Understanding buyers starts with the realization that they purchase benefits rather than services. Consumers don't select toothpaste. Instead, some will pay for a decay preventative. Some seek pleasant taste. Others want bright teeth. Or perhaps any toothpaste at a bargain price will do.

Problem Solving

Similarly, industrial purchasing agents are not really interested in drills. They want holes, they insist on quality appropriate for their purposes, reliable delivery, safe operation, and reasonable prices. Video games are fun. Cars are visible evidence of a person's wealth, lifestyle, or self-perceptions.

ESSENTIAL

You must find out, from their point of view, what your prospective clients are buying—and why. Understanding your clients enables you to profit by providing what buyers seek: satisfactory solutions.

Remember that people don't buy consulting services. They purchase practical advice to solve specific problems. They want accurate information they can use to make more money or have more fun. They want knowledge they can use. They couldn't care less about buying consulting services! Put yourself in their shoes and determine what they want, why they buy, when they buy, and how and where they buy these benefits. Then you will understand how to reach them.

Finding Prospects

A prospect is a prospective client, someone who could potentially use your service but hasn't done so yet. They may not have heard of your service, or they may not know enough about your service to determine its value, or they simply haven't been asked.

Identify

Who is a prospect for your consulting services? Of course, that depends on what service you perform for clients. If you're a consultant who specializes in selecting appropriate pets for clients, your prospects are people who want to find a new pet. To turn these prospects into clients you must first think like they think, only faster. As an example, consumers who are considering a new pet may read classified ads or visit pet shops. The consultant can place an advertisement under "Pets and Supplies" offering advice on pet selection. The consultant could offer a fee for referrals from pet stores.

The U.S. Census Bureau is an excellent source of statistical data for market surveys. Based on the latest decade's census, the bureau divides large cities into census tracts of about 5,000 residents within Standard Metropolitan Statistical Areas (SMSAs). Data on these tracts cover income, housing, and related information that can be valuable to you. Results of the 2000 census are now available. Data from the 2010 census, taken in March, will begin to be released by the end of that year. (Visit *http://2010.census.gov* for specifics.) For this and other market information, contact the Office of Business Liaison, U.S. Department of Commerce, Washington, DC 20230 (*www.commerce.gov /OS/OBL.index.htm*). The U.S. Census Bureau (*www.census.gov*) also offers business statistics, data, and special demographic studies among its services. Canadian census statistics are available online at *www.statcan.gc.ca*.

Tracking

How should you keep track of your prospects? There are many ways, depending on how many prospects there are and how you plan to market to them. Some consulting services business owners use 3"× 5" index cards. A typical prospect card will include both basic information—name, owner, address, telephone number, business, etc.—and qualifying information and notes from prospective contacts.

If you're using a computer to automate your business records, there are contact management software programs that will help you keep track of prospects. They range in price from about $50 for a simple system to $500 or more for a specialized prospecting system that can even help you write personalized sales letters. As an example, a good contact management program will give you standard fields or areas where you can type the firm name, contact name(s), address, telephone and fax numbers, the names of mutual friends or associations, and information about contacts. Some programs can even serve as a simple order entry form. If you're making regular telephone calls to prospects, the program may help you schedule callbacks, maintain records of conversations, and help you write personalized proposals that can be quickly printed for mailing or even faxed to your prospect while they're still thinking about you.

FACT

There are numerous client and contact management software programs available in the marketplace—everything from database programs to integrated network systems. To ensure that client record systems are consistent among all sales people, businesses typically purchase a license to use a contact management program throughout their company. One of the most popular is ACT! by Sage Software (*www.act.com*).

Qualifying

Depending on the service you provide and its cost, you may want to establish a screening or qualifying process for prospects. You cannot afford to spend much time contacting people who will never become clients. You can require a small initial consultation fee or have an associate screen prospects for you. One successful business consultant charges for initial consultation unless the prospect has been in business for at least a year and meets other basic criteria. If qualified, the initial consultation is free.

The majority of your prospects will make first contact with you by telephone or e-mail. They may have read your ad in the newspaper or phone book, visited your website, or heard about you from a mutual acquaintance. In any case, it is vital that you make the most of this first contact, answering their questions while getting answers to your own questions about them.

The prospect wants to know:

- Why should I use your service?
- Are you qualified to offer me effective consulting services?

- Are your services of greater value than the price?
- Are you trustworthy?

You want to know:

- What's your name and how can I contact you?
- How did you hear about my service?
- What do you need to know to make a decision to hire me?

Learn all that you can from the prospect. It not only develops a bond, but also establishes that you are a good listener—an important characteristic for success. In addition, you'll make important inroads into the industry, learning who's hiring and who's laying off, which trades use consulting services and which don't, and many other important facts.

Market Analysis

In analyzing your business concept and the marketplace, you must consider your strengths, weaknesses, opportunities, and threats—commonly called SWOT analysis. It is a strategic planning tool for analyzing business ventures. It is a useful tool that can help you develop your consulting business.

Strengths

In business analysis, a strength is an internal attribute that will help achieve an objective. These are the good things about your business. These are the attributes that make it stronger than the competition. Strengths for a business can include:

- **Brand:** established, recognized
- **Competition:** knowledge, assets
- **Costs:** inventory, employees
- **Creativity:** new products, services
- **Employees:** knowledgeable, credentialed
- **Resources:** location, financial

Your business plan offers a good opportunity for you to list the specific strengths of your venture. What brand, competitive, cost, creativity, employee, and resource strengths does your business venture have? Listing them will help you analyze your business.

Weaknesses

A weakness is an internal attribute that can be harmful to a business's objective. To identify weaknesses, consider the same categories you reviewed for strengths. Is your business name or primary brand unrecognized? Is the competition strong? Will your costs of inventory and employees make it difficult to be profitable?

It may be easier to identify business strengths than weaknesses, but you must make the effort. Your competitors will be analyzing them carefully in order to retain or grow their market share. Look at your business concept as your competitors will. Focus on the internal weaknesses and analyze how you can overcome them. Be proactive.

FACT

The SWOT system of market analysis was developed by Albert Humphrey of the Stanford Research Institute while studying the success of Fortune 500 companies in the 1960s. Humphrey's system has since been taught by all major business schools as a method of analyzing and comparing business and competitive marketing. It has also been successfully applied to other business departments.

Opportunities

An opportunity is an external condition that can help a business meet its objectives. What unique opportunities does your business or the current marketplace offer? The following are common market opportunities:

- **Competitor:** downsizing or redirection
- **Economic changes:** growth, recession
- **Environment:** enhancements, reductions

- **Global influences:** availability, costs
- **Perceptions:** popularity, increased need
- **Technology:** greater features, lower cost

These and other opportunities can offer your business openings to start or grow. The reduced cost of a technology that your business depends on can give your venture a pricing advantage.

Threats

A threat is an outside condition that may be harmful to a business's objectives. Each of the market opportunities available can become a threat to your business venture. For example, your competitor may be poised to expand operations or focus its business more on the clients that you hope to serve. The local perception of your business location may be a negative if the neighborhood is declining. You need to analyze and address this issue.

Developing a SWOT analysis for your consulting business will guide you in defining a target market as well as establishing an effective marketing strategy.

Market Strategy

Some consulting services have longer periods between resales than others. For example, if your business is tax preparation, your service is longer term and you'll be helping the majority of your clients annually. If your consulting business advises homebuyers, the life cycle may be three to five years before your current client buys another house.

The repurchase term of your service and related products is important to your marketing strategy. It will help you develop a business design that will ensure your clients have what you offer when they need it.

Sustaining Sales

Many businesses ensure themselves against erratic selling cycles by offering secondary products or services that help maintain income during the "off-season." Tax preparers offer year-round recordkeeping services. Real estate agents develop referral business to supplement repeat client sales. Product-based businesses offer related services that clients need.

What strategy should your consulting business use to sustain sales? Will you develop an automatic service renewal system? Will you contact existing clients during slower seasons and seek additional or referral sales? Your consulting business design should include the specific goals and steps needed to ensure that what you sell is being offered to the greatest number of prospective clients.

Strategizing SWOT

As you design your consulting business, you should review this analysis and develop specific strategies for taking advantage of these internal and external business factors. The following is an example of strategizing a time management consulting service around its strengths, weaknesses, opportunities, and threats.

STRENGTHS
- Owner's varied organizational experience in corporate and residential environments
- Owner's acquaintance with many individuals in the local corporate world
- Office strategically located in the geographic market
- Low operating overhead
- Competitive pricing structure

WEAKNESSES
- Start-up company with no track record
- No individuals, as yet, identified to fill positions requiring specific organizational skills

OPPORTUNITIES
- Professional organizers are a relatively new professional in the targeted geographic market
- The Internet is increasingly becoming a primary source for seeking goods and services

- Population and economic census data indicate existence and continued growth of the specific types of office and residential clients we will target

THREATS
- Some competition may react with lower price ranges
- Competitors will promote existing client base and experience
- Continued recession in the region may cut into total potential client base for all competitors

Make sure your market analysis considers the SWOTs of your business and those of your competitors. With it, you can proactively prepare for your business's marketplace.

Positioning

Wouldn't it be great if your consulting business didn't have any competitors? You could charge whatever you wanted and not worry about another business taking your clients. However, in the real world, all businesses have competition. If someone does come up with a unique consulting service, chances are it will have competitors popping up by tomorrow afternoon. That means you must accept the fact that your business will face competition. But you don't have to be passive about it.

Positioning is the process of comparing your services favorably with those of your competitors. It is how your target market sees your business. Your market strategy should include specifics on your business' position within the market in comparison to your competitors in reality and through perceptions and differentiation.

Reality

In identifying your primary competitors, you need to determine what market share they currently have. If your position among competitors is strong, you can market your services by comparing it to a known factor, your competitors. For example, if your new personal training service is growing faster than the established personal training service in your marketplace, you can say so: The Fastest Growing Personal Training Service in Anytown!

Positioning also can be geographic. You can locate your new business near a known business, competitive or not, and draw from its position. Shopping malls are built on the premise that small businesses benefit from geographic proximity to big businesses. Your marketing strategy may include a relative comparison with your major competitor or the success of an established business.

Perceptions

Reality is what is true. Perception is what is believed to be true. It is an observation or conviction, often one that is suggested through advertising or other promotion. Politics, especially, relies on perceptions over reality. Each candidate and cause attempts to position himself as the appropriate answer to the current question. Perceptions often depend on emotional messages to sell their position: Everyone *loves* our new line of services.

Perceptions can be effectively used in positioning your business, especially if reality positions aren't successful. Your business can suggest that it offers the friendliest service in town, for example. This is a comparative perception. Your marketing strategy may develop one or more competitive positions based on favored perceptions.

Differentiation

Your consulting service should not only position itself well against competitors, it should also make sure that the marketplace knows the difference. Brand X is better than Brand Z. Who says so? Brand X, of course! However, if it is frequently repeated it becomes a perception. Your market strategy will benefit from a clear differentiation.

Differentiation can be used to favorably compare products, services, brands, competitors, and other business components. The differences can be in quality, price, design, solutions, features, benefits, distribution, availability, popularity, service levels, or other specifics. In each case, the differences are emphasized to draw attention to a specific advantage that will benefit the client. Differentiation is an especially useful marketing strategy in defining and promoting niche markets, specialties within specialties. How is your consulting service unique? What's the difference between you and your competitors? What can your business offer that others don't?

Repositioning the Competition

Repositioning can be an effective counter-strategy for your business. For example, you can strive to change the perception the marketplace has of your competitors. This strategy can be more expensive to implement, requiring additional advertising and promotion to be effective. In a sense, you are building your business's market position by reducing that of a competitor.

You can actually reposition your competitors by comparison and contrast. In advertising and promotion, you can either identify or anonymously refer to your competitors in relation to your own business. You can favorably compare your business to a well-known competitor: "Lower Prices than XYZ." Or you can compare your business to a group of unnamed competitors: "Best Service in Anytown!" By doing so, you are developing a perception that differentiates your business yet favorably compares it to established competitors.

CHAPTER 13

Advertising and Publicity

You are entering the large and expanding market of business or personal consulting. Thousands of businesses have gone before you and established their brands. How can your business clearly identify and differentiate itself in a crowded marketplace? By smart advertising and publicity. You can't depend on word-of-mouth advertising to do it. You must be proactive. This chapter outlines how successful consulting businesses have made names for themselves, then promoted those names to build business with proven techniques. You can do it.

Word of Mouth Isn't Enough

Thousands of consultants have learned that developing the best consultancy in the field doesn't guarantee success. It takes more. It takes referrals from friends, various media, and other trusted resources. It takes hard work, lots of money, and some time. You can't profitably depend on your first client to tell ten others and then each of them to tell ten more. You can't afford to wait for profitable clients. You must be an aggressive promoter of your business.

How Long Does It Take?

What about word-of-mouth referrals? Won't quality service ultimately be rewarded by drawing clients? The short answer is: Yes. In the meantime, your knowledge is getting older waiting to be put to use and your business is paying rent, utilities, and salaries. You must pay these ongoing expenses until clients find you. So the more accurate answer is: Not in time.

ALERT

You must be able to control, as much as possible, what is being said about your consulting business. That means you should be the speaker in business promotion. That doesn't happen with typical word-of-mouth advertising. You're not in control.

How long does it take to build word-of-mouth advertising? There are many factors in spreading the word about your consulting business. Even with advertising, many businesses find that clients will discover their enterprise two and even three or more years after opening day. What can help is determining who the authorities are in your field and making sure they know about your new venture. You also can use proven techniques in this chapter for promoting your business. You can't afford to wait on word-of-mouth advertising to find you more clients.

What Will They Hear?

The other inherent problem with word-of-mouth promotion is that you don't always know what is being said about your business. You are not controlling the conversation. You might have a dynamic and unforgettable mission statement, but few are going to quote it. They will pass along their perceptions, which may be accurate but limited. Or the perceptions may be inaccurate and misrepresent your business entirely. You can't afford to rely exclusively on other people's words.

Will They Hear It Over the Din?

We are bombarded by hundreds and sometimes thousands of consumer messages every day: use this brand, buy from that service, operators are standing by. How can your word-of-mouth referral compete with all these carefully worded messages? Not very well.

Because there are so many messages, most clients simply turn off their internal message receivers, zoning out during commercials and passing over pages of ads in magazines and newspapers without even seeing them. So what chance does word-of-mouth advertising have? Unless passed along by a trusted authority, it has the lifespan of a snowball in the Sahara.

The Value of Word of Mouth

So, what is word-of-mouth advertising good for? It can, at little or no cost, supplement your primary promotional efforts. If it is offered by a respected authority, it can initiate or support a positive awareness of your consulting service in a client's mind.

However, word-of-mouth promotion cannot supplant smart business advertising and publicity. Your consulting business cannot succeed if it must wait idly for clients to discover it. Advertising is a tool that you need to learn to use to grow a successful business.

Advertising 101

Advertising is a paid message intended to get someone's attention. In business advertising, the message calls attention to a product or service. It's a one-way message that invites the receiver to take some action.

Promotion is any effort to influence others toward a desired action. It can be advertising, sometimes called above-the-line promotion (because it is obviously a paid message) or below-the-line promotion, such as endorsement, sponsorship, and product placement. Yes, advertisers actually pay film companies to have movie actors hold their brand of soda during a scene.

Publicity is the promotion of a product or service through filtered information, such as a product announcement or press release. Along with promotion and advertising, publicity is a component of marketing. Marketing is the task of getting products and services chosen by the consumer. Your service business is a vital component of the marketing process.

Before you begin advertising your business, make sure you know what your message is, who you want it to reach, and how you can best reach them. Your business's success greatly depends on your ability to promote—advertise, publicize, market—an accurate and needed message about your service.

What is Your Message?

Every product, every consulting business, every franchise, has a distinct message that it wants the buying public to hear, understand, and act upon. The message is rarely about a product, but about the benefits of a product. Coca-Cola Corporation doesn't sell soda; it sells refreshment.

FACT

Charles Revson, founder of Revlon Cosmetics, said, "In our factory, we make lipstick. In our advertising, we sell hope." What does your consulting business sell? The solution to a specific client problem? People really don't buy products or services, they buy solutions. Make sure you know your message before spending thousands of dollars in advertising.

What is your business's message? It is different from your mission statement, which probably has to do with client focus and profitability. The message is what you want your clients to think, to say, to believe, about your business. It can define your clients ("The Homeowner's Helper") or the services you offer ("Weight-Loss Solutions") or more obvious benefits ("Building Your Small Business"). Make your message memorable. A good place to look for service messages is in the yellow pages of telephone books from other areas, which are available at larger libraries.

To formulate your own business's message, first take a look at your business plan (see Chapter 7). It will offer clues from definitions of your business and your clients. Some business plans outline a unique selling proposition or USP, a list of features and benefits that the business will be designed to provide. However, most USPs are too long to become a business's message. It may take some creative writing to develop a succinct yet easy to remember communication that will be your message. Make your message short and snappy.

Who Is Your Audience?

When your were formulating your business plan, you did research and developed a definition of who your primary clients are. Don't say "everyone;" there are many people within the local marketplace who would never consider buying the services you sell. You can't realistically expect to sell something to everyone who contacts you. You must focus on a specific group of primary buyers who most need what you sell. And you must define them carefully: "Senior adults looking for individual training in personal technology tools," for example.

Of course, you have other client groups as well, depending on what types of services you sell. However, most of your clients will have commonality. They may primarily be of a specific interest group, economic group, education level, or a geographic area. Your business may attract others, but these are your core clients. That's the audience for your message.

How Can You Reach Them?

Because your core clients have commonality, promoting your business is a matter of getting your defined message to your target audience. Of course, it's not quite that easy. You first must figure out what message paths these people have in common. Are they all readers of a specific newspaper's business or leisure section? Do they drive past your office every day?

Promoting Your Consulting Business

As you analyze your business's markets and opportunities, you must consider the best methods of reaching these markets. Do your clients watch television, listen to the radio, read newspapers or news magazines, see billboards, read online pop-ups, or click on web links? More important: how can you cost-effectively reach them with your message at the point where they are considering a purchase of your service? You can buy a thirty-second Super Bowl ad for $2.6 million, but will it earn many times the price in new sales? Probably not. How many of the 45 million viewers need the services you offer and will contact you? Not enough. What are your other options?

Media is the plural of medium, something in the middle position—such as between you and a potential client. Mass media are mediums of communication designed to reach the mass of the people. Mass media include television, radio, newspapers, magazines, billboards, and the Internet. In addition, there are target media or specialized communication mediums that focus on specific groups. A local business newspaper, for example, is a medium designed to reach a specific group of people, such as small business operators in Chicago, Illinois. A website offers instructions, advice, and advertisements on household repairs.

ESSENTIAL

A cartoon in a business journal shows two vultures on a large rock. One says to the other: "To heck with waiting for something to die. Let's go *kill* something!" Sometime a business has to be proactive to survive.

The primary business goal of the media is to make a profit by delivering advertising messages to prospective buyers. The media does so by offering these buyers something they want: news, information, data, music, entertainment, or other benefits. Most small businesses use the telephone book, newspapers, shoppers, broadcasting, and other media to present their messages to potential clients. Your marketing analysis and business plan should consider the most effective media for delivering your message.

Phonebook Advertising

Many consulting services say an ad in the yellow pages is one of their best sources of new business. In most locations, if you purchase a business telephone line you will get a listing in one category of your local telephone book. In some areas, the listing is optional. The listing may be as simple as:

AAA Shipping Services, 123 Main St 555-1234

Or the firm name can be in capital letters such as:

AAA SHIPPING SERVICES
123 Main St 555-1234

Or you can include information on your specialty, and even an alternate telephone number like this:

AAA Shipping Services
Specializing in International Cargo
123 Main St 555-1234
After hours 555-2345

ESSENTIAL

Most telephone books include a few pages with information on how to select a space ad. You'll see terminology like double half, triple quarter, and columns. Many telephone books in rural areas are half-size with only two columns per page. So a triple quarter is three columns wide and a quarter page long; a double half is two columns wide and a half page long.

Many businesses upgrade their listings with space ads. A space ad is simply an advertisement that takes up more space than a line or two and is usually surrounded by a box. To determine the size and cost of an appropriate space ad, check your local telephone book's yellow pages index section under the heading for "consultants." It will list consultant categories and the page number. In your category, look for ads from competitors. When a potential client looks in the yellow pages, which ads stand out best? Which have the greatest eye appeal? Which are easiest to read? Remember that you don't need the largest ad in the phone book; you need the one that's most cost-effective for you.

The firm that produces your telephone book will help you design and write your ad. Then they will supply a layout of the ad and a contract for you to sign. Most listing or space ad contracts are for one year and can be paid in monthly installments with or separate from your telephone bill.

Newspaper Advertising

The task of a newspaper is to make money for its publisher. It does so by developing a relationship of information and trust with its target readers. In fact, it will have numerous target groups, each developed in order to sell advertising to businesses that want to reach them. The paper's sports section offers one target group, the classifieds another.

Newspaper advertising is sold by the column inch or other space measurement. Take a look at your local newspaper. Most have between four and eight columns of text to a page. An advertisement that is one column wide and one inch long is one column-inch (1 c.i.).

Once you've identified the local newspaper and the section of the newspaper that best reaches your target clients, contact the paper's advertising department and meet with an ad rep to get a rate card and discuss campaigns.

Shopper Advertising

A shopper is primarily an advertising publication. Most don't attempt to be objective news sources. Their function is to bring as many buyers as possible together with sellers. Regionally, shoppers are also called penny savers.

One of the big differences between newspapers and shoppers is how they are distributed. Although most newspapers are delivered by carriers, they must limit advertising to qualify for cost-effective USPS second class postal rates. Shoppers, because they are primarily ads, don't get this low distribution rate and are distributed either at retail stores or by more expensive third-class postal rates.

Because newspapers are purchased by consumers and shoppers are not, newspapers are considered more desirable media for advertising. People are willing to pay for them. Shoppers simply come in the mail or are handed out free. However, the advertising rate (also measured in column-inches) is typically much lower than that of area newspapers. As with newspapers, contact your local shopper publications and ask for a rate card and sales rep to learn more about their market and their advantages.

Be aware that, in many markets, newspapers and shoppers may be owned by the same publisher. This may limit your advertising options, but you also may get lower combined rates as opposed to buying space in them individually.

Broadcast Advertising

Radio and television have revolutionized advertising, bringing sound and moving images to the sales pitch. Both types of broadcast media have their advantages. Radio is more portable, found in cars, stores, homes, and devices. Television is more visual, offering additional sensory messages to the advertising process. However, in most markets, television advertising is too expensive for small businesses. A thirty-second advertisement (called a "spot") can cost thousands of dollars to produce and require thousands more in advertising fees to make a significant impression on viewers.

Radio stations play specific types of music or offer news and talk on definite topics for one purpose: to draw a defined audience to listen to ads from their sponsors. The audience for sport talk radio will be different than a hip-hop or an oldies station. Considering the local population, radio stations position themselves to reach—and to sell to—a defined audience that isn't otherwise being reached efficiently.

The point to remember about radio advertising is to select what your clients want rather than what you want. You can be a big fan of PBS, talk shows, or classic rock, but if these local stations don't focus on delivering your message to your prospects, don't advertise on them. Spend your money where it will bring you more money. Advertising must be an investment. Your advertising representative can help you write your business's ads and advise you on who should read them—you or announcers (called "talent").

Magazines

A magazine is a focused periodical. It is published on a regular basis (weekly, semi-monthly, monthly, bi-monthly, etc.) to be read by a specific target market, such as local upscale buyers or contractors interested in news about residential remodeling. Your ad in a magazine has readership as long as the issue is in print; once it is replaced by a new issue, your ad has effectively expired.

Magazine advertising makes sense for niche businesses, those that are focused toward a readership that is similar to that of your target client. It may be a local magazine or one defined by an industry or special interest. Your business plan should identify any magazines and trade (industry) publications that are read by your target market.

Magazine ads are purchased as fractional pages, such as quarter-page, half-page, etc. Rates decrease for the space used as the size goes up. A half-page ad typically costs less than two quarter-page ads. Frequency also earns a discount. An ad in two issues as a rule costs less than twice the single-issue rate. You can save advertising dollars by purchasing a longer-term contract for the most effective size of ad for your business.

Other Media

You've probably already noticed that advertising permeates modern life. It's everywhere. Why? Because it works! Advertisers wouldn't spend thousands, even millions, of dollars on something that doesn't work. They're not philanthropists.

Once you open your consulting business, you will be inundated with media sales reps offering everything from yellow pages advertising to vanity ads. There will be placement ads in regional directories, reps for bus bench ads, pitches for ads in shopping carts, direct mail campaigns, and many others. Which should you consider? Any that will profitably bring you new clients. How can you know if the medium is profitable for your business? You can't.

FACT

Consultants who offer services online can advertise with search engines and on sites of interest to your prospective clients. Google offers AdWords (*http://adwords.google.com*) and Yahoo sells search ads (*http://searchmarketing.yahoo.com*) that you can purchase to promote your consulting service. You also can search for "internet advertising agency" to find businesses that can help you identify where to promote your services online.

The easiest way to determine where you can profitably advertise is to carefully study your best competitors. They know. They've probably spent many thousands of dollars on advertising that doesn't return a profit. Follow their lead. Eventually, you will discover profitable media they are missing, but don't try to reinvent business advertising just yet. Follow the leaders.

Seminars and Public Speaking

Besides advertising, there are numerous ways you can make positive impressions on prospects. One time a management consultant developed and presented a low-cost Saturday seminar on managing time for success. Admission was $25 at the door, which covered the room rent, coffee, donuts, and printed handouts offered to participants. Of course, the consultant offered additional services, including copies of her book on time management.

In addition, consultants can speak to other groups on a variety of employment topics. Kiwanis, Rotary, Lions, and other service organizations are always looking for informative (and free) speakers. Just remember that it must be informative, not just an opportunity to sell. Also consider speaking to special-interest clubs within your field of experience. You will be building your credentials as an expert.

Many consultants who speak at seminars supplement their income by selling books or tapes before or after their presentation. This is called back-of-the-room selling and gives you an opportunity to promote your business and meet prospective clients. If your consulting service will be built with seminars and public speaking, consider this opportunity.

Publicity Opportunities

There are many effective ways that you can advertise your consulting services at little or no cost. Exactly which methods you use depends somewhat on your specialization.

Business Cards

Once you have your business card printed, carry a stack of them with you wherever you go. Pass them out to anyone who may be or know a prospect. As you stop for lunch, put your business card on the restaurant's bulletin board. Do the same if you stop at a local market for anything: put your card on their bulletin board. All it costs is the price of a business card. In fact, order separate business cards for your specialties.

Press Releases

Many consulting services overlook one of the best sources of free advertising—publicity. As you start your business, write a short article—a press release—and give copies to your local newspaper, radio stations, shoppers, and other media. Include information about your business such as names of owners, experience, affiliations, background, expertise, purpose of the business, location, target market, and contact name. If your market is across an industry rather than a geographic area, send this press release to magazines in that particular trade, called trade journals.

Expert Columns

You can promote your business and get free advertising by offering to write a newspaper or trade journal column on your specialty in exchange for an ad in the publication. A memory development consultant can offer a column on how to use memory to get ahead. A shipping consultant can write a column in a trade journal that reaches those who use shipping services.

Radio and TV Shows

If you're personable and would be comfortable doing so, offer to host a radio call-in talk show on your specialty. Or you can become a regular guest on someone else's talk show. The publicity will make you a local celebrity as well as an authority in your specialty.

Cable TV also offers opportunities for consultant owners who want to creatively market themselves. Talk with your local cable operator about current and upcoming channels that may need your services.

Donations and Awards

Consider establishing an award or scholarship at a local high school, trade school, or community college in your business's name. Not only will you be able to deduct the award as a legitimate business expense, you can also use the award to promote your business in the local media.

One more proven idea—seek awards. Join professional and business associations, entering all applicable business contests. If you win anything, from first place to honorable mention, use the award as an opportunity to promote your business through local and national media.

Client Referrals

Let's get back to word-of-mouth promotion. It is one of the best and least expensive methods of promoting your consulting business. As you know, it also takes the most time to develop and it sometimes doesn't present the message you want to distribute. How can you take advantage of on-message word-of-mouth promotion? By helping your client refer more clients to you.

To refer is to report. A referral is a report about something to someone. Your goal is to entice clients into giving good reports about your business to their friends and acquaintances. Be proactive in getting clients to report good things about your business. How? You can ask them for referrals! Here are some ways to get referrals:

- Ask clients, "Do you know any of your friends who might need help solving this problem?" If so, ask them for a referral.
- Give discount coupons to current clients, one for themselves and one for a friend.
- Give clients discount coupons that they can redeem when they bring a friend.
- Honor your best clients publicly, such as in your client newsletter. Your proud clients will tell others about it.
- Make sure your business has signage that reminds clients to "Tell a Friend about Weight-Down Services."
- Whenever a client mentions friends in conversations, ask the client for a referral.

The best way to profitably build your business is to clone your best clients. Referrals can do this. They are the most effective word-of-mouth promotion your consulting service can earn.

Many successful consulting services develop much of their business through referrals. That is, they sell their services to those who work with people looking for jobs: counselors, human resources departments, businesses, employment offices, and executive placement centers.

Of course, you can enhance word-of-mouth advertising by developing testimonials. That is, when you have a client who expresses satisfaction with your service, you ask the client to write you a testimonial letter. The letter, on business stationery, will describe how professional your service is and how well you respond to the needs of clients.

Unfortunately, only a small percentage of those who say they will write a testimonial letter will actually do so. But the problem isn't sincerity, it's time. Most clients just don't have the time to write such a letter. Some consulting services offer to write a draft of the letter themselves and send it to the client for approval and typing on their letterhead. A well-written testimonial from a well-respected person will be worth literally thousands of dollars in new business to you. You will copy it and include it with your brochure, quote from it in advertisements, and pass it out to prospects. It will be your best form of advertising. Of course, make sure you have a client's written permission to use any testimonials you quote in advertising.

FACT

You don't have to depend on just your clients to get you referral business. You can work with other businesses in the area. In merchant association meetings, give members some of your brochures or other collateral that tells about your business and what you offer. Also learn what others are selling and ask for reciprocal referrals.

To encourage satisfied clients and their testimonials, some consulting services establish and promote a policy of satisfaction guaranteed.

CHAPTER 14

Working by Priority

So much to do; so little time. That's how you'll feel as you start your consulting business. How are you going to get everything done? Professional consultants know the answer: work by priority. This chapter offers proven methods of establishing your goals, planning execution, scheduling your work day, and making things happen based on their importance to your business.

Importance of Priorities

Whether your clients know it or not, you are being paid based on the time you spend helping them. And you're being paid well for that time. Therefore, you must work by priority: most important tasks before least important tasks. By breaking down your job into specific tasks and scheduling each one, you can help ensure that all tasks are completed on time.

You can also prioritize your jobs into most important, less important, and least important to make sure that you're always doing what's most valuable to your business. A most important job is one with the shortest deadline, the quickest payout, the most important client, the greatest opportunity for your consulting services firm.

Of course, this doesn't mean that any of your clients are less important than any other. All have equal potential for helping your business succeed either through the jobs they hire you to complete or through other clients they bring you. But the full-fee client who must have a special report for her Tuesday staff meeting probably has a greater need for your services than does the client who wants to start planning next year's financial strategy. So you prioritize your work based on the client's need as well as your own. The success of your business depends on it.

Planning for Success

Success in consulting isn't an accident. It's deliberate. You must *plan* for consulting success. That planning requires that you establish professional goals, from how many hours a day you spend prospecting to how many new clients you must locate each month. Your ultimate goal may be to earn a specific amount of money, but it takes these other goals—and many more—to achieve your financial goal. One of the advantages of consulting over many other professions is that you'll have more control over your own goals.

Understanding Goals

A goal is an objective, an intent put into action. Many people have problems with goals simply because they don't understand what goals are and how to use them. Instead, they drift from one situation or desire to another without ever deciding and acting on their aspiration. They don't actually set goals.

The profession of consulting teaches you the requirements and benefits of setting goals. As you discover this powerful tool, you may begin seeing applications within your personal life. It doesn't mean that your life will be filled only with activities intended to meet specific goals. It does mean that you will learn to prioritize your actions better because you can visualize how these actions result in meeting goals.

Using Goals

You cannot set only one primary goal. You must set smaller goals, groups of interrelated objectives that work toward your personal life goal. For example, earning $100,000 a year offering weight-loss solutions is an admirable goal, but it's not your primary one. Your life goal will involve your values, your relationships, and your needs and desires. It may be to enjoy your life in all its facets as well as you can. It may be to help reduce world hunger or find a solution to another larger problem. It may be to make sure that your family gets opportunities that you didn't have. Whatever your life's goal is, your career and specific job goals are components. They are means to an end.

Acting on Goals

Goals are just desires until they are acted upon. To someday visit Rome, you must first decide how to get there, fund the trip, and plan what you will do when you arrive. In a small way, those decisions can begin your action toward the goal. However, it will take greater actions to make the event happen. You will need to get a passport, purchase a ticket, make arrangements for accommodations, and perform related tasks. To enhance your trip, you will want to learn some Italian. You probably will buy and study a travel book on visiting Rome. These are specific actions toward your stated goal.

Your consulting goals require action as well. Reaching $100,000 in annual sales is just a desire until you act upon it, learn what it takes to arrive, make specific plans for your business, and learn what skills you will need to make it happen. You must take action on your desires to make them goals. You must set your goals.

Setting Your Goals

A goal is an objective. It can be physical (such as visiting Rome), financial, or personal. To be a true goal it must meet three criteria. It must be specific, measurable, and time-targeted.

For example, a goal of earning $100,000 in consulting fees in the coming year is specific, measurable, and time-specific. It's a goal—if you take the action required to initiate it. For example, you arrange your work day to see more prospective clients. You upgrade your consulting skills to match those of people who make that much in a year. You take specific actions appropriate to the measurable goal you've set.

Your goal also must be realistic. That's where some goals fall apart. If this is your first year in consulting and it looks like $50,000 in fees is a more realistic number, setting a goal of $100,000 will discourage and frustrate you. Your goal, instead, may be to increase your income level by 10 or 20 percent, a more modest goal. That doesn't mean you can't modify the goal later and even surpass it. It does mean that your frustration will be less.

The time component of goals is also important. There are long-term, short-term, and project goals. Each has its own set of requirements. In addition, you will have personal goals that parallel or supersede your income goals.

Long-Term Goals

A long-term goal is relative. It can have a duration of six months, a year, five years, or more. In most business situations, a long-term goal is three to five years. Rarely are long-term goals for business longer than five years in duration. Few experts can predict business conditions and the economy for more than five years with any accuracy.

Your long-term career goals will be less specific than other goals. They are intended to guide you. For example, your long-term consulting career goal may be to have a staff of three associates within five years. There are no financial specifics in this goal because it is difficult to project five years ahead in many volatile business environs. Even so, such a long-term goal can help you focus your short-term and other goals better because you have a long-range plan.

Short-Term Goals

Short-term goals typically have a duration of a year or less. If your long-term goal is to have three associates within five years, your short-term objective may be to find and hire your first associate within one year. Or it may be to enhance your formal education with courses that can help you in your management role.

Short-term goals can be more specific. A goal of earning $100,000 in fees in the coming year is more explicit. The goal can be even more specific, noting how many new clients you will need, or how you expect to achieve the goal. Remember that successful goals are both specific and measurable.

Project Goals

As you continue your consulting career, you will be involved in a variety of projects. They may be longer or shorter term, though most will be less than a year. However, a specific result rather than a date often defines the length of a project. For example, the goal of a project may be to find an appropriate location for the latest in a chain of fast-food restaurants. There may be a vague time measurement, but, in truth, the project isn't complete until the goal is achieved.

If your consulting service involves large projects, setting goals is a little different because the criteria may be an event or a decision rather than a date. The definition of "success" must be more measurable than a dollar amount. If finding a profitable business location is the project, the criteria must include specifics about territory, market, costs, profitability, and other factors. Project goals require more specifics.

Personal Goals

In addition to your career goals, you will develop personal goals. For many people, they are vague: to be happy or to be rich. As you're learning in your consulting career, goals must be specific and attainable, whether the goals are business or personal. For example, you may develop a long-term personal goal of funding your children's college education within five years. Or it may be to travel to India for a least one month in the next two years. You can have personal projects, too, such as restoring a classic car before your fiftieth birthday. The benefits of learning the craft of consulting can stretch beyond your professional life. It also can teach you how to set and reach personal goals, develop better communication skills, and enhance relationships through listening.

Goals require that you get rid of conflicts. You cannot have the goals of spending all your time at work and all of your time bowling. They aren't compatible, nor are they attainable—unless you're a professional bowler. Instead, you must analyze what compromises you can make in each goal to satisfy the other. If the potential conflicts aren't evident, they will soon become so. Proactively eliminating or reducing conflicts among goals can help you prioritize them.

Prioritizing Goals

Goals are wonderful tools for organizing your career and your life. However, you will soon have an excess of goals. Some will guide your long- and short-term success; others will direct your business and personal projects. What can you do to make sure that you are working on the most important goals? You can prioritize them.

ALERT

Many professionals begin with their life's goals and make sure their career goals fit within them, rather than the other way around. If your life goal is to nourish and enjoy relationships with your family, obviously this will conflict with the time requirements of your career's long- and short-term goals. You must establish a balance.

A priority is something that is prior to another thing. The priority can be based on time, such as dressing before you leave for the office, or it can be set by importance to your long-term goals, such as earning an advanced degree before you launch your business. In your life, there will be conflicts among goals, but most often time will be the telling factor. That is, you have twelve business and personal priorities for a Thursday, but you know you can't get to them all. Which ones should you tackle first? What about the others? Making those decisions is prioritizing, following a list of tasks in order of importance.

How can you prioritize the goals of your career? By determining their relative value to you. Is earning $100,000 more important than serving as many clients as possible? Is advancing your education more important than spending an extra hour on the phone each day? These can be tough questions, especially as you mix in goals from other aspects of your life.

ALERT

Many professionals begin with their life's goals and make sure their career goals fit within them, rather than the other way around. If your life goal is to nourish and enjoy relationships with your family, obviously this will conflict with the time requirements of your career's long- and short-term goals. You must establish a balance.

One effective exercise is to list your personal and professional goals, determine what the requirements are, then analyze how each is important to your life goal. From this you can develop a list of goals in order of importance. Prioritizing isn't easy, nor is it an exact science. Your priorities today will surely be different from those of a year from now. Also, some goals and priorities will be thrust upon you by clients, family, and others. A financial downturn in your field or a medical emergency at home can shuffle your priorities in a moment. But that doesn't mean you shouldn't have priorities; just use them as guidelines for planning your days. Goals are aspirations, not requirements.

How can you ensure that your career goals support instead of subvert your life goals? Communicate. If your life goals involve family, talk with the members, asking them to help you prioritize your time and assets. What do they need from you to meet their own goals? If they don't know, help them understand the importance of goals in your life. Have the same conversation with yourself. What do you need? With such an understanding, you can better prioritize your career efforts to balance your life.

Keeping Score

Imagine a baseball, football, or golf game where no one kept score. What's the point? What would motivate the players and the fans? How would everyone know who won?

The same is true in consulting. Keeping score helps you measure your progress toward your goals. How you keep score depends on the specifics of the goals: prospects, clients, projects, fees, etc. For example, if your goal is to increase the number of new prospects you see each month, then your score card will measure prospects. If the goal is a specific level of income, the goal will be counted in dollars.

Measurable Goals

As you establish goals, make sure that they are measurable. "A fantastic consulting career" isn't a measurable goal. "Earning $100,000 a year advising parents of slow learners" or "Becoming the most respected transportation consultant in Sacramento within three years" are measurable goals. You will know when you arrive—just as a football player knows he's in the end zone.

QUESTION

How can I make my goals measurable?
Make your goals measurable by stating them in terms of your objectives. That is, if the objective is financial, state the goal in financial terms. If it is in a measurable amount of prospects, clients, or problems solved, state the goal in that quantity. This makes it easier to keep score and to identify when you've won—or how close you are to your goal.

As you set goals, remember that various games have different ways of keeping score as well as different definitions for winning. For example, football, baseball, and many other sports use open-ended scores; the team with the highest score at the end of the playing period wins. Other games, such as volleyball, are played until one player or team reaches a specified score. Set your goals and keep your own score based on either the greatest number within a period (as many new clients as possible in the next year) or as a set amount (dollars in fees). Just make sure that your consulting goals are measurable.

In Writing

New Year's resolutions often melt before the snow does. As life moves on, it can be difficult to remember resolutions you made just a few days or weeks ago. It's important that you write them down.

As you make your income, career, and life goals, record them somewhere. Write them as specific and measurable as possible. List them by priority. Include specific plans with them on how you expect to achieve these goals.

Also, be sure that you frequently refer to them as reminders. For example, post them as your computer screen saver or on the front page in your daily planning book. Remind yourself to read them daily or as often as you need to.

Commitment

Having a to-do list doesn't mean things will get done. That requires action. And action requires commitment. Commitment is a pledge or promise. When you commit to a relationship, you make a promise. When you commit to a goal, you make a pledge to take needed action.

ESSENTIAL

Professional consultants advise that as your daily life begins to seem like an out-of-control roller coaster, make a fresh commitment to your life and career goals. They can be anchors that help you see the bigger plan in your life and how it relates to your daily activities. Your goals can keep you on track toward your values.

One motivator for helping you develop commitment to a goal is to visualize the results of that goal. For example, if your goal is to increase your consulting income this year by 25 percent over last year, imagine the benefits of doing so. Picture yourself being able to take more or better vacations, of giving your family more security or better things, or of purchasing something you've always wanted. Use your desire to see results as motivation to make an appropriate commitment to your goals.

Revising Goals

Life changes on a daily basis. Some of those changes can have an impact on your goals. Should you be rigid or flexible about changing those goals as life changes? It's a good question.

The answer depends on the value of those goals and what type they are. For example, life situations may cut your available time to develop new prospects. You may need to revise your weekly goal of helping one new prospect. If the problem is longer-term, you may have to modify your goal of helping fifty new prospects this year. This is a performance goal.

Other goals are not tied to performance, but to knowledge. Your goal may be to increase your understanding of computers so that you can better solve business problems. This is a learning goal. Though important, learning goals often are secondary to performance goals in consulting careers.

Should you be messing with your goals? Only if it's necessary to accomplish longer-term goals. That is, if events threaten one of your longer-term goals, consider revising specific shorter-term goals. If your goal is $100,000 in commissions this year and, because of an economic downturn, you'll need sixty new prospects in the year instead of fifty, adjust your short-term goal of one prospect a week to five a month.

Keep in mind that the function of goals is to take you to a desired destination. It may be to visit Rome or to secure a position of greater wealth and authority. You may need to adjust smaller goals to meet larger ones. That's okay. In fact, it's expected. Life changes on a daily basis and those who adapt have the greatest opportunities to succeed.

Scheduling for Success

A schedule is a list of time-based details. It can be a schedule of appointments, meetings, phone calls, tasks, or other events, each with either a time or a priority level. Your daily efforts as a consultant will require scheduling or planning tasks and events by date and time. In addition, it must have sufficient room to manage unscheduled events. Learning to manage your schedule is a critical part of being a successful consultant.

Calendars

Most schedules are recorded on calendars of some type. It can be a simple printed calendar book available at office supply stores or it can be an electronic device such as a personal digital assistant (PDA) or software on your computer. Exactly what the tool will be depends on what works best for you. If you do most of your work on a laptop or a PDA, putting your scheduling calendar on it makes sense. If your scheduling requirements are limited, a simple pocket calendar book may be sufficient.

ALERT

Who manages your schedule? In most cases, you will. However, depending on what support staff you have, a gatekeeper—secretary, assistant, clerk—may be in charge of setting up your schedule and helping you to meet appointments. If there is more than one source for scheduling, make sure it is coordinated.

Monthly and Weekly Planning

Scheduling books and programs often use a filter-down method of planning. That is, if a client says, "Call back in March," you record it as an event for March with no specific date. Once you begin planning for March, you select a date for the follow-up and record the specifics in your calendar for that date. Alternately, you may place it within a specific week and not make final plans until you are ready to start planning that week in detail.

FACT

If you don't make consulting calls by appointment and only have a few scheduled events, purchase a printed calendar book. It may be sufficient and it's much easier to carry with you in a pocket, purse, or briefcase. In addition, most calendar books include an address book and maps to help you keep track of people and places on the job.

Computer planning software can be helpful. It allows you to quickly note a March appointment for a specific client and it will help you schedule it. The notation can also include a link to your notes on the prior conversation as well as client info from a database. If the next meeting requires that you check some facts or take some other action, the program can help you identify and even schedule those efforts.

Daily Planning

Professional consultants use the past to plan the future, but they live only in the "now"—as does everyone. Your planning and scheduling serves a single purpose: To help you take appropriate action on specific days. It's Tuesday and your schedule says you have client meetings at 9:00, 10:30, 11:15, 1:00, 2:20, and 4:00. That's your primary schedule for the day. Before, after, and in between you'll be preparing for and traveling to those meetings. If one meeting is short, you may get additional time to work on other priorities. If a meeting goes long, you may have to adjust other meetings or delay secondary priorities.

Notice the word "priority" coming up frequently. A priority is a preferential rating. Consulting for a fee is a higher priority than paperwork. Both are necessary, but if you must make a choice, you'll do so in favor of the higher priority task. That's working by priority. You do that many times a day as you review your schedule and prioritize your tasks as a professional consultant.

Calendar Feedback

Feedback is output used to adjust input. You see that the faucet you turned on is flowing too fast (output), so you turn the faucet handle back (adjusting the input). The process is called feedback and you use it in a hundred ways every day as you drive, speak, eat, and work. You make correcting changes in the input to alter the output to a desired level. Eating lunch, you feel full (feedback) and stop eating.

Scheduling your day gives you specific outputs. For example, you meet with Bob at 3 P.M. and learn that he is prepared for your one-hour meeting and it only takes a half hour. So, when scheduling your next meeting with him, you plan it for a half hour. Other adjustments are made in your scheduling based on feedback. You learn that taking a new highway cuts off thirty minutes in your commute and you can start the day earlier. Or you discover that Monday traffic delays you in getting to your afternoon appointments. These adjustments are common and necessary. By making note of them, you can schedule your valuable time more efficiently.

Advanced Time Management Tips

Set up a regular work schedule. It may be from 7 a.m. to 6 p.m. or 8 a.m. to 5 p.m., or 6 a.m. to 6 p.m. Whatever it is, try to stick to it. If you have one time of the day that seems more productive for you than others, plan your most important functions around it.

Consider using one of the popular time management planning systems to help you get the most out of your day. They include Day Timer (*http://daytimer.com*), Day Runner (*www.dayrunner.com*) and Planner Pads (*http://plannerpads.com*). These and other systems give you a place to record appointments, daily to-do lists, special projects and their steps, and names and addresses. If you spend most of your time in the office at a computer, there are numerous contact management and scheduling programs that will help you manage your time.

ESSENTIAL

Having trouble staying motivated in your consulting business? As your consulting career grows, you will discover new relationships with people in your trade. Some will become your mentors. At the very least, you may get a sympathetic listener who understands the problems that you face and can hear you out. Don't give up. Ask for help.

What about travel and waiting time? Take work with you in a briefcase or purchase a laptop computer or PDA that you can use to be productive every minute. As your time management skills improve, you'll learn how to do more than one thing at a time. You'll multitask. You could be making job notes, talking with a key employee, or gathering information on an upcoming project while you're waiting to talk with a client.

CHAPTER 15

Profitability

Money certainly isn't everything in life. But it is a convenient way of keeping score. In most cases, you will be rewarded monetarily in relation to the service you provide to others. The more you help, the more you earn. How much of that you keep depends on how well you manage your money. This chapter will help ensure that you gain and keep an appropriate amount of money for what you do. It covers profits, profitability, ways to increase profits, and the vital topic of cash flow. It also offers proven methods of increasing profits by retaining clients.

Understanding Profit and Loss

"My consulting service is a nonprofit business. It wasn't designed that way, but that's how it's working out!"

Too many businesses get so busy that they forget to make a profit. They don't quite understand what "profitability" really means or how to seek and maintain it. Profit is simply the amount of money you have left over once you've paid all of your expenses. If you have more expenses than income, you have a loss. It seems pretty simple.

Of course, there's much more to profit and loss than numbers on paper. Your business can actually show a profit on paper, yet not have any cash. In fact, many profitable businesses go out of business each year because of negative cash flow.

How can you keep your consulting business profitable and the cash flowing? By clearly understanding profitability—especially gross and net profit—how to reduce expenses and how to increase income. Later in this chapter, you'll learn how to manage cash flow.

Profits

Profit is income less expenses. It's what's left over after you've paid the bills. Because you have some options as to how you price your services, earn income, and pay expenses, you also have choices in profitability. Certainly, you want the highest profits your business can consistently earn. The problem is that if your profits—based on your prices—are too high, they will develop market opportunities for competitors. If you sell a service at $120 an hour that a competitor profitably offers for $80 an hour, you will lose some business to that competitor.

As you develop your consulting business, you should study competitors to determine what their profitability is. This will help you see how your business can be at least as profitable in the long run. You may decide to offer some services at prices lower than the competition—called loss leaders—to draw clients who may also purchase more profitable services. You may learn that a competitor works on an average profit of twelve percent. You may then decide that you can beat the competition with a profitability of 10 percent. In addition, you will offer some loss leaders at no profit and others at 20 percent profitability. You don't have to get into the specifics just yet, but you should develop a profitability goal for your business early on. Otherwise, when you finally do come to the question of profits, you may find that the business model you developed won't support sufficient profits.

ESSENTIAL

If you can, purchase stock in your competitor's business to find out what their profits are. If the business is a franchise, become a candidate for the franchise and learn what level of profitability is required to maintain the franchise opportunity. Alternately, ask a business consultant who can do the research for you and offer a fairly accurate estimate of the competitor's profitability.

Profitability

Profitability is the bottom line. It is why you spent time determining the appropriate pricing for what you sell. If your business isn't profitable, you won't be able to serve your clients for very long.

Profitability is the ability to make a profit. Profit is income less expenses. Sell $200,000 worth of services with expenses of $150,000 and your profit is $50,000. The primary purpose of your business—any business—is to make a profit for its owner(s) and investor(s).

Of course, calculating a profit isn't quite that easy. Gross profit or net profit? Before taxes or after? Which taxes? Are there tax credits available? Is the profit retained by the business or passed on to the investors? The following topics will analyze profitability.

Gross Profit

Gross profit is the difference between revenue and the cost of providing a service before deducting overhead expenses and taxes. If your consulting service takes in $5,000 for a project and must pay $1,000 in direct expenses, the gross profit is $4,000. Those direct expenses can include research, unreimbursed travel, and any expenses that are tied directly to that project. Depending on the business, gross profit is also called sales profit or gross operating profit. It typically doesn't include expenses of operating the business, called indirect or overhead expenses.

Net Profit

Net profit deducts overhead from gross profit. Overhead includes the costs of your office operation, staffing, and any other expenses that are required to keep your business open, such as telephone service. Net profit is the amount of money left over after all fixed and variable expenses are paid except one: taxes. Net profit is also known as pre-tax profit; once taxes are paid, the amount becomes profit after taxes. If no profit was made, it is loss after taxes.

Increasing Profitability

As your business grows, you will discover opportunities to increase profitability. You will find cost-effective ways to increase sales, reduce overhead, reduce taxes, and offer profitable discounts and allowances. Anything that increases your gross margin—the difference between sales and costs—offers potential profitability.

How can you increase profitability for your consulting service? The three primary ways are to increase services, reduce costs, and adjust pricing.

Increase Services

Your business may begin by offering one or two primary services or solutions to clients. However, you may soon discover related services—or even products—that your clients need and are willing to pay for. Increasing services can increase profitability.

For example, a restaurant consultant helps clients better manage their business by analyzing business ratios, labor costs, and other cost accounting activities. Once established, the consultant may discover that there is a need for food management services: how to purchase and store foods while minimizing waste and loss. It's a related service that existing clients need and, with research, the consultant can provide. Income increases. Because the consultant doesn't have to go out and find new clients for this service, costs are down. Expenses barely increase. Higher income with lower expenses equals greater profits.

Reduce Costs

Reducing fixed and variable costs can also help your new or growing business increase profits. If a specific service costs you $1,000 a day to provide and you find a way of reducing that cost by 10 percent, you also are increasing your profits. In fact, if you only made $100 profit on a unit and you now earn a $200 profit, you have doubled your profits!

QUESTION

Should I cut employee salaries to reduce costs?
All businesses benefit from reducing costs. Many attempt to cut wages and related costs. However, they often find out that the quality of service diminishes and sales are lost. Instead, find ways to reduce costs by increasing employee productivity. Analyze how you can make your employees more effective by using training and technology to get more from their time.

Adjust Pricing

Pricing is an important issue in your consulting business. Your pricing policy should include measurements to ensure that services are priced for profitability. If your competitors lower prices, you may need to adjust yours. Or you may decide that the gross margin on these products isn't sufficient, so you refocus on offering products with higher margins.

In addition, you will continue to use cost accounting to know what your services are costing you to produce. As needed, you can adjust pricing to remain profitable.

Improving Client Profitability

Once your new or growing business attracts clients, how will you keep them? Client retention is a vital component of business success. For example, if you calculate that it costs you $100 in advertising and other promotions to earn a single client and just $20 to retain that client, it's a smart business decision to invest in retaining your existing clients.

That's why business experts suggest that you "lose a sale if you must, but never lose a client." If a client needs something that you don't have, make it your goal to satisfy and retain the client by making a referral, even to one of your competitors. You may lose $50 in profits on the sale, but you will probably retain the client, who will come to you first for future advice. Again: Lose the sale, but don't lose the client.

ESSENTIAL

If you don't know where to start in determining how you will keep clients, look first to your competitors. Then determine what method will work best for your business depending on whether you want to avoid or beat your competitors. Also anticipate future competitors as well as redirections from current competitors. Stay ahead of them to stay in business.

Retaining By Price

Individual buyers and market groups often buy commodity products based on price. ABC Stores has Crust Toothpaste at $2.95 a tube, but XYZ Mart offers it at $2.55. If your consulting business offers a commodity (common or mass-produced) service, be prepared to sell it based on competitive pricing. Any one of your competitors can cut his price and take some of your business away.

Most small businesses don't attempt to retain clients based on the lowest price. They often cannot compete with large competitors who can automate services and can sell them for less than your business can produce them.

Retaining by Service

Service is helping others. Whether your business sells a product or a service, service is involved. Representatives of your business—yourself or employees—directly or indirectly assist clients in solving problems. Service is an action that benefits others. By considering your client's needs and fulfilling as many of them as possible, you are providing a service. Your unique insight into your client's needs and your ability to help clients are what make your service unique and less subject to competition.

Retaining by Selection

Many consulting businesses capture and retain clients by offering a selection of services that is wider than those available from your competitors. Consider the many needs of your core clients. What related needs do they have? Which of these needs can you fulfill with your knowledge and experience? What further services can you develop that will benefit your clients? Can you somehow make your business a one-stop resource for your core clients?

ALERT

> You can improve client income—and profitability—by improving your services. It can be as simple as having fresh, quality coffee in the waiting room; meeting clients near their home or office; or offering a free initial consultation. Whatever you can do to earn your client's business can help your business' profitability.

Many small consulting businesses are niches, or specialized businesses within specialties. Small businesses often start up in this category. The primary reason is diversity. If a well-funded competitor enters the market and takes some of your clients, you still have segments of your business that can be expanded to compensate. In addition, many of your clients will appreciate the wide selection and buy from you even though your prices may be higher than price competitors. Identifying and analyzing your individual clients can help you determine the best ways to find and retain your best clients with a wider selection.

Cash Flow

Making a profit is a good thing. Being able to spend it is better. Too many profitable new businesses have difficulty because their profits are all on paper and not in the bank. They are cash-poor.

Your consulting business must have a healthy flow of working capital to survive. Cash flow is the amount of working capital available in your business at any given time. It is your income less expenses, in cash. To keep tabs on cash flow, forecast the funds you expect to receive and disburse over a specific time. Then you can predict deficiencies or surplus in cash and decide how best to respond.

Cash Flow Forecasting

A cash flow forecast serves one other very useful purpose in addition to planning. As the actual information becomes available to you, compare it to the monthly cash flow estimates you previously made to see how accurately you are estimating. As you do this, you will give yourself on-the-spot business training in making more accurate estimates and plans for the coming months. As your ability to estimate improves, your financial control of the business will increase.

ALERT

Every time you have to purchase on credit, you add interest costs to your business. If you had more cash, you would be able to save more on interest expense. For this and other reasons, you can reduce your costs—and increase profitability—by increasing cash flow.

The cash flow forecast identifies when cash is expected to be received and when it must be spent to pay bills and debts. It shows how much cash will be needed to pay expenses and when it will be needed. The cash flow forecast enables you to plan for shortfalls in cash resources so short-term working capital loans or a line of credit may be arranged in advance. Also, if you have excess cash, it allows you to put this cash to productive use and earn a return. It allows you to schedule purchases and payments so you can borrow as little as possible. Because not all sales are cash sales, you must be able to forecast when accounts receivable will be cash in the bank as well as when regular and seasonal expenses must be paid.

Budgeting

The cash flow forecast may also be used as a budget, helping you increase your control of the business through comparing actual receipts and payments against forecasted amounts. This comparison helps you identify areas where you can manage your finances even better.

A cash flow forecast or budget can be prepared for any period of time. However, a one-year budget matching the fiscal year of your business is the most useful. Many successful consulting services prepare their cash flow forecasts on a monthly basis for the next year. It should be revised no less frequently than quarterly to reflect actual performance in the previous three months of operations and verify projections.

Importance of Cash

All businesses, no matter how small or large, function on cash. Many businesses become insolvent because they don't have enough cash to meet their short-term obligations. Bills must be paid in cash, not potential profits. Sufficient cash is, therefore, one of the keys to maintaining a successful business.

Consulting services face a continual cycle of events that may increase or decrease the cash balance. Cash is decreased in the acquisition of equipment or supplies. It is reduced in paying off the amounts owed to suppliers (accounts payable). Services are sold and these sales generate money owed from clients (accounts receivable). When clients pay, accounts receivable is reduced and the cash account is increased. However, the cash flows are not necessarily related to the sales in that period because clients may pay in the next period.

Net Working Capital

Consulting services must be continually alert to changes in working capital accounts, the cause of these changes, and their implications for the financial health of the company. The change in the cash can be readily determined if you know net working capital and the changes in current liabilities and current assets other than cash.

Let:

NWC = net working capital
CA = change in current assets other than cash
CL = change in current liabilities
Cash = change in cash

NWC is the difference between the change in current assets and current liabilities:

$$NWC = CA + Cash - CL$$

This relationship shows that if we know the net working capital, the change in current liabilities, and the change in current assets less cash, we can calculate the change in cash. The change in cash is then added to the beginning balance of cash to determine the ending balance.

At any given level of sales, it's easier to forecast the required accounts payable and receivable than net working capital. To forecast this net working capital account, you must trace the source and application of funds. Sources of funds increase working capital. Application of funds decrease working capital. The difference between the source and application of funds is the net working capital.

Balancing Cash Flow

The following calculation is based on the fact that the balance sheet is indeed in balance. That is, the total assets equal total liabilities plus owner's equity.

Current Assets + Noncurrent Assets + Retained Earnings = Current Liabilities + Long-term Liabilities + Equity

Rearranging this equation:

Current Assets – Current Liabilities = Long-term Liabilities + Equity– Noncurrent Assets – Retained Earnings

Because the left side of the equation is working capital, the right side must also equal working capital. A change in either side affects the net working capital. If long-term liabilities and equity increase of noncurrent assets decrease, net working capital increases. This change would be a source of funds. If noncurrent assets increase or long-term liabilities and equity decrease, net working capital decreases. This change would be an application of funds.

Typical sources of funds or net working capital are funds provided by operations, disposal of fixed assets, issuance of stock, and borrowing from a long-term source. The typical applications of funds or net working capital are purchase of fixed assets, payment of dividends, retirement of long-term liabilities, and repurchase of equity.

ALERT

Experienced consultants advise that managing cash flow is one of the most critical business skills they must develop. Some use spreadsheets; others rely on computerized accounting systems to track income and expenses. To minimize borrowing on credit, smart consultants make sure that there is always sufficient incoming cash to pay expenses when due. Your business's future depends on cash flow.

Developing Business Credit

Credit is simply someone's faith that the client will keep a promise. You buy a computer system on credit, and the lender believes that you will pay back what you've borrowed. Or, in the case of secured loans, you have assets that can be sold to cover what you've borrowed. So how do you build credit? Easy. You borrow a small amount, pay it back, borrow a larger amount, and pay it back, and so on.

A good way to start building your business credit is to use personal assets—signature, real estate equity—as collateral for your business. One enterprising consulting service owner simply applied for a credit card in his business name from the same company that sponsored his long-standing personal credit card. He asked for a small credit limit, used it and paid it off, then asked for an increased credit limit. In the meantime, he used the credit card as a reference for a new account with a supplier. Other new business people use equity in their homes or investment land as collateral for credit with banks and suppliers.

To increase your business's profitability, understand and track income, expenses, and—especially important—cash flow. Your consulting business must not only be profitable, it must manage cash to minimize the cost of credit.

CHAPTER 16

Financial Records

Businesses keep score of their success with financial records. They track income and expenses, make sure that assets and liabilities are in balance, manage interest and the flow of cash, and use financial ratios to improve financial planning. Your success as a consultant will depend on how well you can manage the money coming in versus the money going out.

Tracking Income and Expenses

As the owner of a consulting services firm, you need accurate information on a regular basis to ensure that your business is running smoothly. As a single-person firm, you may have all the information you need in your head. But as your firm grows, you will need various data daily, weekly, or monthly. Let's take a look at what you will need and when.

Daily Reports

In order to manage your consulting firm, you will want the following information on a daily basis:

- Cash on hand
- Bank balance
- Daily summary of sales and cash receipts
- Daily summary of money paid out by cash or check
- Correction of any errors from previous reports

You can either prepare this information yourself, have an office employee prepare it for you, or rely on your accountant. While daily records will not show trends, they will help you get a feel for the level of business that you're doing. You'll also be able to spot problems before they become serious.

Weekly Reports

Once a week, you or one of your employees should prepare a weekly report on your firm. While they are still not sufficient for long-term planning, weekly figures will help you make small corrections in the course your business is taking. Weekly, you'll want the following reports:

- Accounts receivable report, listing accounts that require a call because they are more than sixty days past due
- Accounts payable report, listing what your business owes, to whom, and if a discount is offered for early payment
- Payroll report, including information on each employee, the number of hours worked during the week, rate of pay, total wages, deductions, net pay, and related information

- Taxes and reports required to be sent to city, state, and federal governments

Your weekly reports should be prepared by the end of business each Friday so you can review them over the weekend or early Monday morning.

Monthly Reports

Once a month, you will want to review a number of pieces of information that have accumulated through your daily and weekly reports but were too small to analyze clearly. Now that they are part of a full month, information about cash flow, accounts receivable, and other parts of your business make more sense and can be more easily acted upon. Here are some of the reports and information you will want to see every month:

- Monthly summary of daily cash receipts and deposits
- General ledger, including all journal entries
- Income statement showing income for the prior month, expenses incurred in getting the income, overhead, and the profit or loss received
- Balance sheet showing the assets, liabilities, and capital or current worth of the business
- Check reconciliation showing which checks were deposited and which were applied by payees against your business checking account, and verifying that the cash balance is accurate
- Petty cash fund report to ensure that paid-out slips plus cash equals the beginning petty cash balance
- Tax payment report showing that all federal tax deposits, withheld income, and FICA, state and other taxes have been paid
- Aged receivables report showing the age and balance of each account (thirty, sixty, ninety days past due)

Let's cover three of the most important documents you'll review monthly: your income statement, your balance sheet, and your cash flow forecast.

Your Income Statement

An income statement is a tally of the income from sales and the expenses incurred to generate the sales. It is a good assessment tool because it shows the effect of your decisions on profits. It is a good planning tool because you can estimate the impact of decisions on profit before you make them. The following is a typical income statement for a new consulting business:

INCOME STATEMENT	
Income	
Consulting services	82,000
Income from speaking, writing	13,250
Gross income	95,250

Expenses	
Owner's salary	48,000
Payroll	20,000
Payroll taxes	4,100
Rent	9,000
Office equipment and supplies	3,500
Telephone and utilities	2,800
Insurance	1,200
Miscellaneous	1,100
Total expenses	89,700

Net Profit (before income taxes)	**5,500**

Your income statement includes four kinds of information:

- Sales information lists the total revenues generated by the sale of your service to clients.
- Direct expenses include the cost of labor and materials to perform your service
- Indirect expenses are the costs you incur even if your service is not sold, including salaries, rent, utilities, insurance depreciation, office supplies, taxes, and professional fees
- Profit is shown as a pre-tax income (important to the IRS) and after-tax or net income (important to you and your loan officer)

Your Balance Sheet

A balance sheet is a summary of the status of your business—its assets, liabilities, and net worth—at an instant in time. By reviewing your balance sheet along with your income statement and your cash flow forecast, you will be able to make informed financial and business planning decisions. A typical balance sheet for a new consulting service may look like this:

BALANCE SHEET	
ASSETS	
Current Assets	
Cash	8,278.15
Accounts receivable	6,511.19
(Allowance for doubtful accounts)	(651.12)
Inventory	819.20
Prepaid expenses	1,160.00
Total current assets	16,117.42
Fixed Assets	
Land	0
Building	0
(Allowance for depreciation)	(0)
Total fixed assets	0
TOTAL ASSETS	16,117.42
LIABILITIES AND EQUITY	
Current Liabilities	
Accounts payable	4,191.00
Owner's equity	11,926.42
TOTAL LIABILITIES AND EQUITY	**16,117.42**

The balance sheet is drawn up using the totals from individual accounts kept in your general ledger. It shows what you have left when you pay all your creditors. Remember: Assets less Liabilities equals Capital or Net Worth. The assets and liabilities sections must be equal or *balance*—hence the name. It can be produced quarterly, semiannually, or at the end of each calendar or fiscal year. If your record keeping is manual you will be less likely to develop a frequently updated balance sheet. Many accounting software programs can give you a current balance sheet in just a couple of minutes.

While your accountant will be most helpful in drawing up your balance sheet, it is you who must understand it. Current assets are anything of value you own, such as cash, inventory, or property that the business owner can convert into cash within a year. Fixed assets are things such as land and equipment. Liabilities are debts the business must pay. They may be current, such as amounts owed to suppliers or your accountant, or they may be long-term, such as a note owed to the bank. Capital, also called equity or net worth, is the excess of your assets and retained earnings over the amount of your liabilities.

Improving Cash Flow

As you can see, to grow your consulting services business you need cash. Chapter 15 introduced the concept of cash flow and your cash flow forecast. Once you've analyzed cash flow and determined you need more of it, what can you do? Depending on the type of business you own, you can find increased cash in your accounts receivable and in your inventory.

ALERT

Failure to closely monitor late payments ties up investments and weakens profits. The more overdue accounts become, the greater is the danger that they will be uncollectible and will have to be written off against profits.

Accounts receivable represent the extension of credit to support sales. In your business, the types and terms of credit you grant are set by established competitive practices. As an investment, the accounts receivable should contribute to overall return on investment (ROI).

Excessive investment in accounts receivable can hurt your return on investment by tying up money unnecessarily. One good way to judge the extent of accounts receivable is to compare your average collection period with that of rivals or the industry average. If your average collection period is much higher than your competitors' or the industry norm, your accounts receivable may be excessive.

If they are excessive, it may be that you're not keeping tight control of late payers. You can check this by developing an aging schedule. An aging schedule shows the distribution of accounts receivable with respect to being on time or late.

If the aging schedule does not reveal excessive late accounts, your average collection period may be out of line simply because your credit policy is more liberal than most. If so, it should translate into more competitive sales and greater profits. Otherwise, you should rethink your credit program.

Managing Loan Interest

Money is a commodity, bought and sold by lenders. Just like other products, you can often save money by shopping around. Here are some points to consider as you shop for money.

First, are there any loan fees or other charges required to set up or service the loan? Some lenders will require that a loan fee of 1 percent, 2 percent, or more be paid in advance. Others will even roll the loan fee into the loan, allowing you to pay interest upon interest. Others will deduct a monthly service fee from each payment as it is made. This arrangement is not necessarily bad; after all, the lender must make his profit from you in some manner. Just make sure you understand what the actual cost of the loan is before you agree to it. You also need to know actual interest rates as you compare rates between lenders.

Second, consider whether your best option is fixed rate or variable rate interest. Fixed rate interest means the interest rate charged by the lender is the same throughout the life of the loan. Variable rate interest can vary during the term of the loan based on some outside factor. This factor is usually the cost of the money to the lender. Most variable or adjustable interest loans have caps specifying a maximum amount the rate can rise, both annually and through the life of the loan. The difference between the lender's cost to get the money and what he charges you is called the spread. From that spread comes his sales costs, office overhead, salaries, and profit. The spread is also based on the amount of risk he is taking in loaning the money to you. Higher risk means a higher spread. There are numerous indexes used to establish the cost of money. Review all of the options with your lender, ask which one makes the most sense for your needs, and get a second opinion.

Variable rate interest reduces the amount of risk the lender is taking, especially on long-term loans. He is virtually assured that, unless the money market goes crazy and goes over the cap, he will get his margin of profit from every dollar you send it. Lower risk means lower rates. The point is that you shouldn't disqualify variable rate loans from consideration. In many cases, they cost less than fixed rate loans and many lenders are more willing to make them.

ALERT

To make sure that you pay the best interest rate available, don't jump into the arms of the first loan officer that comes to you. Shop around and compare. You may eventually decide to take that first offer, but only because you've found nothing better.

But don't worry about getting the absolute lowest interest rate available. You may want to accept your regular lender's loan terms, even though it's a quarter of a percentage point higher, in order to maintain a mutually profitable relationship. That quarter point may only mean a few dollars to you and will reinforce your business relationship with your lender.

Offering Credit to Clients

Offering advice in which people must trust you requires that you trust them as well. This means extending credit to your clients. Some consultants require prepayment for the initial consultation or purchase, then place the client on a net-thirty-days credit policy.

Common terms of payment for consultants include:

- Payment on receipt of weekly, biweekly, or monthly invoice
- Advance payment of weekly or monthly retainer, offset against weekly or monthly invoices for actual time
- Advance payment equal to a percentage of total fixed fee
- Total fee payable on completion of job

Many offer payment by credit or debit card. Using credit card services, such as Visa, MasterCard, American Express, and Discover, can transfer bad debt problems to others and increase cash flow for your business. However, consider that you will need to pay an initial set-up cost and ongoing service charges. The credit card service will charge you between 2 and 5 percent on each transaction. Talk with your banker about offering your clients the option of paying for services with their credit card. Ask about a merchant account.

Improving Financial Planning

Financial planning affects how and on what terms you will be able to attract the funding you need to establish, maintain, and expand your business. Financial planning determines the human and physical resources you will be able to acquire to operate your business. It will be a major factor in whether you will be able to make your hard work profitable.

The balance sheet and the income statement are essential to your business, but they are only the starting point for successful financial management. The next step is called ratio analysis. Ratio analysis enables you to spot trends in a business and to compare its performance and condition with the average performance of similar businesses in the same industry. To do this, compare your ratios with the average of other consulting services as well as with your own ratios over several years. Ratio analysis can be the most important early warning indicator for solving business problems while they are still manageable.

QUESTION

How can I know what my financial statements should look like? Members of trade associations will often share their balance sheet, income statement, and management ratios with other members through studies and reports published by the association. These percentages can help you to determine whether your consulting services business is being operated as efficiently as other firms in your industry.

Ratio Basics

The language of business is math. Mathematics is used to measure income, expenses, profits and losses, taxes, and every other aspect of conducting business. So it is no surprise that ratios are also important.

A ratio is the relationship of two or more measurable things. Ratios help you compare. Imagine that your business ratio of sales to profits is 10:1 (ten to one). On average, every $10 in sales earns $1 of profit. You now want to know how that ratio compares to the sales-to-profit ratio for similar businesses. Going deeper, you may want to compare the COGS ratio or the sales expense ratio for your business to others.

Just as important, investors and other financial people look to ratios to diagnose your business. They may decide to only invest in businesses that have a specific earnings ratio or asset ratio. So it's important that your business understands how ratios work. Important balance sheet ratios measure liquidity (a business's ability to pay its bills as they come due) and leverage (measuring the business's dependency on creditors for funding). Liquidity ratios indicate the ease of turning assets into cash. They include the current ratio, quick ratio, and working capital.

Current Ratio

The current ratio is one of the best known measurements of financial strength. It is calculated as follows:

$$\text{Current Ratio} = \frac{\text{Total Current Assets}}{\text{Total Current Liabilities}}$$

The main question this ratio answers is: Does your business have enough current assets to meet the payment schedule of its current debts with a margin of safety? Let's say that you or your lender decides your current ratio is too low. What can you do about it?

- Pay some debts.
- Combine some of your short-term debts into a long-term debt.
- Convert fixed assets into current assets.
- Leave in earnings or put profits back into the business.

- Increase your current assets with new equity (bring more cash into the business).

Quick Ratio

The quick ratio is sometimes called the acid test ratio and is one of the best measurements of liquidity. It is calculated as follows:

$$\text{Quick Ratio} = \frac{\textbf{Cash + Securities + Receivables}}{\textbf{Total Current Liabilities}}$$

The quick ratio is a much more exacting measure than the current ratio. By excluding inventories (typically small in consulting services businesses), it concentrates on the really liquid assets with value that is fairly certain. It helps answer the question: If all sales revenues should disappear, could my business meet its current obligations with the readily convertible quick funds in hand?

Working Capital Ratio

Working capital is more a measure of cash flow than a ratio. The result of the following calculation must be a positive number:

Working Capital = Total Current Assets – Total Current Liabilities

Lenders look at net working capital over time to determine a company's ability to weather financial crises. Bank loans are often tied to minimum working capital requirements.

Debt Ratios

Nearly all businesses borrow money or have other forms of debt. Investors and bankers are often interested in what the level of debt to assets is for the business. Debt ratios measure the business' ability to repay long-term debt. A couple of popular debt ratios are:

$$\text{Debt Ratio} = \frac{\textbf{Total Liabilities}}{\textbf{Total Assets}}$$

$$\text{Debt-to-Equity Ratio} = \frac{\text{Long-Term Debt} + \text{Leases}}{\text{Owner's Equity}}$$

There are many other debt ratios useful in business. Your accountant and banker can suggest the best ones for your business.

Profitability Ratios

Profitability ratios are useful for ensuring that assets and expenses are well managed. Gross margin is a profitability ratio. Other useful ones include:

$$\text{Net Profit Margin} = \frac{\text{Net Profits after Taxes}}{\text{Sales Revenue}}$$

$$\text{Return on Equity} = \frac{\text{Net Profit}}{\text{Equity}}$$

$$\text{Return on Investment} = \frac{\text{Net Income}}{\text{Total Assets}}$$

Profitability is the lifeblood of business. Profitability ratios can help you quickly take a business's pulse.

You can make a ratio out of any two numbers in your business. You can use a ratio of the people who call your business in comparison to those who buy your services. You can establish a ratio of newspaper to radio advertising dollars. The question is: Is it useful in measuring and managing your business? If it is, use it.

CHAPTER 17

Growing Your Business

Once you've established your successful consulting business, you will face additional challenges. One of the first is how to encourage and manage growth. You'll need to better understand business cycles, learn to control expenses, and, most important, use advanced techniques for problem solving. Your consulting business is built on helping others solve problems; you must start with your own business. Managing business growth is an important component of success.

The Challenges of Growth

Growth is good, right? Especially when your consulting business is the topic. Actually, no, growth isn't always good. Growth of expenses without improving profits isn't good. An increase in losses certainly isn't good for business. Growth by your competitors isn't necessarily good for your business. It's managed growth toward business goals that benefits your business. Like a living plant, your business must be fed, nurtured, and trimmed as needed to produce fruit: profits. If a plant grows into a tall stalk or doesn't have sufficient leaves or buds, it won't be as healthy as one that is cared for. Your consulting business is similar. Feed it well, keep it trimmed, and watch it grow.

QUESTION

How should I know when to grow my consulting business?
Successful consultants don't move their businesses to the next level of profitability because they don't recognize what's needed for managed growth. They don't see the overall changes because they are lost in the details. More importantly, they don't control them. Make sure you use data to identify trends and don't allow the data to be your goal.

Unmanaged Growth

Your consulting service will grow every day it is in operation. Your list of prospects will grow, sales will (hopefully) grow, expenses will probably grow, and the image your clients have of your business will develop. If these elements are managed well, profits will grow.

At the same time, problems will develop in your business. New opportunities present themselves and must be considered. Client or employee issues will crop up and require your attention. New laws, taxes, and other business requirements will attempt to pull your business in new directions.

How can you manage growth for your consulting business?

- Keep focused on your business objectives.
- Identify problems that keep your business from growing.
- Resolve problems with minimal effort.

These are three important tasks for managing the growth of your consulting business. They are vital responsibilities for the owner/manager.

Focus on Your Objectives

Consider this old adage: "When you're up to your neck in alligators, it's difficult to remember that your intent was to drain the pool." The consulting business is like that. Modern consulting is much more complex than it was just twenty years ago. Most of the complexity comes from the new power that computers present to consultants—and to clients. Yes, they are supposed to make management easier, but in reality they just give managers a level of detail and communication that was not available before.

A major technique for managing business growth is to stay focused on your objectives rather than on the details that can overwhelm your days. For the moment, ignore that the printer driver on your computer is keeping you from printing the monthly reports. Fix the problem, but don't take it as an omen of impending doom. Hire a computer consultant or read the reports on screen. Don't get frustrated and locked into the problem so that it gets blown out of proportion. Instead, focus on your business objectives, as defined in your business plan. Spend your time on identifying and resolving your business's primary problems.

Identify the Problems

In the pool example, the problem seems to be that alligators are in the pool. That's the immediate—and significant—problem. Draining the pool will come later, as will checking its pH level. Even figuring out how they got into the pool in the first place can be held off for a few minutes. For right now, the problem definition is: hungry alligators in the pool.

In your consulting business, sometimes the most difficult task can be to clearly identify the underlying problem. Not having enough clients is a symptom. What's the problem? Are the business hours insufficient? Is advertising reaching your target market? Has a major competitor taken them from you? Clearly identify the problem and you're halfway to a solution.

Consider Your Options

As you are up to your neck in the pool, a number of solutions will come to you quickly. They include:

1. Fight the alligators off with every ounce of energy you have.
2. Distract the alligators with food (other than your arm).
3. Swim like the dickens.
4. Yell for help.
5. Accept your fate.

Of the quickly considered options, option 2 sounds the best, followed closely by option 3 and option 4. Option 1 seems futile and option 5 defeatist. The final decision depends on your proximity to food. If none is readily available, maybe a simultaneous application of options 3 and 4 is the best choice.

Of course, few business problems require the immediate action of swimming with alligators. If the business problem is that a major competitor is taking your clients, your options may include:

1. Develop an aggressive advertising campaign that targets your competition.
2. Offer your clients more compelling reasons to hire your business.
3. Build your business to replace lost clients.
4. Hire a specialized consultant to advise you on ways to counter the competition.
5. Sell your consulting business.

Again, option 2 sounds like the best, followed closely by options 3 and 4. Option 1 seems too aggressive and option 5 is giving up. Your business always has options. Your job, as the owner/manager, is to determine what they are and make the best decision you can relative to the business's goals.

Growing in the Right Direction

It's increasingly vital to your business's growth that you step back once in a while and take an objective look at your business and its operations and results. This your chance to resolve any problems that keep the business from offering its best to your clients, your employees, and to you. It's also vital that you make sure your business objectives grow as your business does. Over time, what you sell, how you sell it, and to whom you sell it will be modified. Your goal is to control the modification rather than be controlled by it. That is, consciously adjust how you do business rather than allow outside factors to make the adjustments for you. Be a proactive manager.

To adjust your business toward a better business model, you must first identify your initial model. That's what your business plan is all about: defining how you do business. Of course, the business plan is written before you get into the actual operations of your consulting business. Once the doors open, you may determine that the business plan isn't fully accurate in addressing what your clients need or to how you will manage it. It's okay to revise your business plan as long as the revision brings you a better definition of what works.

The problem for some consultants can be that the business model is revised too often. Offering weight-loss advice today is replaced by selling widgets next month. It can be confusing to clients. The problem of a volatile business model is that there probably wasn't a clearly defined model in the first place. That's why it's so important to do market research before opening your consulting business. Research after the doors are open should help focus your business, but it shouldn't take your business in a radically new direction. That's an identity crisis.

The key to growing your consulting business in the right direction is 1) having a well-defined direction and 2) making only mid-course corrections rather than deciding on new destinations.

Solving Common Business Problems

As the owner of your own consulting services business, you deal with clients' problems on a daily basis. Learning how to effectively solve your own business problems can dramatically affect the growth and success of your business. Most business owners solve problems by intuition. By learning the necessary skills, you will become more comfortable with solving problems and reduce the inherent stress of your job.

What is a problem? A problem is a situation that presents an obstacle to your desire to move ahead. Here are a few examples:

- A client threatens to sue you for the results of advice you gave.
- Your industry is declining rapidly because of a new law.
- A computer program doesn't function as it should.
- A part you need for your copy machine is unavailable.
- An employee is undermining your authority with clients.
- New business income is down.
- You're two payments behind on a lease.

Where do problems come from? Problems arise from every facet of human and mechanical functions as well as from nature. We cause some problems (hiring an untrainable employee) ourselves. Other problems, such as tornadoes, are caused by forces beyond our control.

FACT

Problems are a natural, everyday occurrence of life. However, if a problem is mismanaged, it causes tension and frustration that only compounds the situation. Successful business people must learn how to deal with problems in a logical, rational fashion.

Steps to Solving the Problem

The solutions to some problems, such as how to plan a heavy workload next week, are typically simple and require only a few moments of contemplation and planning. However, other problems, such as how to increase income by $50,000 in the next six months, are more critical to your operation and will require more time and effort. In fact, for critical problems, you may want to set aside a full day for analyzing the problem and finding the best solution.

Recognize the Problem

Before you can solve a problem, you must first recognize that it exists. Here is where your approach to problem solving is crucial. You should not allow the problem to intimidate you. Don't take it personally. Approach it rationally and remind yourself that every problem is solvable if it is tackled appropriately.

Fear of failure can block your ability to think clearly. You can overcome this natural fear if you:

· Follow a workable procedure for finding solutions
· Accept the fact that you can't foresee everything
· Assume that the solution you select is your best option at the time
· Accept the possibility that things may change and your solution may fail

Define the Problem

Once you recognize that a problem exists, your next step is to identify or define the problem itself. You can do so by asking yourself such questions as:

· What exactly happened?
· What started the problem?
· Did something occur that wasn't supposed to?
· Did something break that was supposed to operate?
· Were there unexpected results?

Determine the Type of Problem

Ask questions that help you identify the nature of the problem:

· Is this a personnel, equipment, or operational problem?
· What product or service does it involve?
· Is the problem tangible or intangible?
· Is the problem internal or external to the firm?

Evaluate Significance

How important is the problem to the scheme of things? Ask yourself:

· Is this problem disrupting operations?
· Is this problem hampering sales?

- Is this problem causing conflict among people?
- Is this problem affecting personnel and their productivity?
- Is this problem affecting business goals and, if so, which ones?
- Is this problem affecting clients, suppliers, independent contractors, or any other external people?

Estimate Frequency

Some problems are 100-year floods that don't occur often enough to warrant extensive attention. Ask these questions:

- Is it a problem that occurred in the past and the main concern is to make certain that it doesn't occur again?
- Is it a problem that currently exists and the main concern is to clear up the situation?
- Is it a problem that might occur in the future, and the basic concern is planning and taking action before the problem arises?

The answers to these questions will help you focus on the true problem. You can't effectively research the causes of a problem until you have a clear definition of what the problem is. Sometimes, managers spend many hours on a problem only to learn, after seeking the causes, that they've been focusing on the wrong issue.

Selecting the Best Solution

As you answer these questions, you can begin developing a list of possible solutions. Go through this list and cross out those that obviously won't work. The best ideas are sometimes those that are revised from ideas that won't work.

Break the remaining solution down into its positive effects and negative effects. To do this, write each solution on a separate piece of paper. Below the solution, draw a vertical line down the center of the sheet. Label one column "advantages" and the other column "disadvantages." Analyze each facet of the solution and its effect on the problem. List each of the advantages and disadvantages you can think of.

Role Playing

One way to help you think of the advantages and disadvantages is to role play each solution. Call in a few of your employees or trusted business associates and play out each solution. Ask them for their reactions. Based on your observations and their feedback, you will have a better idea of the advantages and disadvantages of each solution you're considering.

After you complete this process for each primary solution, select those solutions that have the most significant advantages. At this point, you should be considering only two or three.

Selection

In order to select the most appropriate solution, consider:

- Cost-effectiveness
- Time constraints
- Availability of manpower and materials
- Your own intuition

Evaluation

Before you actually implement the chosen solution, you should evaluate it further. Ask yourself:

- Are the objectives of the solution sound, clear, and simple?
- Will the solution achieve the objectives?
- What are the possibilities that it will fail and in what way?
- How can I reduce the possibility of failure?

Taking Action

Finding the solution doesn't mean the problem is solved. Now you need to design a plan of action so the solution gets carried out properly. Designing and implementing the plan of action is just as important as finding the solution. The best solution can fail because it isn't well implemented.

As each phase of your plan of action is implemented, you should ask yourself whether your goals were achieved, how well they were achieved, and whether they worked smoothly. To check your own perceptions of the results, get as much feedback as possible from your managers and employees. What you may think is working may not be perceived the same way by those closer to the action. Always remember that clients and employees are your most valuable resources in successfully carrying out your solution.

ESSENTIAL

Design a plan of action chart that includes all the details you need to consider to implement the plan and when each phase should happen. Keep in mind, though, that even the best plans have setbacks. A key person may be out sick, a supplier may ship materials late, or a change at the client's site may require that the timetable be changed.

Dealing with Business Cycles

No businesses are truly recession-proof. All businesses have cycles where sales become easier or harder to make. Consulting services are subject to the same business cycle that most businesses face. Even so, there are steps you can take to minimize the market's downswing and extend its upswing.

Identify Cycles

First, determine the business cycle for your industry or market. Reviewing income and financial records from prior years or checking with the local chamber of commerce, you can draw a chart illustrating the local business cycle. In your region, it may be that most of the market for your service occurs in the spring and summer. Or the cycle may be fairly equal across the year, but alternate years may fluctuate up or down. The first step to coping with recessions in the local business cycle is to determine exactly what and when that cycle is.

Plan for Cycles

The next step is to begin planning for it. That is, if you're coming up to a typically slower period, determine what you need to do. In past years, how much has income dropped? For how long? Can you find income sources in other specialties where the cycle is moving up? What expenses can you cut? Do you have an employee who would like a seasonal layoff so he can catch up on other interests? Maybe you need to drastically cut back on your expenses and debts for this period. If so, list them out now and determine which will naturally diminish and which will need to be reduced. If you aren't into your slow season yet, you can also talk to your lender about building a line of credit now that will help you get through the tougher times ahead.

Build Assets

Another source of cash to tide you through a recession is a second mortgage on your building, your home, or another large asset. Speak with your lender about this opportunity. Even if you decide not to take out a second mortgage, you will be ready if and when you need to do so.

Market Expansion

Consider widening your market. That is, travel to a nearby metropolitan area and study whether you can expand your services to reach it. If so, you can pick up additional sales by either subcontracting your services or by promoting your services in the expanded market. It certainly beats starving at home.

Locating Reducible Expenses

Growth often means that your business's expenses will go up. Managing these expenses can help you thrive during growth periods as well as survive times when your consulting business isn't growing.

Your income statement provides a summary of expense information and is the focal point in locating expenses that can be cut. For this reason, the information should be as current as possible. As a report of what has already been spent, an income statement alerts you to expense items that should be watched in the present business period. If you get an income statement only at the end of the year, you should consider having one prepared more often. The end of each quarter is usually sufficient for smaller firms. Larger consulting services should receive the information on a monthly basis.

Two Income Statements

The best option is to prepare two income statements. One statement should report the sales, expenses, profit and loss of your operations cumulatively for the current business year to date. The other statement should report on the same items for the last complete month or quarter. Each of the statements should also carry the following information:

- This year's figures and each item as a percentage of sales
- Last year's figures and the percentages
- The difference between last year and this year—over or under
- Budgeted figures and the respective percentages
- The difference between current year actuals and the budgeted figures—over or under
- Average percentages for similar businesses (available from trade associations and the U.S. Department of Labor)
- The difference between your annual percentages and the industry ratios—over or under

This information allows you to locate expense variations in three ways:

1. By comparing this year to last year.
2. By comparing expenses to your own budgeted figures.
3. By comparing your percentages to the operating ratios for similar businesses.

The important basis for comparison is the percentage figure. It represents a common denominator for all three methods. When you have indicated the percentage variations, you should then study the dollar amounts to determine what kind of corrective action is needed.

Variable Expenses

Because your cost cutting will come largely from variable expenses, you should make sure they are indicated on your income statements. Variable expenses are those that fluctuate with the increase or decrease of sales volume. Some of them are overtime, temporary help, advertising, salaries, commissions, and payroll taxes. Fixed expenses are those that stay the same regardless of sales volume. Among them are your salary, salaries for permanent employees, depreciation, rent, and utilities.

When you have located a problem expense area, the next step is obviously to reduce that cost so as to increase your profit. A key to the effectiveness of your cost-cutting action is the worth of the various expenditures. As long as you know the worth of your expenditures, you can profit by making small improvements in expenses. Keep an open eye and an open mind. It is better to do a spot analysis once a month than to wait several months and then do a detailed study.

Taking Action

Take action as soon as possible. You can refine your cost-cutting action as you go along. Be persistent. Results typically come slower than you might like. Keep in mind that only persistent analysis of your records and constant action can help keep expenses from eating up profit.

Reducing Overhead

Business overhead is simply the cost of keeping your doors open. If your consulting services business is located in your home, overhead costs are probably small. But if you have an office and office personnel, your overhead is greater. It's also large if you have high debt to banks, suppliers, and backers.

Start Small

Depending on your consulting services market, start with an office in a corner of your home. If you build the client's perception of quality with your product, you won't have to maintain impressive offices.

Manage Supplies

You can also reduce overhead by carefully watching the costs of supplies. Printed stationary is an excellent way to promote the quality of your business, but you don't need printed notepads unless the client will see them.

Manage Travel

Travel expenses can easily get out of hand without good record keeping. Develop a simple system for tracking transportation, lodging, meals, phone, and other costs.

Labor cost is one expense that can quickly eat at away the profits of a small consulting services business. Don't hire an office manager or a secretary until you absolutely must. It's more profitable to do the required filing and office functions yourself after normal business hours or on weekends. Or you can ask the help of a spouse or older child who could be put on the payroll as soon as your business can afford it.

ALERT

Buy supplies in quantity if you can, but don't buy more than you will use in three to six months unless you're certain that they won't become out-of-date. Pens that include your business name and phone numbers are generally inexpensive. But don't buy so many that you still have hundreds when you change your address or phone number and can no longer use them.

Hire Temp Help

Some small consulting services use temporary help or outside services rather than hire employees and deal with all the taxes and records that come with it. Records can be kept by a bookkeeping or accounting service, office cleaning can be done by a janitorial service, telephones can be answered by an answering service, and correspondence and retyping service can be performed by a secretarial service. Consulting jobs that the owner can't handle are contracted out to other consultants. The complexity of regulations and taxation is endlessly multiplied when the first employee is hired—so avoid hiring anyone until your success requires you to do so.

Telephone Expenses

Long-distance phone calls can quickly add to your expenses and cut into your profits, especially when they are personal calls made by employees. Many successful consulting services use a telephone call record to keep track of long-distance calls, then compare the report with the monthly phone bill. Calls not listed on the report are assumed to be personal calls and should be checked out.

Keeping an Eye on the Future

As your consulting service grows, your task of managing a successful business becomes more complicated. You must consider and plan for the loss of a key person or the business structure. You must remind yourself to enjoy what you're doing. You must review your options if the business fails. You must consider the long term and begin planning for retirement. Planning well for tomorrow can reduce your worries today.

Growth Plans

A business plan can help an existing business grow. Your forestry consulting business has been in operation for a few years and now needs to expand to be competitive. Your etiquette school is considering adding more classes or more teachers and needs to borrow some cash. Your wedding business is so successful that you are considering franchising it. These are growth opportunities.

Expand Your Current Business

Once your business is up and running, you will be making decisions that impact the growth of your venture. Most of these decisions will be small and self-funded. You have sufficient profits and capital to add a new line. But what if you need more money than you have? You discover an opportunity to double your business by moving it into a new business complex. Then you probably need to write a new growth business plan, updating your existing plan and describing the opportunity and costs.

Build a Second Business

In growing marketplaces, you may discover an opportunity to set up a clone of your successful business. It may be in a similar business center in a nearby town or community. Or it may be a related business, operated independently by the same owners.

Your growth business plan will use the success of your first business to design the second one. If financing is required, the growth plan will show investors how you plan to profit—and pay back your loans. If you are hiring a manager for the second location, a business plan can help you attract and train qualified candidates.

FACT

Business plans don't expire, but they can become out of date. Decide right now to update your business plan at least once a year. You might discover a rare opportunity and have to act quickly. Someone may walk in and ask to buy your business for a good price—if you can document your success.

Build a Purchased Business

As your first business succeeds, you may see the opportunity to buy out one of your competitors. Or you may opt to venture into business by buying an existing business where a plan is already in operation. What you will write in each case is a growth plan. You will show yourself and others how you plan to expand and operate an existing business.

Sell Your Business

If you someday decide to sell your business, you don't really need a start-up business plan, which is a goal document. You need a results document. Guess what?! An up-to-date business plan can serve as your offering memorandum, a document that tells prospective buyers about your business. By changing the perspective of the document and its readership, you will have a paper that will guide prospective buyers in understanding the value of your business.

Growth business plans are different from start-up plans because of perspective, but the components are essentially the same and both answer the same business questions. In addition, they have similar components.

CHAPTER 18

Managing Employees

Employees can magnify the profits—or the losses—of your consulting service. That's why it's critical to the success of your business that you learn to choose, hire, promote, and fire employees and independent contractors. Your decisions regarding employees can be some of the most critical ones you will make as a small business owner. In this chapter, you will learn from the pros how to hire and manage employees.

Hiring Good Employees

Hiring an employee is a critical decision. To make the best decision, you need to determine whether you really need an employee, what that person will do, where to find qualified candidates, and how to test candidates. The future of your consulting business depends on smart decisions.

ESSENTIAL

> As you start and grow your consulting service, continually look for opportunities where you can profit from hiring and managing employees. Consider what related services your clients need as well as how you could work more efficiently if you had qualified help.

Do You Need an Employee?

Should you add an employee? Experts say: Only if you are certain you will increase income by at least three times the employee's wages or salary. For example, to hire an employee at $30,000 a year (about $15 an hour), make sure the employee's services will bring you at least $90,000 in business during the coming year. That's a minimum. Some service businesses use multipliers of four or even five to determine whether they can afford to hire additional staff. Remember that about 40 percent of your income will go toward labor costs. For an employee, that's wages (30 percent of increased sales) and benefits (10 percent of increased sales). Keep in mind that to increase sales you will have to reduce your billable time, thus reducing your business's income.

Job Description

The best way to hire the right person for the job is to clearly define what skills are needed. Once you know what it takes to do the job, you can match the applicant's skills and experience to the job's requirements. This step will probably be easy for you if you're hiring an associate, but how about office help or other support functions?

Once you have a job description on paper, decide what skills the person must have to fill the job. Then, estimate the value of this service to your business. Finally, determine how much other employers in your area are paying for these skills.

When you know the kinds of skills you need in your new employee and her market value, you're ready to contact sources that can help you recruit job applicants. Make sure you offer a living wage.

QUESTION

What is a living wage?
It is the cost of living in your community based on the size of the living group (one adult, two adults with one child, etc). If you've decided to pay your employees a living wage, visit *http://livingwage.geog.psu.edu* online to calculate what that amount is for your location.

Employment Resources

Each state has an employment service (Department of Employment, Unemployment Bureau, or Employment Security Agency). All are affiliated with the U.S. Department of Labor Employment & Training Administration (*www.doleta.gov*), and local offices are ready to help businesses with their hiring problems. The state employment service will screen applicants for you by giving aptitude tests if any are available for the skills you need. Passing scores indicate the applicant's ability to learn the work, so be as specific as you can about the skills you want.

ESSENTIAL

Consider hiring a military veteran. Many have extensive training and experience in their fields of expertise as well as discipline. For more information, contact the U.S. Department of Labor Veterans' Employment & Training Service (*www.dol.gov/vets*). VETS also offers retraining services to prepare veterans for new jobs.

Private employment agencies will also help with recruitment. However, the employee or the employer must pay a fee to the private agency for its services. This fee can be from a month's to as much as a year's salary. Large employment agencies include Manpower (*http://manpower.com*) and Kelly Services (*www.kellyservices.com*).

Newspaper advertisements are another source of applicants. You reach a large group of job seekers, and if you use a blind box address, you can screen them at your convenience. If you list an office phone number, you may end up on the phone with an applicant instead of with a client.

Job applicants are readily available from local schools. The local high school may have a distributive or cooperative education department where the students work in your office part-time while taking trade or business courses at school. Many part-time students continue with their employer after they finish school. Consider local and regional business schools as well. The students are often more mature and more motivated than high school students.

You may also find job applicants by contacting friends, neighbors, clients, suppliers, current employees, local associations, service clubs, or even a nearby armed forces base where people are leaving the service. However, don't overlook the problems of such recruiting. What happens to the goodwill of these sources if they recommend a friend you do not hire, or if you have to fire the person they recommend?

Your choice of recruitment method depends on what you're looking for, your location, and your method of managing your business. You have many sources available to you. A combination may serve your best needs. The important thing is to find the right applicant with the correct skills for the job you want to fill, whatever the source.

Employment Tests

A good employee is one who is skilled, reliable, and trustworthy. You may be the best judge of the applicant's skills, but how do you test reliability? Fortunately, there are standardized tests you can administer to measure potential of substance abuse, courtesy, maturity, conscientiousness, trustworthiness, commitment, and attitudes toward safety.

Wonderlic Personnel Tests, Inc. (*www.wonderlic.com*) offers a variety of employee selection, assessment, training, and development tests for small and medium-sized businesses. The tests are available in paper and computerized versions. Wonderlic also offers productivity testing to ensure that employees are working efficiently. Such tests can help you find and manage better employees.

Employee Benefits

Employee benefits play an important role in the lives of employees and their families, and they have a significant financial impact on your business. Consulting services cannot be competitive employers if they don't develop a comprehensive benefit program. However, if not managed, an employee benefit program can quickly eat up a small firm's profit.

Comprehensive Benefits

A comprehensive employee benefits program can be broken down into four components: legally required benefits, health and welfare benefits, retirement benefits, and perquisites.

Legally required benefit plans are mandated by law and the systems necessary to administer such plans are well established. These plans include social security insurance (FICA), worker's compensation insurance, and unemployment compensation insurance (FUTA).

FACT

For information regarding FICA, contact the U.S. Social Security Administration (*http://ssa.gov*). Information about worker's compensation insurance is available from your state's employment offices. Information about FUTA is available online at *www.doleta.gov* and through your state's employment offices.

Health Benefits

Health and welfare benefits can be viewed as benefits provided to work in conjunction with statutory benefits to enhance employees' financial security. Health and welfare plans are perhaps the most visible of all the benefit program components. They include medical care, dental care, vision care, short-term disability, long-term disability, life insurance, accidental death and dismemberment insurance, dependent care, and legal assistance.

When purchasing a health and welfare plan, select an insurance professional whose clientele is made up primarily of small businesses. In fact, if you can find one in your area, select one that is used and recommended by other consultants. Your insurer needs to be aware of the special problems that face small businesses, especially in your trade. Generous plans that look attractive and logical today may become a financial burden for your growing company. Remember that it is much easier to add benefits than it is to take them away.

ALERT

For regularly updated information on the status of federal health insurance laws and plans, contact the U.S. Department of Health & Human Services (*http://hhs.gov*) and its Agency for Healthcare Research and Quality (*www.ahrq.gov*).

Medical plans are usually the greatest concern of employers and employees. There are essentially two kinds of traditional medical plans. Major medical plans cover 100 percent of hospital and inpatient surgical expense as well as a percentage (typically 80 percent) of all other covered expenses. Comprehensive medical plans cover a percentage (again, generally 80 percent) of all medical expenses.

In both plans, the employee is usually required to pay part of the premium, particularly for dependents, as well as a deductible. A comprehensive medical plan is typically less expensive because more of the cost is shifted to the employee. Any plan you design should include features for containing costs.

As an alternative to a traditional medical plan, an employer may contract with a Health Maintenance Organization (HMO) to provide employees with medical services. The main difference between a traditional medical plan and an HMO is that the traditional plan allows employees to choose their medical providers while HMOs often provide medical services at specified clinics or through preferred doctors and hospitals. HMOs trade this flexibility for lower costs that are often passed on to the employees through reduced or eliminated deductibles or lower rates.

Retirement Benefits

Retirement plans are established to help ensure that employees are able to maintain their accustomed standard of living upon retirement. Retirement benefit plans basically fall into two categories: defined contribution plans, which provide employees with an account balance at retirement, and defined benefit plans, which provide employees with a projected amount of income at retirement.

Retirement benefit plans are either qualified or unqualified plans. A plan is qualified if it has met certain standards mandated by law. It is beneficial to maintain a qualified retirement plan because contributions are currently deductible, benefits earned are not considered taxable income until they are received, and certain distributions are eligible for special tax treatment.

Of the various qualified plans, defined benefit plans, 401(k) plans, and profit-sharing plans are the most popular.

Defined Benefit Plans

A defined benefit plan promises participants a benefit specified by a formula in the plan. The focus of a defined benefit plan is the retirement benefit provided instead of the contribution made. Plan sponsors must contribute to the actuarially determined amounts necessary to meet the dollar amounts promised to participants. Generally, benefits begin at retirement and are paid over the remainder of the employee's life, so a defined benefit plan guarantees a certain flow of income at retirement.

ESSENTIAL

As a business owner, you can establish your own retirement plan, called a Self-Employed Pension (SEP) plan. Contact the IRS (*www.irs. gov*) for a booklet (Self-Employment Pension Plans, publication 560) on how to start and manage these plans.

401(k) Plans

In a 401(k) plan, participants agree to defer a portion of their pretax salary as a contribution to the plan. In addition, the sponsoring employer may decide to match all or a portion of the participant deferrals. The employer may even decide to make a profit-sharing contribution to the plan. As the employee works, the money he sets aside from his paycheck accumulates. After he reaches age 59½, he is allowed to start withdrawing money from the account. The 401(k) plans are popular because they allow employees the ability to save for retirement with pretax dollars and they can be designed to be relatively inexpensive.

Profit-Sharing Plans

A profit-sharing plan is a defined contribution plan in which the sponsoring employer has agreed to contribute a discretionary or set amount to the plan. Any contributions made to the plan are generally prorated to each participant plan account based on compensation. The focus in a profit-sharing plan, and in defined contribution plans, is on the contribution. What a participant receives at retirement is a direct function of the contributions. Profit- sharing plans are favored by employers because they allow employers the ability to retain discretion in determining the amount of the contribution made to the plan.

Insurance

Group life insurance is a benefit employees have come to expect in many regions and trades. Such insurance is usually a multiple of an employee's salary. Be aware that an amount of insurance over a legally specified amount is subject to taxation as income to the employee.

Recent legislation provides that employers who maintain medical and dental plans must provide certain employees the opportunity to continue coverage if they otherwise become ineligible through employment termination or other causes. In addition, new rules state that if a firm's health and welfare plan discriminates in favor of key employees, the benefits to those employees are taxable as income. Talk to your plan administrator about current laws and requirements.

Perqs

Perquisite benefits, or perqs, are any other benefits an employer promises, such as a company automobile or truck, professional association or club membership, paid tuition, sabbatical, extra vacation, expense account, credit cards, or financial counseling services.

ALERT

Disability insurance is an important but often overlooked benefit in small businesses. Disability insurance prevents a drain of financial resources to support a principal in the event that she cannot continue working. For more information, contact the Social Security Administration (*http://ssa.gov/disability*) or the U.S. Department of Labor (*http://dol.gov*).

Selecting the Right Plan

Designing and implementing an employee-benefit program can be a complicated process. Many small businesses contract with employee benefit consulting firms, insurance companies, specialized attorneys, or accounting firms to assist in this task. As you establish your program yourself or with a professional, ask yourself:

- What should the program accomplish in the long run?
- What's the maximum amount you can afford to spend on a program?
- Are you capable and knowledgeable in administering the program?
- What kind of program will best fit the needs of your employees?
- Should you involve your employees in the design and selection of the benefit program? If so, how much and at what stage?

Certain plans are more suitable for consulting services, based on the employees' financial situations and the demographics of the employee group. Employers who are not confident of their future income may not want to start a defined benefit plan that will require a specific level of contributions. However, if the employees are fairly young, a profit-sharing plan or a 401(k) plan can result in a more significant and more appreciated benefit than a defined benefit plan. Remember that while a qualified plan has many positive aspects, the qualified retirement plan area is complicated and well monitored by the government. Make sure you have adequate counsel before you decide on the most appropriate plan for your business.

Hiring Temporary Help

How does your consulting business cope with unexpected personnel shortages? Many businesses face this question, whether the cause is seasonal peaking, several employees on sick leave, or an unexpected increase in business. For some skills, many consulting services hire and use independent contractors. They may also use them in the office to fill a void or provide additional services. For office work, a growing number of businesses also hire help through temporary personnel services. In fact, many new consulting services will start up their business renting part-time temporary office personnel or independent contractors instead of hiring full-time employees.

Using a Temporary Personnel Service

A temporary personnel service, listed in your phone book's Yellow Pages under "Employment Contractors—Temporary—Help," is not an employment agency. Like many service firms, it hires people as its own employees and assigns them to companies requesting assistance. This means that when you use a service, you're not hiring an employee; you're buying the use of their time. The temporary personnel firm is responsible for payroll, bookkeeping, tax deductions, workers' compensation insurance, fringe benefits, and all other similar costs connected with the employee. You're relieved of the burden or recruiting, interviewing, screening, and basic skill training.

Most national temporary personnel companies also offer performance guarantees and fidelity bonding at no added cost to their clients. Equally important, you're relieved of the need for government forms and for reporting withholding tax, social security insurance, and unemployment compensation insurance.

If you need temporary personnel for a period of six months or more, it's usually more cost-effective to hire a full-time employee. Also, if the task requires skills or training beyond basic office skills, it may cost you less to pay overtime to an employee who has those skills.

Using Independent Contractors

An independent contractor is a self-employed person who performs a service for you. Because an independent contractor is not an employee, you cannot dictate the hours in which the service is performed nor, in many cases, where it will be performed. The advantage of an independent contractor is that they are not on your payroll.

A contract with an independent contractor should state clearly that the person is an independent contractor and not an employee. Otherwise you may have to pay social security and other payroll taxes on their services to you.

Many consultants expand their services by using the service of other consultants on a contract basis. These collaborations can help a consultant reach a new market with additional services without the expenses of adding staff. If you do establish a collaboration, make sure there is an equitable sharing of revenue based on who found the client, who will do most of the work, and who brings more to the collaboration.

Using Temporary Employees Efficiently

The key to successful use of temporary employees lies in planning what type of help you will need, how much, and when. The accurate information you give to the temporary service firm will improve its efficiency in supplying the correct person for your needs.

Before your temporary employee arrives on the job, there are a few things you should do. First, appoint one of your permanent employees to supervise the temporary employee and check on his progress. Be sure this supervisor understands the job and its responsibilities. Next, let your permanent staff know that you're taking on extra help and that it will be temporary. Explain why the extra help is needed and ask them to cooperate with the new employee in any way possible.

Have everything ready before the temporary employee arrives. The work to be done should be organized and laid out so he can get right to it, minimizing the time he has to spend adjusting to the job and the surroundings. Also, don't set up schedules that are impossible to complete within the time you allot. Try to stay within the time limits you gave the temporary help service, but plan to extend the time period if necessary, rather than hurry the employee.

Finally, furnish detailed instructions. Describe your type of business and the services you offer. Help the temp feel comfortable and part of your team. Most temporary employees have broad business experience and can easily adapt to your requirements—if they know what they are.

Using Co-Employment Services

All states allow employees to be hired by a professional employer organization (PEO) as the employer of record. Technically, your employees work for the PEO. Practically, you manage the employees as if they were your employees.

The obvious advantage to co-employment is that your small consulting business doesn't have to be burdened by the paperwork of employment, payroll taxes, and worker's compensation insurance. The PEO typically advises you throughout the hiring process.

The downside can be the cost. Many co-employers will charge you a flat percentage over and above the employee's wage. The rate can vary depending on the PEO and services, typically ranging between 25 and 35 percent.

Unfortunately, not all PEOs are reputable. Some will send you any warm body and the bill. There is no pre-screening. In fact, they may be taking deductions for payroll taxes but not passing the money on to the government. You can be in a worse mess than if you'd just handled your own payroll. Make sure that the PEO you select is reputable. Your business banker or accountant may be able to recommend such a service to you. Also, look for membership in professional organizations like the National Association of Professional Employer Organizations (*www.napeo.org*).

Managing Payroll Records

Quarterly and yearly reports of individual payroll payments must be made to federal and, in many cases, state governments. Each individual employee must receive a W-2 form by January 31 showing total withholding payments made for the employee during the previous year.

Payroll Summary

A payroll summary should be made each payday showing the employee names, employee numbers, rates of pay, hours worked, overtime hours, total pay, and amount of deductions for FICA, Medicare insurance, state and federal withholding taxes, insurance, pension, savings, and child support, as required.

To ensure that you maintain adequate records for this task, keep an employee card or database record for each employee of your firm. This should show each employee's full legal name, social security insurance number, address, telephone number, name and address of next of kin, marital status, number of exemptions claimed, and current rate of pay. A federal W-4 form completed and signed by the employee should also be attached to the employee card or record.

Also maintain a running total of earnings, pay, and deductions for each individual employee. If your business employs union members, you may have additional deductions for union dues, pensions, and other fees.

ESSENTIAL

Many small consulting services with minimal employee requirements use temp agencies for temporary help. The agencies take care of the payroll requirements for them. Other businesses use co-employment services for longer-term employees. Co-employers help you hire and pay employees, including taxes and salaries. You write a single check and don't have to worry about payroll taxes.

Payroll System

To begin your payroll system, contact the Internal Revenue Service (*www.irs.gov*) and request the Employer's Tax Guide (Circular E) and get a nine-digit Employer Identification Number. The IRS will then send you deposit slips (Form 8109) with your new ID number printed on them. Use these deposit slips each time you pay your payroll taxes. Payroll taxes are paid within a month of the ending of a quarter; that is, January 31, April 30, July 31, and October 31. As your business grows, you may be required to pay payroll taxes more frequently. By then, you will need an accountant to help you determine your needs.

The IRS often doesn't provide EINs to sole proprietorships. Instead, it requires that the business use the social security number of the owner. Contact the IRS for the latest rules and requirements.

In addition, you will probably have to pay payroll taxes to your state and/or municipal government. Contact them to determine payroll requirements. It may be worth hiring an accountant to advise you on how to establish a payroll system that complies with regulations.

Employee Appraisals

The majority of employees in the labor force are under a merit increase pay system, though most of their pay increases result from seniority and other factors. This approach involves periodic review and appraisal of employee's performance.

When designing the plan of action, consider:

- Who will be involved in the solution?
- How will they participate?
- Who will be affected by the solution?
- How will they be affected?
- What course of action will be taken?
- How should this course of action be presented to employees, clients, suppliers, and others?
- When will the action start and be completed?
- Where will this action happen?
- How will this action happen?
- What's needed to make it happen?

Performance Reviews

An effective employee appraisal plan improves two-way communication between the manager and the employee, relates pay to work performance and results, and helps employees understand job responsibilities and expectations and areas for improvement. An employee appraisal plan also provides a standardized approach to evaluating job performance.

Such a performance review helps not only the employee, but also the manager, who can gain insight into the organization. An open exchange between employee and manager can show the manager where improvements in equipment, procedures, or other factors might improve employee performance. Try to foster a climate in which employees can discuss progress and problems informally at any time throughout the year.

ALERT

To get the best results, use a standardized written form for appraisals. An appraisal form should cover the results achieved, quality of performance, volume of work, effectiveness in working with others in the firm and with clients and suppliers, in initiative, job knowledge, and dependability. Employment services, trade associations, and some office supply stores can provide standardized performance appraisal forms.

Annual Reviews

To keep your pay administration plan in tune with the times, you should review it at least annually. Make adjustments where necessary and don't forget to retrain supervisory personnel. This isn't the kind of plan that can be set up and then forgotten.

During your annual review, ask yourself if the plan is working for you. That's the most important question. Are you getting the kind of employees you want or are you just making do? What's the employee turnover rate? Do employees seem to care about the business? Most importantly, does your pay administration plan help you achieve the objectives of your business?

CHAPTER 19

Managing Business Risk

Business is legalized gambling. No matter how much of a "sure thing" a business opportunity seems to offer, there always is a chance of losing some or all of what you invest. This chapter guides you in analyzing, understanding, and minimizing risk in your consulting business with smart planning. It can help you develop a risk/reward structure that is tolerable. In business, no risk equals no reward.

Understanding Risk

Building a consulting business is hard work. It should be rewarded. Unfortunately, the world doesn't always work that way and a successful business can be out of business in a month because of an unrecognized risk. How?

- An employee is injured on the job and sues you.
- An employee runs off with money stolen from your business.
- A fire or flood wipes out your office, equipment, and important records.
- A partner in your business files bankruptcy and the courts attach your business.
- The local economy goes sour and you can't find enough work for six months or more.
- A business partner is involved in a divorce settlement and business assets must be sold to meet a court order.
- The IRS comes after you for a large tax bill they think you owe them and takes over your bank account until everything is resolved.

ESSENTIAL

A consulting service business owner may decide that the firm can afford to absorb some losses, either because the frequency and probability of loss are low or because the dollar value of loss is manageable. Maybe your consulting services business owns an older vehicle and your drivers have excellent safety records, so you decide to drop the collision insurance.

The list goes on. There are many ways that an otherwise profitable service business can quickly be thrown into a situation where the business's future is in jeopardy. What can you do about it? First, you can make sure you understand the risks involved in your business. Second, you can take precautions to ensure that the risks are minimal. They will never go away, but through smart risk management you can minimize them and prepare for the worst.

As you plan for a new or growing consulting business, you know you're taking some kind of a risk, but what does that mean exactly? And how can you keep the risk to a minimum?

As you develop your consulting business, you will discover that there typically is not much time spent on the topic of risk. Though risk is an underlying factor within all businesses, it isn't a popular topic. No person wants to consider the inevitability of death; likewise, few businesses consider catastrophic risks.

Degrees of Risk

Risk is an important topic in managing your consulting business. But the question of risk isn't answered by yes or no. There are degrees of risk. And the degrees are relative; that is, they may be at one level today and another level six months from now under new conditions. How can you define the level of risk involved for various components of your business? With knowledge and research.

Identifying Risks

What are the important risks in your business venture? What internal and external factors offer significant risk to your business goals? Each business concept has a unique set of risks. However, most businesses share types of risk. The risks common to most small businesses include:

- Competition
- Cost structure
- Distribution
- Employees
- Errors and omissions
- Financing
- Industry cyclicality
- Industry maturity
- Interdependence
- Management
- Natural catastrophes

- Production
- Profitability
- Regulatory environment
- Suppliers
- Technology

The underlying question of risk is: What can go wrong? The list includes the most common things that can go wrong in businesses. Add to it any risks that are primary in your industry or venture.

Next, prioritize those risks. In some service businesses, the greatest risk is that a new technology will adversely damage your market. In another enterprise, new regulations or loss of key employees could be a major problem that could impact the future of your business. Or competitors may be a foremost risk factor. Also, consider both the external and internal risks that your business faces. Some are outside of your direct control and others allow you more control of the conditions and the outcome.

Rating Risk

There are numerous ways of rating risk levels for an opportunity. The ratings can be on a numbered scale of one to five, on a pre-defined scale, or by a defining statement. For example, the risk of profitability for your business can be rated as a three, moderate or "relatively high for the value."

ALERT

Don't assume you've identified and accurately rated all primary risks for your business venture. Share your risk analysis with a knowledgeable and trusted business advisor. Don't be defensive; listen. There may be risk factors you haven't considered or your ratings may not reflect all aspects. Ultimately, you will decide what goes into your consulting business.

Rate each of your primary business risks on whatever scale works best for you. Many use the four-step scale: lowest risk, moderate risk, higher risk, maximum risk. You also can rate risks by probability in percentage, such as 0, 20, 40, 60, 80, or 100 percent chance of loss.

Because risk ratings often are subjective, categories often work better than specific numbers. In addition, ask a trusted advisor to help you verify the risk factors and ratings before including them in your consulting business.

For example, your plan may state, "the risk of a major competitor taking a significant portion of our clients is rated as low" or ". . . is rated as a 15 percent probability." You may later, through your management efforts, reduce this probability to a lower level. For now, however, you need to analyze the various risks of your business and rate them as accurately as you can. Once they are identified, ranked, and rated, you can develop plans to reduce or eliminate risks.

Weighting

Some risks are more critical to the success of your business. For example, your business opportunity may be subject to higher than normal risks from competitors, costs, distribution, employees, financing, industry cyclicality or maturity, interdependence, management, natural catastrophes, production, profitability, regulatory environment, suppliers, technology, or other factors. How can you factor these unequal risks into your consulting business and management? You can use category weighting.

Weighting is setting the relative value of various elements. In business statistics, you can calculate that, of ten types of risks, some are more important to your success than others. For example, risk from competitors may be less than one-tenth or 10 percent, so you set it at 5 percent. However, changes in technology could have a greater impact on your business, so you give it more than one-tenth, such as 20 or even 30 percent. You weight the risk factor.

Weighting is an educated guess; you don't know for certain that changes in technology will have three or four times the impact on your business as competitive risks can. However, weighting the risks can give you a more accurate picture of total risk than simply assigning equal value to all business risks.

If you are using a numeric scale for calculating risks, you can interpolate or combine risk factors. For example, if technology risk is 60 percent with a weight of 20 percent of the total risk, then technology risks comprise about 12 percent (.60 × .20) of the total risks that your business faces. That's significant.

Rationale

Why did you rate your business profitability risk at 35 percent? Why do you believe there is a 15 percent chance that a major competitor could take your primary clients and sales? What is your rationale?

A rationale is an underlying reason. A risk rating system can be useful and efficient, but sometimes it doesn't offer the completeness that an investor—or a manager—needs to decide about the risks of your business venture. They need more information.

Rationales should be included in your business planning for all primary risks that your venture faces. It is vital to your success and to your investors' understanding that you analyze, rank, rate, and, as needed, rationalize your decisions about the risks that it faces. You cannot rely on "luck" (unknown circumstances) to somehow converge to make your business successful and prosperous. Your venture may receive some luck, but you cannot depend on it—especially as you spend large amounts of time and money on starting or growing a small business.

Minimizing Risk

All of your efforts in understanding, ranking, rating, weighting, and rationalizing your business's inherent risks will now come to fruition as you discover what you can do to minimize them. Minimizing risk is a vital step in your development of a consulting business that will answer questions raised by owners, partners, managers, and investors. What are the primary risks of your venture and how will you respond to them?

To minimize business risk, you first need to determine what they are—the topic of the first part of this chapter. Once identified, you need to consider the causes and components of the primary risks, then look for ways of reducing the impact of those components. Finally, you need to continue watching primary risk components so that they don't threaten your business's success.

Determine Primary Risks

As you develop a consulting business, it is critical that you determine your venture's primary risks. A small consulting business in a downtown area will have different risks than a wholesale import company. It's time to get specific. List your business's primary risks, rank them and, if possible, weight their relative value to the success of your venture. For example:

Risk	Level	Rating	Weight	Percent of Total Risk
Competition	4	50%	2	67%
Industry maturity	1	20%	0.2	6.7%
Suppliers	2	10%	0.2	6.7%
Technology	3	20%	0.6	20%
Total	100%	100%	3	100%

In the example, competitive risks are calculated as two-thirds of the total of all risks the business faces, distantly followed by technology risks. Industry maturity and supplier risks are relatively insignificant. This exercise can help you identify your venture's primary risks.

Identify Risk Reductions

Once you've clearly defined a problem, solutions become more evident. For example, to minimize the risk of loss due to competition, a cruise vacation consultant can:

- Specialize in cruises that competitors don't sell
- Serve a specialized group of clients that you know better than your competitors do
- Offer a superlative level of individual service to clients
- Identify weaknesses of specific competitors and respond to them

Track Primary Risks

Once the primary risks are identified and solutions offered, your business must carefully track them to ensure that they are being minimized. For example, if you have a primary competitor who could, on short notice, capture a significant client, you must keep an eye on that competitor. Who is it? What is it doing today? What is it planning for tomorrow? How can you further reduce the risk that it presents to your business?

Your consulting business must identify and respond to the threats your venture faces. It must maximize the rewards by minimizing the risk. Like the professional gambler, it must consider the odds and either bet or pass depending on which action has the greatest chance of ultimate success.

Risk Management

Once business risks have been identified and assessed, what can you do about them? How can you manage them? Your consulting business should include specifics on risk management involving clients, competition, marketing, pricing, profitability, suppliers, and other vital categories.

Professional business managers use one of four primary techniques in managing risk:

- Avoidance
- Reduction
- Transfer
- Retention

These responses are available to you in your consulting business. The following are some proven guidelines for risk management in small business.

Risk Avoidance

In business, risk avoidance can be effective. For example, if you believe competitors can ruin your business, find a niche where you will have no competitors. Of course, you must also verify that it will have sufficient clients to support your services.

In building your consulting business, consider the primary risks that you've identified and consider whether avoidance is a viable option. What can you do to avoid these risks?

Risk Reduction

Risk reduction minimizes the chances of risky events occurring. This chapter has focused primarily on risk reduction: how to identify and lessen the potential risks to your business. In most business situations, it is the easiest path to lowering inherent risks. Identify and mitigate. If there is a danger that erroneous advice can damage a client, perform due diligence (research and analysis) to ensure the advice you give is accurate. If new technologies may challenge your business, find ways of reducing the challenge through absorbing some technologies to mitigate potential damage.

FACT

For additional information on risk management, visit *www.risk-management-basics.com*. In addition, the Small Business Administration (*www.sba.gov*) offers online resources on risk management that focuses on the problems faced in business start-up and growth. You can also find courses on risk management at colleges and universities.

Risk Transfer

In some cases, you can make your problems someone else's—for a fee. The entire insurance industry is built on this premise. Concerned that an unintentional error will wipe out your assets? Buy an insurance policy that covers errors and omissions.

Insurance isn't the only way to transfer risk. You also can pass it on to clients, suppliers, landlords, and others with whom you do business. For example, if the cost of collecting on accounts receivable is cutting into your profits significantly, you can transfer at least some of the loss by changing a late fee or by requiring clients to make a deposit on services.

Risk Retention

In some cases, the best thing to do about risks of loss is to brace yourself. That is, if you expect that 5 percent of your accounts receivable will be uncollectable—and that's the best you can do—then accept the loss as part of your cost of doing business. All risks that are not avoided, reduced, or transferred are retained.

Business Insurance

For many consulting businesses, risk management includes risk transfer—buying appropriate insurance. Depending on your service business, it can include fire, automotive, liability, and workers' compensation insurance.

ALERT

Consider purchasing an umbrella business insurance policy that covers numerous risks in one policy. Many have a liability limit of $1 million, $3 million, or $5 million. The premium is usually cheaper than individual policies and can cover you for risks you may not have considered. Speak with a business insurance agent regarding risk and the costs of risk transfer.

Fire Insurance

Fire insurance covers the risk of loss of assets because of a fire or related events. Special protection other than the standard fire insurance policy is needed to cover the loss by fire of accounts, bills, currency, deeds, evidence of debt, and securities.

You can add other perils—such as windstorm, hail, smoke, explosion, vandalism, and malicious mischief—to your basic fire insurance at a relatively small additional fee. Even if you have several policies on your property, you can still collect only the amount of your actual cash loss. Most insurance policies have fine print stating that all the insurers share the payment proportionately.

In most cases, to recover your loss you must furnish within sixty days a complete inventory of the damaged, destroyed, and undamaged property, showing in detail quantities, costs, actual cash value, and amount of loss claimed. If you and your insurer disagree on the amount of the loss, the question may be resolved through special appraisal procedures provided for in the fire insurance policy.

Automobile Insurance

Does your consulting business need auto insurance? The answer depends on whether there is a company car, who uses it, and why. Note that when an employee uses a car on your behalf, you can be legally liable even though you don't personally own the car or truck.

Automobile insurance pays for medical claims, including your own, that come from vehicle accidents, regardless of the question of negligence. In most states, you must carry liability insurance or be prepared to provide a surety bond or other proof of financial responsibility when you're involved in an accident. In addition, you can purchase uninsured motorist protection to cover your own bodily injury claims from someone who has no insurance. In most policies, personal property stored in a car or truck and not attached to it is not covered under an automobile policy.

ALERT

If you use your personal car for business travel, discuss coverage with your auto insurance agent or company. You may need additional coverage, depending on use. It will also depend on whether the vehicle is used exclusively, primarily, or occasionally for business. Of course, it also depends on who owns the vehicle—you or your company or corporation.

Liability Insurance

Liability insurance is necessary for most businesses, especially those that deal with property or advice that can be misused by a client. Property liability insurance is important if your business has a physical location, such as an office, that is visited by clients or suppliers. You may be legally liable for damages even in cases where you used reasonable care. Under certain conditions, your business may be subject to damage claims even from trespassers.

Note that most liability policies require you to notify the insurer immediately after an incident on your property that might cause a future claim. This holds true no matter how unimportant the incident may seem at the time it happens. Even if the suit against you is false or fraudulent, the liability insurer pays court costs, legal fees, and interest on judgments in addition to the liability judgments themselves.

Workers' Compensation Insurance

Federal laws require that an employer provide employees a safe place to work, hire competent fellow employees, provide safe tools, and warn employees of existing danger. Whether an employer provides these things, he is liable for damage suits brought by an employee and possible fines of prosecution.

State law determines the level or type of benefits payable under workers' compensation insurance policies. However, not all employees are covered by workers' compensation insurance laws. The exceptions are determined by state law and therefore vary from state to state.

You can save money on workers' compensation insurance by seeing that your employees are properly classified. Rates for workers' compensation insurance vary from 0.1 percent of the payroll for safe occupations to about 25 percent or more of the payroll for very hazardous occupations. Office workers employed by consultants typically have very low accident rates and workers' compensation insurance rates are appropriately low. Your business insurance agent can help you determine workers' comp rates and how to keep them low.

Risk is a significant part of doing business. Analyzing and managing risk is a major component of starting and growing a business. Make sure your consulting business identifies its risks and explains how your business will avoid, reduce, transfer, or retain them.

CHAPTER 20

The Future of Your Consulting Business

Wouldn't it be great to have a crystal ball that could show you the future of your new business and your life? Not really. It would take the challenge out of day-to-day operation and dampen feelings of success. Instead, your consulting business should offer enjoyment, support your personal life, and offer the satisfaction of real success. If it doesn't, consider how you can avoid burnout—or plan for the sale of your business. These topics are covered in this final chapter.

Enjoy What You Do

Life is too short to be doing something that isn't enjoyable—at least some of the time. In fact, you probably chose consulting because it sounded like pleasant work. You saw the opportunities to make an income, build equity, and have some fun. But maybe the reality of mundane tasks and the frustration of working with a few ill-tempered clients has taken its toll and you're having serious second thoughts. The alligators are showing their teeth. What can you do?

You're not the first consultant to lose the fun. It's easy to misplace it in the tedious tasks that make up the consultant's day: trying to solve difficult problems for others, training apathetic employees, dealing with delinquent accounts. Consultants are just as vulnerable to negative feelings about their jobs as any other work group. In most cases, it's not the work that's an issue, but the attitude toward work. It happens to employees, household managers, students, and just about anybody breathing.

So what's the solution? Many people find that a periodic reality check, reviewing your initial goals, and finding things to enjoy can put the fun back into nearly any duty. Consulting is no exception.

Reality Check

There are two ways to listen to news reports:

1. "Oh my God, the world is falling apart."
2. "Thank God that isn't happening to me."

The difference? Attitude. Yes, the world does seem to be falling apart and, yes, it probably isn't happening to you. Unfortunately, you won't hear many news reports that start with "Today, 352,000 children were born into the world, bringing joy and hope to parents and friends." Even so, it happens. That's the reality.

The reality of your consulting business is that it provides a valuable service to clients and community, a place for employees to earn an income and grow as people, and a place for you to profit from your skills and efforts. There are problems, of course. Most of them are solvable. In fact, by even starting a consulting business you've solved hundreds of problems successfully. You'll solve even more every day—if you don't get lost in the overwhelming feelings of not having control of your life. You do. That's the reality.

ESSENTIAL

For some consultants, being able to offer employees affordable health care and a safe work environment are mandates, not options. In any case, offering employees better working and living conditions than the big firms provide is a satisfying measurement of business success.

Take a deep breath. Find enjoyable activities inside and outside your consulting business. Remember that most problems are solved by time more than effort—and certainly not by worry. Have some fun. Chill!

Reviewing Goals

At least once a week, step back from what you are doing and take a look at the wide picture. It will not only help your mental attitude, it can be a productive exercise for any business owner. The details and decisions of each day can sometimes make inadvertent changes to your long-term goals. Do you want them to? Maybe. But don't let those decisions—by you and by others—make big changes without your approval.

Reviewing your business goals can be done in many ways. For example:

- Reread your business plan, or at least the executive summary.
- Start a sanity journal that begins with your business concept and adds your weekly notes on how reality is stacking up against goals.
- Meet periodically with a trusted business advisor to discuss your business's goals and progress.

Enjoying the Day

Every day as a consultant is a new adventure—or an adversary. The facts of the day are often the same, but the attitude is different. Find ways to enjoy your day. Review your days as a consultant and determine what you enjoyed the most. Client contacts? Employee interactions? Prospecting? Travel? Recordkeeping? Then make sure you give yourself these little pleasures each day you're at work. Eventually, you may find that the fun of some jobs will carry over to the not-so-fun jobs you must do.

Sometimes the problem can be chemical. Too much—or too little—coffee in the morning. Maybe it's that Big Mac for lunch or junk food throughout the day. If your system is sensitive to what you eat, find foods that make you feel better rather than worse. If you need your coffee but are obviously getting too much caffeine, switch to decaf or herbal teas after that first cup or two. Delicious donuts can dump carbohydrates and sugars into your system and shut down an otherwise active brain. Busy consultants soon discover that good eating can build good attitudes.

Keeping Your Life

Is there life after consulting? Yes, definitely. You had a life before you opened your business, and it's even more important that you have one now. The pressures of small business management can be immense without a periodic reality check and the rewards of life. Fortunately, successful consultants have found proven ways to balance work and life. The following are some suggestions.

- Spread the difficult tasks throughout your day and work week.
- If possible, find a quiet place in your office or a nearby cafe where you can relax and think about something besides business.
- Give your day some variety. Eat at a different restaurant or bring lunch from home. Take another route to the bank. Visit a friend before or after work.
- Take a person break. Find someone in your day, a client or employee, and learn what you can about her life outside the office. Share your own nonbusiness life with others.
- Give something unexpected to someone. Offer candy to clients. Give a free sample or consultation coupon to a postal employee, a meter reader, a walk-in, or some other random person. Hand a dollar to a homeless person.
- Take a break. Built up stress can be released with a walk around the block, a beverage, a few minutes listening to your favorite music or reading a few pages in a novel, or a moment of meditation.

- If you work alone in the office, use less busy times to call a friend, take a moment to meditate or pray, or do some stretching and light exercising.
- Involve friends in your business, inviting them into your office or out to lunch with you.
- Involve family in your business, hiring youngsters for appropriate jobs.
- Get more involved in your community and local professional or merchant associations.
- Use some of your profits to benefit your local charity, using your name for publicity or donating anonymously just to give yourself a little boost.

You can probably come up with dozens of other ways to integrate your life with your consulting business, and vice versa. Unlike a franchise, your small consulting business reflects who you are and what you want your life to be. Share it.

FACT

Stress in a service business can seem overwhelming. It is a pressure developed by a constraining force and it is caused by conditions or events that are seemingly uncontrollable. Releasing the pressure or removing the forces can resolve stress. Mental stress is relieved by mental efforts.

Measuring Success

As your consulting business grows and begins celebrating anniversaries, you'll wonder whether your business is a success or not. There are many ways to measure success, so the answer is not an easy one. Some people suggest that success is a destination, while others see it as a journey. Every day can be a success.

How do you measure consulting success? Are you a success if you have the largest service agency within a twenty-five-mile radius? Do you want to be named the local businessperson of the year? Is success achieving a specific annual salary or taking in a partner? Many successful consultants measure their achievements in terms of personal, client, employee, and community profits and satisfaction.

Personal Profit

Certainly, one of the major reasons for starting a consulting business is personal profit. You want to make a living at a rewarding job and, hopefully, build equity and goodwill that you can someday trade in for cash.

Your small business's success can be measured, in part, by personal profits. You want a salary that will fund the other parts of your life: food, shelter, fun. First, it must fund your business: research tools, expertise, overhead, taxes. You'd also like to build the assets of your business—furniture, fixtures, goodwill, cash in reserve—toward someday passing the business along to a relative or selling it. Whatever these personal goals are, moving toward them is an indication of success. Your progress is a measurement of success. That doesn't mean financial setbacks or even losses are failures; it just means it will take some more management skills to produce success. Profits will return.

Client Profits

For your clients, success means finding what they want. They benefit from the successful operation of your consulting business. For some consultants, serving clients is the most important measure of success. They believe that service to others is the greatest profit. They add to the value of others' lives by serving their needs for solutions.

Client profits are more difficult to quantify than financial profits. However, they are still measurable. Because the opinions of clients are important to verify this success, the owner must be in constant touch with them, asking how the business benefits individual clients. The results can be quantified by looking at sales levels. If one in two clients express their appreciation for your business and it serves ten clients a day, at least five clients clearly benefit from what you do. That is client success.

Employee Profits

It is increasingly difficult to find a job that is both satisfying and pays a living wage. Many consultants take pride in what they can offer their employees. With capital and smart management, consultants can hire the best employees in the area, ones who recognize the rewards of offering genuine service to others. Whether you hire employees now or are building your business to hire some later, you can measure success by how you improve the lives of current and future employees.

ESSENTIAL

Consulting services with key employees should consider life insurance payable to the firm on the death or disability of these people. How much life insurance? It should be an amount sufficient to offset financial losses during the readjustment period, to retain good credit standing, and to assure clients and suppliers that the company will continue as usual.

Community Profits

Your community benefits from your decision to start and run a successful consulting business. In addition to offering clients a trusted place to find solutions and employees a superior place to work, your business does other things for the community. It pays taxes. It upgrades the professional community. It makes donations to local charities. It enhances local pride.

You should take pride in the services you provide to your community. Whether your business is in a downtown area, a professional building, or a large shopping mall, your community benefits from your efforts—as do you, your clients, and employees. These are very good indications of success.

Avoiding Consultant Burnout

You've probably talked with a consultant who is grumpy or angry and not handling the day well. It happens to all consultants at some point: burnout. They are tired, worried, or afraid and it comes out as anger. Maybe a challenging client, a slow-to-learn employee, or a late payment pushes the button. Burnout is the problem. What's the solution?

Recognition! Unfortunately, consultants who blow up at a client, employee, or delivery service haven't yet recognized they are burned out; they don't see the signs and stop them before they become overwhelming. If their boiling point is 212°F, they don't recognize that they're already operating at 210°F. A common and otherwise minor event—a client request, an employee question, or a late payment—adds a few degrees and everyone gets scalded.

How can you avoid burnout? Recognize the signs and take action toward lowering the temperature. Taking a break is a primary step in avoiding burnout. In addition, you can consider what it is that has increased your operating temperature. Is there a conflict at home? Are you frustrated by your lack of control over a business or personal situation? Is there a health or diet issue that is making you volatile? Recognition of the components that can lead to burnout is the first step in minimizing it.

Taking a Break

Have fun, enjoy your work, recognize your contributions, avoid burnout. What if none of this advice works? You need a Break with a capital B. You need to get away from the office. You've either been in it or thinking of it for months and you're getting burned out. It's time to take a Break.

How long? Where? What will you do? You can answer these initial questions with some help from other consultants. Here are some of their suggestions:

- The length of a Break isn't as important as the depth. A true weekend Break can be more renewing than a week away with worry.
- Either find a trusted employee to run the office or close the business for a few days (maybe around a holiday or slow period).
- Instead of calling you if there is an emergency, ask your employee to call a friendly consultant to help solve the problem.
- Change habits. If you typically eat out, make your own meals instead. If you don't get to read many novels, do so. Don't even look at any business books.
- Find a place where you can stare at the horizon: mountains, sea shore, desert.

- Don't have a "busman's holiday," visiting competitive offices on your Break. It's not relaxing.
- Take in a play at a theater, listen to live music, stroll through an art gallery or museum.
- Meditate. Spend some time each day connecting to whatever level of life force is comfortable.
- Train your mind to set aside problems and focus on the positive aspects of your life.

In fact, you may discover that Breaks don't require that you drive or fly somewhere else. You can take Mini-Breaks just about anywhere and any time. It's a process: clear your mind, suspend your worries, enjoy the moment. A ten-minute Mini-Break can refresh your work day. Your problems will still be there when you get back from a Break or Mini-Break, but you will be more ready to prioritize and solve them.

Selling Your Consulting Business

When is a good time to retire from your profitable consulting services business? When you want to. Some consultants will hold off retiring until they are no longer able to work their trade. Others make plans to retire at a specific age, say when they turn sixty-five. Still others give their business ten or twenty years to grow, then sell it and semi-retire or move to a different trade. Some work their children into it, then gradually turn it over to them. A few will sell or give their equity in the business to a more distant relative. Other successful consulting business owners will sell their shares to a partner or to a corporation. Some will sell out to key employees or to competitors.

How much can you get for your business? Of course, much depends on how successful your business is. Once it is established and shows a profit for three years or more, a consulting service will typically be valued at the replacement cost of tangible assets plus 0.75 to 1.25 times gross annual billing.

For example, a successful consulting service billing $500,000 a year from an office with assets valued at $25,000 will typically sell for $400,000 ($500,000 \times 0.75 + 25,000$) to $650,000 ($500,000 \times 1.25 + 25,000$). Quite a range. As it probably took you nine to eighteen months to build your consulting business to a point of profitability, the price should repay you for this lost income as well as the physical assets the business has acquired. How much above or below this guideline you get depends on the value of your business's name in gaining new clients. If your consulting business is on the threshold of expansion, you will get more in the sale than if it is just paying its bills.

You can fund your retirement or future activities by selling your business on a contract. Depending on the buyer, you may want 25 percent down and the balance paid over five to ten years. Or you may opt to take a smaller purchase price and require an annual royalty on gross billings or on net profits. Once your consulting business gets to this point, you'll have a better idea of what you want and how you want it.

QUESTION

What are my options if my business partner dies?
Unless there is a written agreement to the contrary, the death of a partner automatically dissolves the firm. In the absence of such an agreement, surviving partners have no right to buy the deceased's partnership interest. Surviving partners cannot assume the goodwill or take over the assets without consent of the deceased partner's estate.

In selling your consulting business, the paperwork can be simple or complex. In fact, if there is no real estate involved, a handshake can seal the transaction. However, if you are selling a business worth $50,000 or more, you will want a nondisclosure agreement, an offering memorandum, a sales agreement with a noncompetition clause, and maybe a promissory note. Corporate sales will require more paperwork and should involve an attorney.

Nondisclosure Agreement

The first document that potential buyers should sign for you is a nondisclosure agreement. It says they will not disclose or use the proprietary information you supply to them in a way that will harm your business. Otherwise, a potential buyer could learn the valuable information you've developed about the local market and your business operations, then open a consulting service nearby and take your clients.

FACT

Generic nondisclosure agreements are available at office supply stores and in books that focus on selling your business. Unless you're knowledgeable in business law, you should have an attorney draw up the nondisclosure agreement or at least review the form you will use.

Offering Memorandum

Your business's offering memorandum outlines what your business is, what it does, how it does it, and the results: profits. It is a summary of how your business works. It's a valuable document that costs you thousands of dollars in efforts to develop. It's the result of your business plan. Don't let anyone see it without signing a nondisclosure agreement first.

A typical offering memorandum for a consulting service will include:

- Executive summary
- Business description
- Business history
- Services offered
- Sales and marketing procedures
- Competition
- Operations
- Facilities
- Personnel
- Goodwill
- Growth potential
- Industry overview
- Financial information
- Reasons for selling
- Price and terms
- Contact information

Additional documents, including profit and loss statement and balance sheet, can be provided as the prospective buyer is ready to move to the next level. Most buyers will want an independent audit or verification of the facts before proceeding.

Sales Agreement

The sales agreement outlines how the sale is structured. This can be important not only to the buyer and seller, but also to the tax collector. Yes, you will probably have to pay income tax on the sale of your business. Whether the tax is based on ordinary income or capital gains depends on how the sale is structured and reported. You'll need a tax advisor to help you set up the sale to benefit the seller while meeting the requirements of the buyer.

The typical asset sale agreement will include:

- Names of seller(s) and buyer(s)
- List of assets being sold by seller
- List of liabilities being accepted by buyer
- Sale price, typically broken down by type of assets
- Value of goodwill; how it is determined
- How accounts payable will be paid
- Terms of sale: deposit, payment at closing, promissory note (if any)
- How seller's debts and obligations will be handled
- Seller's representations
- Buyer's representations
- Covenant not to compete
- How disputes will be handled
- Governing law

The covenant not to compete typically says that the seller will not start or work for a similar business within a specific geographic area for a specified time. This covenant is not easily enforceable in many jurisdictions if the seller must find employment after the sale.

Promissory Note

In many sales, the buyer has all cash or has financing. In others, the seller agrees to finance a portion of the sale under a promissory note and security agreement. The security agreement says that the business assets—and any buyer assets that are agreed—serve as security for the note. If it is not paid as agreed, the security can be sold to collect the balance.

The promissory note outlines the terms of payments. Equal monthly payments are commonly made over a three- to five-year period at a specified interest rate, often from 8 to 12 percent, until paid off. A large payment during or at the end of the note, called a balloon payment, may be required.

ALERT

If you are selling your business on a promissory note, it is especially important to have legally binding documents. Use an attorney to draw up all the documents or, at the very least, to review form documents you have drawn up yourself.

You've come full circle, from considering the opportunities of a consulting business to making sure you enjoy it and your new life. Now it is time to take action. If consulting is for you, read this book again and start building your own consulting business, tailored to your skills and goals. Consulting can be a rewarding business for those who sincerely enjoy helping others solve problems.

Consulting Business Glossary

The consulting business has a unique language. This glossary of business terms can help you understand and be understood in the world of business and personal consulting.

Accounts payable: Money that you or your business owes to others.

Accounts receivable: Money owed to you or your business.

Accrual: An accounting term for the increase over time of expenses incurred by your business. They are accrued up until the time they are paid.

Acid-test ratio: A measurement of how well a business can meet its short-term financial obligations without selling any inventory.

Added value: The process of going the extra mile with a client. Added value also is used to describe when products and services include additional features beyond what is generally desired by the client at no additional cost.

Advocates: Those people in the client's organization a salesperson works with who support the recommendation being offered.

Agent: A person who has the authority or is empowered to represent a company or a company's products and services.

AIDA: Attention, Interest, Desire, Action.

Asset: Things of value. Tangible assets include cash, receivables, inventory, and buildings. Intangible assets include goodwill.

Atmosphere: The physical characteristics and surrounding influence of a business that is used to create an image in order to attract clients.

B2B: A sales organization whose primary effort is selling to and doing business with other businesses.

B2C: A sales organization whose primary effort is selling to and doing business with consumers, or with individual users.

Base salary: The guaranteed portion of a salesperson's monetary compensation. Base salaries reward salespeople for their accumulated experience and overall selling efforts.

Benefit: The value experienced by the client as a result of the purchase of a product or service. Salespeople who focus on communicating benefits and aligning those benefits to a client's business objectives increase the likelihood of gaining a sale.

Bill of lading: A contract between a freight company and a shipper regarding transportation that includes the exact contents of the delivery.

Blue law: Rules created to restrict particular activities to certain days or hours. Many blue laws have been removed from the books or are no longer enforced.

Body language: The gestures, body movements, and mannerisms by which a person communicates his outlook or frame of mind.

Bonus: In sales compensation, a type of incentive payment typically awarded when the salesperson or sales team achieves pre-determined financial objectives.

Brainstorming: A methodology undertaken by a person or a team to solve a problem or to generate ideas by rapidly listing a variety of possible solutions and approaches.

Brand: A name, term, or symbol used to identify the products and services of the selling organization and to differentiate them from those of competitors.

Break-even point: The point in business where the sales equal the expenses. There is no profit and no loss.

Brick and mortar: A business that is in a building as opposed to an online shopping destination, door-to-door sales, kiosk or other similar site not housed within a structure.

Business cycle: A sequence of economic activities typically characterized by recessions, recovery, growth, and at times, decline.

Business plan: A detailed document describing the past, present and future financial and operational objectives of a company.

Buyer: The person who purchases or procures a product or service. This person may also be the decision maker, but not necessarily.

Buying office: A central office where buyers purchase products or services for all businesses owned by the parent company.

Buying process: The steps a client organization or a buyer takes in making a purchase for a product or service.

Buying signal: A statement or indication from a prospect or client that suggests he is considering making a purchase.

Call: A visit or meeting with a client or prospect.

Canvas: Another word for the activity of prospecting for clients.

Capital assets: Long-term assets used to produce income, such as buildings and equipment.

Cash discount: A percentage reduction in price for payment within a specified period of time.

Cash flow: The movement of money in and out of a business and the resulting availability of cash.

Centralized buying organization: Company in which all buying decisions for all the locations in the company are made by one central office.

C-Level Executive: An executive in the organization whose title often is preceded by the word "chief," e.g. CEO, COO, CIO, CFO, etc.

Close: The point at which the salesperson asks for a commitment to purchase the product or service being evaluated.

Closed questions: Questions that provide the client with a choice among alternatives. Often these are brief answer, yes-no questions.

Cold call: A visit made to an organization without having an appointment.

Commission: In sales compensation, a type of payment or revenue sharing resulting from achieving a sale or attaining a given sales level. Commissions are typically expressed as a percentage of the selling price for the product sold.

Commodity: Competing products or services that bear the same or similar characteristics.

Competitive advantage: Those areas deemed to have preferential value to a client versus a similar competitive product.

Confidentiality agreements: Agreements between two parties affirming that the information exchanged during a relationship is maintained within the confines of the agreement, and not shared beyond the agreement.

Consultant: Someone who sells advice to someone who needs it. The advice must be useful, of value, and assist the client in solving a specific problem.

Consultative selling: A selling methodology where the client is seeking advice from the selling organization.

Contact management system: The use of technology to track client contact information, activity, and history.

Contribution margin: The difference between total sales revenue and total variable costs. The term is applied to a service line and is generally expressed as a percentage.

Conversion ratio: Used in sales organizations where gaining sales is a function of taking away business from competition, this ratio is usually a measure of the number of targeted opportunities secured versus the number of opportunities pursued.

Conversion: The methodology used to convert a client's use of one product or supplier to another.

Corporation: A legal entity that can buy, sell, and enter into contracts as if it were a person.

Cost-Benefit Analysis: The method a client (or sales organization) follows to assess the viability of a recommendation, by examining the total amount of money, time, and resources used relative to the value being received.

Cost of sales: For sales compensation purposes, the percentage calculation of total sales generated by the sales force divided by the total compensation costs of the sales force.

Coupon: A promotional tool in the form of a document that can be redeemed for a discount when purchasing goods or services. Coupons feature a specific savings amount or other special offer to persuade consumers to purchase specific goods or services or to purchase from a specific business.

Cross-selling: A methodology in selling where a client need lends itself to a possible need for another product or service.

Client profile: A document that outlines the critical information about a particular client.

Client relationship management (CRM): The process used internally to manage client relationships.

Decision maker: The person most responsible for deciding the outcome of a salesperson's or selling organization's proposal.

Demographics: Characteristics of a specific group of people, such as potential clients.

Demonstration call: A client call involving a salesperson and a manager, in which the manager's role is to teach and show the salesperson a technique or approach the salesperson wishes to improve.

Desire: A longing, a wish. Strong desire drives ambition and performance.

Differentiation: The process of distinguishing services or products through design.

Direct marketing: The process of marketing directly to an end user. The most known form of direct marketing is direct mail.

Discount: A reduced amount (typically from standard price) that is offered by the seller or the selling organization to encourage purchase of a product being offered.

Distributor: An indirect sales channel that markets or sells a product or service. Distributors are used by selling organizations to capitalize on the distributor's local presence and capacity to support the manufacturer.

Double entry: An accounting system that requires two balancing entries, a debit and a credit, to be made for each transaction.

Draw: In sales compensation, a cash advance in anticipation of future sales performance.

Durable goods: Products that can be used frequently and have a long life expectancy, such as furniture, jewelry, and major appliances.

E-Business: Conducting business via the Internet.

Economic benefit: The financial value of a product or service. This is tied closely to the term ROI, or return on investment.

Electronic shopping: Shopping over the Internet or through a TV cable channel.

Elevator speech: Sales slang for a short, 20-second overview of who your company is, what it does, and what you do, with the intent of gaining an individual's interest to learn more and seek further discussion.

Empathy: The ability to communicate and understand someone else's situation and feelings.

Employer identification number: Also known as a Federal Tax Identification Number, is used to identify a business entity.

Executive summary: Often considered the first page or first several pages in a business plan, summarizing the key issues, solution and value a client will receive by implementing the recommendation.

Farmer: A slang term in sales referring to a salesperson whose primary job is to maintain and grow business with existing clients, versus acquiring new clients.

Feature: A characteristic of your product or service. The distinct parts of your product or service that can be described.

Focus Group: A small group selected to participate in open discussions on a topic, in order to solicit the participants' opinion about that topic or area.

Forward stock: Merchandise that is kept on the selling floor.

Free on board (FOB): Shipping term used to indicate who is responsible for paying transportation charges. FOB factory means the buyer must pay shipping from the factory.

Gatekeeper: The person who controls access to someone you are trying to meet with.

Goal: The end toward which a salesperson or sales organization is headed. The ability to set and execute against ambitious yet realistic goals is considered the essential foundation to a sales organization's success.

Golden Rule Selling: Selling as you want to be sold. Applying what you know as a buyer to becoming a better seller. See *The Everything Sales Book* by Dan Ramsey (Adams Media, 2009).

Goods: Tangible products for sale that can be held or touched.

Grade labeling: Product labeling that includes a quality rating for the product.

Gross income: Total income derived from a business.

Gross leasable area (GLA): Total floor space available for sales.

Gross margin: The difference between the cost of goods sold and the price at which they were sold.

Gross profit: Profit calculated after deducting all costs of merchandise, labor, and overhead.

Hot buttons: Those areas that can be used to position solutions to align with a decision maker's most important criteria for selection.

Image: The impression clients have of a company or service.

Incentives: Any form of compensation or reward made to a salesperson or sales team to influence sales results: bonuses, commissions, trips, catalog award points, etc.

Influencer: An individual who has sway over how a decision is made, but is not the direct decision maker.

Inquiries: Those individuals or organizations who contact your organization to find out more about what you do. When qualified, they become a qualified lead.

Key performance indicator (KPI): The primary measures an organization uses to determine its own internal performance.

Key players: The men and women inside an account who are essential to the selling organization gaining a positive decision.

Keystone pricing: A method of marking merchandise for resell to an amount that is double the wholesale price.

Leave-behind: A sample or piece of written material about your product or service that you leave with a client during or at the end of a call.

Level of influence: The degree of influence an individual has on the decision-making process.

Liabilities: Amounts that a business owes to suppliers and other creditors.

Loss leader: A product or service that is discounted significantly from list price and used, typically for a limited period, to influence buyers to purchase other products.

Loss prevention: The act of reducing the amount of theft and shrinkage within a business.

Margin: The difference between the cost of a product and its selling price, expressed as a percentage or dollars-per-unit.

Markdown: Planned reduction in the selling price of an item, usually to take effect either within a certain number of days after seasonal merchandise is received or at a specific date.

Market area: Geographic area from which a business draws its clients.

Market penetration: The ability to enter and gain a share in a specified market, generally measured in percentage terms.

Market share: An organization's portion of the total market, typically expressed as a percentage.

Marketing calendar: A tool used by businesses to show what marketing events, media campaigns and promotional efforts are happening when and where, as well as the results.

Marketing: The process followed by organizations to satisfy the needs, wants, and demands of their clients through the application and promotion of products and services that satisfy those client requirements.

Markup: The amount added to the cost price of a product or service to determine its selling price.

Mission statement: An organization's purpose for being. Mission statements typically communicate what an organization values.

Needs analysis: The process of formally evaluating a client's needs and requirements.

Net lease: Lease in which the tenant pays the base rent plus property taxes. Also known as a single net lease.

Net-net lease: Lease in which the tenant pays the base rent plus property taxes and building insurance. Also known as a double-net lease.

Net-net-net lease: Lease in which the tenant pays the base rent plus property taxes, building insurance, and maintenance. Also known as a triple-net lease.

Networking: The process of developing and maintaining alliances externally and internally with a wide variety of contacts that can provide information, insight, help, and access to others.

Niche market: A unique segment of the market a selling organization is targeted toward. This unique segment, if served well, can provide areas of distinctive competitive value.

Objection: A term often used in sales when a client challenges or rejects a salesperson's idea or suggestion, or when the client communicates issues that will prevent the sale from moving forward.

Open-ended questions: Questions that encourage the client to respond freely. They include questions with what, why, and how that require more information from the client than a simple yes or no answer.

Operating expenses: The sum of all expenses associated with the normal course of running a business.

Opportunity: A situation, need, condition, or circumstance where you have the potential to meet a client's business requirements.

Partnership: Two or more people own a business together.

Price: A price is the monetary value placed on a product or service.

Pricing practices: The methods and strategies an organization uses to price its products and services in the marketplace.

Probability: The likelihood that a given event will occur.

Problem analysis: The process of examining the symptoms, conditions, and possible causes of a problem in order to define alternatives for possible resolution.

Process: A series of steps bringing about a desired result.

Profit margin: A ratio of profitability calculated as earnings divided by revenues. It measures how much out of every dollar of sales a business actually keeps in earnings.

Pro-forma: The process of preparing a hypothetical income statement for a client, based on a given set of assumptions.

Project management: The science and discipline of planning, organizing, overseeing, managing and tracking projects in an organization.

Proposal: An offer that is made, both verbally and in written form, between the selling organization and the client organization in order to initiate business activity.

Prospect: A potential buyer or client for your products and/or services.

Prospecting: The process of searching for and finding qualified clients for your product or service.

Qualify: The process of assessing whether or not a client or an opportunity represents a potential fit for your product or service.

Referral: A client's direction or recommendation to another party, internal or external, that may benefit from your product or service.

Request for proposal (RFP): Used by clients to assess who will respond, and evaluate solutions being posed.

Retention: The science and practices used to keep a client.

Return on investment (ROI): The amount, expressed as a percentage, earned by an investment.

Returns percentage: The relationship between returns and allowances, and sales, calculated by dividing returns and allowances by gross sales.

Run of paper (ROP): A newspaper advertising term referring to an advertisement that may be placed anywhere within the paper.

Run of schedule (ROS): A broadcasting advertising term referring to an advertisement that may be placed anywhere within the broadcast schedule.

Segmentation: The division of a market into separate units with similar characteristics.

Service: A product/service mix that offers only a service, with no accompanying product needed or wanted, such as an insurance policy.

Sole proprietor: One person (or a married couple) who owns a business.

Stall: When a client avoids making a decision and, in essence, puts the sales process on hold.

Strategic selling: A selling methodology considered by some to represent the most complex type of sale, because of the number of people who are typically involved in the sales process, or the nature and scope of the relationship.

Strategy: The planning of all the resources available to a company or a salesperson to achieve a stated goal or purpose.

Supportive services: Free services offered to clients to increase convenience, make shopping easier, and entice clients to buy more.

Suspect: A prospect that has not been qualified as a potential client yet.

Target market: The set of clients or organizations that you deem most viable for your product or service.

Test market: The process of evaluating the appeal of a product or service by selecting cities, clients, and locations in which to introduce the product or service, and monitor how receptive the intended users are to it.

Testimonial: A verbal or written expression of the value a client received by having used or purchased your product, service, or overall solution.

Trade credit: An open account with suppliers of goods and services.

Trade discount: A discount on the list price given by a manufacturer or wholesaler to a retailer or service business.

Value: The relative worth, utility, importance, or financial benefit that is assigned by a buyer to the product or service an organization sells.

Vertical market: A market characterized by certain unique characteristics.

White paper: A document, typically less than 12 pages in length, that describes your organization's point of view in areas that may be of interest to the client.

Widget: An unnamed product or service used as a hypothetical example.

Word of mouth: A powerful method of selling products by creating interest, desire, or incentives on the part of current users to promote the use of your product and service to others.

Index